NATIONAL GEOGRAPHIC
TRAVELER
Romania

NATIONAL GEOGRAPHIC
TRAVELER
Romania

Caroline Juler
Photography by Steve Weinberg

National Geographic
Washington, D.C.

Contents

**Page 1: A boy in Vlahiţa,
Transylvania, during the
annual Narcissus Festival
Pages 2–3: Morning sunlight
streams into Biserica
Stavropoleos in Lipscani,
Bucharest
Left: A fiddler in Valea Mare
reviving the Căluş, a pagan
Whitsuntide ritual for
success and fertility**

How to use this guide

See back flap for keys to text and map symbols

The *National Geographic Traveler* brings you the best of Romania and the nearby imperial palaces in text, pictures, and maps. Divided into three main sections, the guide begins with an overview of history and culture. Following are eight regional chapters with featured sites selected by the author for their particular interest and treated in depth. Each chapter opens with its own contents list for easy reference.

The regions, and sites within them, are arranged geographically. A map introduces each region, highlighting the featured sites. Walks and drives, plotted on their own

maps, suggest routes for discovering an area. Features and sidebars offer detail on history, culture, or contemporary life. A More Places to Visit page rounds off each regional chapter.

The final section, Travelwise, lists essential information for the traveler—pre-trip planning, getting around, communications, money matters, and emergencies—plus a selection of hotels, restaurants, shops, and entertainment.

To the best of our knowledge, site information is accurate as of the press date. However, it's always advisable to call ahead.

Color coding

116

Each region is color coded for easy reference. Find the region you want on the map on the front flap, and look for the color flash at the top of the pages of the relevant chapter. Information in **Travelwise** is also color coded to each region.

Muzeul Naţional de Istorie a României

- 49 E1
- Calea Victoriei 12
- 021 315 0782
- Closed Mon.
- $
- Metro: Piaţa Unirii 1

Visitor information

for major sites is listed in the side columns (see key to symbols on back flap). The map reference gives the page where the site is mapped. Other details are the address, telephone number, days closed, entrance fee ranging from $ (under $5) to $$$$$ (over $25), and the nearest metro stop or transportation options. Visitor information for smaller sites is provided within the text. Admission fees are based on the prices foreigners pay.

Hotel and restaurant prices

An explanation of the price bands used in entries is given in the Hotels & Restaurants section beginning on p. 244.

TRAVELWISE

TRANSYLVANIA — Color-coded region name

🏨 **GASTHOF CLARA**
$$ — Hotel name & price range

STR. RÂULUI 24
TEL 0269 222 914
FAX 0269 206 071
www.gasthofclara.ro — Address, telephone and fax numbers, & website

This upmarket pension, situated on a busy street across the river from the old town, is about a 10-15 minute walk from the main square. — Brief description of hotel

🛈 6 🅿 🚫 🚭 ⚑ — Hotel facilities & credit card details

🍴 **LA PIAZZETTA**
$$ — Restaurant name & price range

PIAŢA MICĂ 15
SIBIU
TEL 0269 230 879 — Address & telephone number

This Italian pizzeria serves the best pizzas in Sibiu and possibly all of Romania. Only 25 seats, so reservations are necessary on weekends. — Brief description of restaurant

🪑 25 🚫 ⚑ — Restaurant closures & credit card details

REGIONAL MAPS

- A locator map accompanies each regional map and shows the location of that region in the city.
- Adjacent regions are shown, each with a page reference.

WALKING TOURS

- An information box gives the starting and finishing points, time and length of walk, and places not to miss along the route.
- Where two walks are marked on the map, the second route is shown in orange.

DRIVING TOURS

- An information box provides details including starting and finishing points, time and length of drive, places not to be missed along the route, and tips on terrain.

NATIONAL GEOGRAPHIC

TRAVELER

Romania

About the authors & photographer

Caroline Juler is a writer and artist. She first visited Romania in 1993 on the trail of a performance art festival in the Carpathian mountains. Having fallen in love with the country, she has been back once or twice every year since then. In 1998 she completed work on the first edition of *Blue Guide Romania*, and another book on Romania, *Searching for Sarmizegetusa*, appeared in 2003. She has taken part in a campaign organized by locals to prevent the development of a gold quarry in the Apuseni Mountains and is currently refurbishing a traditional Romanian house, to be used by friends and visitors on her guided tours.

For more than 15 years, **Steven Weinberg** has extensively photographed the countries of Central Europe and the former Soviet states, with their emerging market economies, as a retrospective commentary on a new era in world history. His work is represented by Getty Images and is continuously published worldwide by several *Fortune* 500 companies. The U.S. Embassy in Tbilisi, Georgia, has sponsored a traveling solo exhibit of Steven's work, and Nikon highlights his images as part of its "Legends of the Lens" photographer series website.

Travelwise was compiled and written by **Mark Baker,** a freelance journalist and travel writer based in Prague. He's a frequent contributor to *National Geographic Traveler* magazine, and his articles have appeared in the *Wall Street Journal,* among other publications. He's a former long-time editor and correspondent for Radio Free Europe and has worked for Bloomberg News and the Economist Group.

History & culture

The Romanian flag at dusk at Bucharest's Arcul de Triumf

Romania today

HIGHLIGHTED BY THE STRIKING CARPATHIAN MOUNTAINS, WHICH PARADE across the country from the southwest corner and up its eastern heartland, Romania is a land of timeless beauty. Isolated from development for much of history, this unspoiled realm showcases rolling farmlands and rugged peaks, fir forests and bird-filled marshes. The majority of Europe's brown bear and lynx populations prowls its forestlands. Here, traditions run deep, life goes on in many places as it has for centuries, and painted medieval monasteries, wooden churches, fairy-tale castles and palaces, and Roman ruins whisper secrets of the past. Since the revolution and Ceaușescu's overthrow in 1989, however, Romania has been striding toward modernity, the most recent stepping-stone being admission into the European Union (EU) in January 2007. Change is in the air in this ancient land, and now's the time to take it all in.

BUCHAREST—LEADING THE CHARGE

Bucharest is the hub of Romania's most dynamic changes. Home to ten percent of the population, the city was modeled on Paris, evident in its Arch of Triumph, palaces, and notable museums. Ceauşescu attempted to obliterate as much of Bucharest's past as he could by cutting a swath through its center. He raised a gigantic palace to his own glory, flattening several square miles of historic buildings for his bleak vision of triumphant modernity.

Since the 1989 revolution, the capital city has acquired a gleaming financial plaza, and

glass-and-chrome high-rise buildings are sprouting everywhere. Advertisements hang like veils off every facade, and the exhaust from an ever increasing number of cars pollutes the air. Faithful jalopies and top-end limousines jostle for position at traffic lights, their drivers honking as they race along, scattering pedestrians in their path. Overhead, the sky is latticed by a jungle of wires that cluster round every available pillar and lamppost. But off the bustling arteries you find a different, more nostalgic world with hints of the country's Ottoman past and powerful accents of eastern Christianity (the city has about 300 Orthodox churches). Plant-festooned balconies, arabesque arches, secluded courtyards, cobbled roads, majestic trees that give ample shade during the hot summers, and a proliferation of parks and gardens belie baleful descriptions of Bucharest as a wasted city, while its "leisure opportunities" (hotels, cafés, bars, restaurants, theaters, cinemas, and clubs) are expanding every year. At times confusing, and even exasperating, Romania's capital is never dull.

KEEPING TRADITION ALIVE

Thanks to its historical circumstances, Romania was so isolated that in some places medieval lifestyles have survived to the present. Few other places in Europe offer such an intimate link with the Old World. Throughout the country's rural landscape, smallholders still drive horse-drawn carts, grow their own vegetables, breed their own livestock, and make their own clothes. They work close to the land and know its moods.

At the same time, the signs of change can be seen even in the far reaches of the countryside. They are manifest in the increase in privately run guesthouses as well as in the recognition of the commercial value of crafts: Every self-respecting ethnog-

Enjoying the wide open space of Piaţa Unirii, Timişoara. This university city in western Romania is often described as the most cosmopolitan city in the country. It was also the first European city illuminated with electric street lights.

raphy museum now has a shop that promotes the work of individual craftspeople.

Perhaps a greater trend, however, are the demographic changes that are occurring. Since 1989, many young people have moved off the land, shifting the balance from country to town. These days, many urban families retain a village smallholding or plot, often tended by themselves and grandparents on weekends and holidays. The contrast between urban and rural is sharply apparent as new-model cars tear through little villages, heedless of speed limits, people, and farm animals in their way.

A TREASURE-TROVE OF REGIONS

Romania covers a large territory, and within its confines there is a wide choice of things to see and do, whether you're interested in culture, history, wildlife, or recreational activities. Most first-time visitors start in the capital city of Bucharest, but there the possibilities have only just begun.

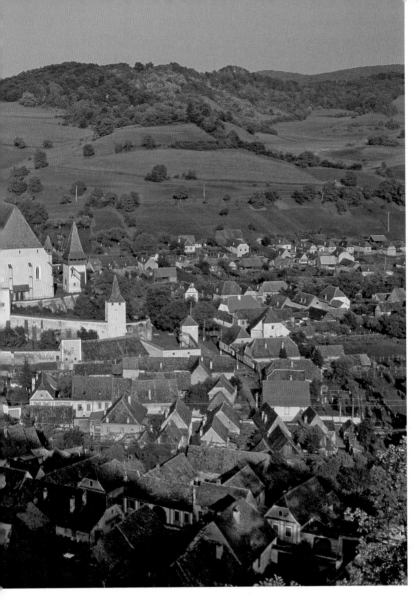

Often overlooked by foreign visitors, Oltenia (the western half of Wallachia) is endowed with spectacular monasteries, historic spas, and charming villages. The most beautiful of the villages lie in the Carpathian Mountains, whose beech-drenched foothills become a riot of gold in the fall. The landscape is also riddled with caves—Muierilor and Polovragi, to name a few. Oltenians are known for their straightforward openness, individuality, and archaic beliefs.

Biertan is one of the first German settlements in Transylvania, dating from 1224. Saxon villagers built Biertan citadel church in the 15th century to protect themselves from their Turkish and Hungarian enemies.

Ringed by the Carpathian Mountains and graced with extraordinary cities and delightful villages, Transylvania always looks just a bit more advanced than the rest of

Romania. Historically this was due to the presence of industrious northern Europeans, especially Germans (known as Saxons), who cultivated the land and developed thriving businesses. In medieval times, the Saxons built fortified churches, many of which still stand. Here, too, you'll see romantic castles and manor houses dotting the countryside. The Romanian winter can be enjoyed in such resorts as Predeal and Poiana Brașov. The legend of Count Dracula has its origins in Transylvania; Bran Castle, built by the Knights of Teutonic Order in 1212, is considered by many to be Dracula's castle.

Maramureș, a deeply rural area in northwest Romania too remote for the Romans to invade, is a haven of traditions. Plowing, harvesting, and haymaking are still done by hand. It is famous for its hand-hewn wooden architecture and especially its tall-spired churches with double roofs.

Tucked away in the northeast of Romania,

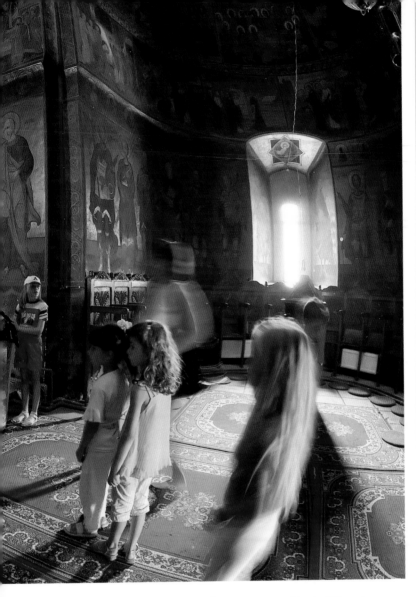

where the steppe rolls up into the forested Carpathian Mountains near the border with Ukraine, the historic area of Bucovina contains some of Romania's most astonishing architectural treasures. The sturdy but elegant painted churches of the 15th and 16th centuries are enveloped in kaleidoscopic Byzantine paintings both inside and out. They are a must for anyone with an interest in art, but their romantic rural setting makes them especially noteworthy.

A school group visits the 17th-century monastery of Căldărușani, 19 miles (30 km) northeast of Bucharest. While its influence has diminished in recent years, religion still plays a central role in the lives of many Romanians.

THE ROMANIANS

Chaotic, emotional, and irreverent, but also deeply religious and respectful of authority: These are some of the generalizations that are used to describe Romanians. The history and

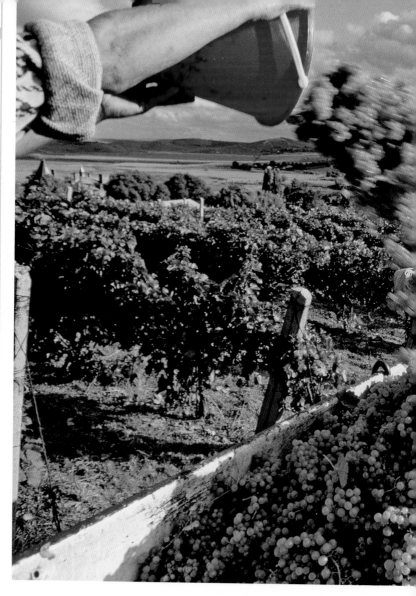

origins of the Romanian people go some way to explaining why.

Poised at the crossroads of three regions—Central Europe, Eastern Europe, and the Balkans—and subject to constant invasions and occupations, Romania is a melting pot of cultures. Today, ethnic Romanians make up 89 percent of the country's population. Hungarians are the next largest group, with 6.6 percent, followed by the Roma (Gypsies) at 2.5 percent (though many believe this official tally is too low), Ukrainians and Germans at 0.3 percent each, and Russians and Turks at 0.2 percent each. Germans and Hungarians live mostly in Transylvania, while Ukrainians and Russians reside for the most part near the Danube Delta, and the Turks cluster along the Black Sea coast.

The nation has 17 official ethnic minorities, the largest and by far the most colorful of which is the Roma, 500,000 of whom reside throughout the country.

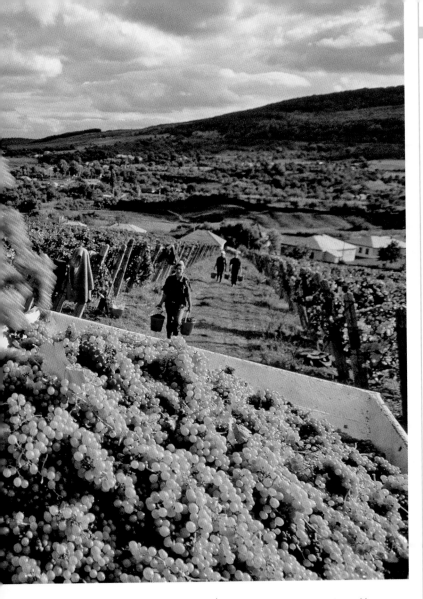

Many of the country's mountain dwellers claim that their forebears were the Dacians, a Thracian tribe that preceded the Romans, but the Romanian language derives mainly from the street Latin spoken at the time Hadrian's legions ruled the fertile provinces north of the Danube in the 2nd century A.D. Romanian developed into something like its modern form by the tenth century, absorbing many words from the languages of the Slavs, who had arrived earlier.

The Greeks introduced winemaking to present-day Romania 3,000 years ago. The country's grape-friendly soil and climate have helped earn its ranking as one of the largest wine producers in the world.

More than half of Romania's 22 million people live in towns and cities. (The country has 30,000 towns, each no more than 40 miles/64 km from the next—a fact that dates back to feudal times when

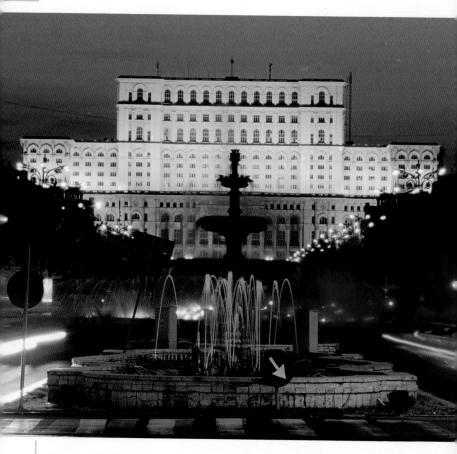

Ceaușescu's 1,100-room, 12-story-tall former palace in Bucharest is now the country's parliament building. It's the second largest administrative building in the world, after the Pentagon.

horses and carts could only travel that far between sunrise and sunset.) The average population density is 59 per square mile (98 per square kilometer), less than a third of India's, and three times more than in the United States.

Most Romanians are members of the Romanian Orthodox church, an autonomous branch of Eastern Orthodoxy. A sizeable minority belongs to the Uniate or Greco-Catholic faith, an amalgamation of Orthodoxy and Roman Catholicism introduced to Transylvania in the early 18th century. Other minority religions include the Hungarian Reformed, Jewish, Muslim, and Protestant.

Although Romania is still a religious country, like elsewhere in Europe fewer people are attending church services than in the past.

AFTERMATH OF DECEMBER 1989

More than a thousand people died as a result of the 1989 revolution, and memorials to them can be found in most of the country's larger cities. A great deal has changed since the end of communism. For one thing, the teenagers and students who drove the revolution have grown up. Their generation regards speaking out as natural—something their parents and grandparents would never have dared to do. They are enthusiastically taking up the challenge of leading their country into a better future.

At the same time, expectations and fears abound—while many Romanians look to the West as their only hope for political and economic advancement, others see EU rules and regulations as an obstacle to natural, organic growth and self-expression.

In the past, Romania has been oriented toward the East as well as to the West. One only has to look at the life stories of its various princes—Vlad Țepes, Constantin Brâncoveanu, Vasile Lupu, and many others—to see that, while fighting for independence, they were either forced or found it expedient to look for connections and sometimes assistance from their non-Christian neighbors. Several of the Byzantine emperors did much the same, occasionally relying on Arab support against their own Christian enemies.

Some Romanians today believe that the country would be better off both politically and economically if it made alliances with other Eastern European and Near East neighbors. In 1992, Romania joined the Black Sea Economic Cooperation (BSEC) along with 11 other countries, including Bulgaria, Georgia, Greece, Russia, and Turkey. The ultra-right-wing nationalist politician Corneliu Vadim Tudor was widely condemned for accepting expensive gifts from Saddam Hussein in the 1990s, but his actions highlight the fact that Romania's survival has always depended on a balancing act, and that its actions have not always been approved by Western powers.

Having only just joined NATO (in 2002) and the EU after a particularly shaky passage from the communist period, the country is still teetering on the tightrope, looking for safe ground. It is not surprising that it sometimes appears to be lurching from one seemingly contradictory position to another, as it searches to find what policies work best.

Finding a firm financial and governmental footing is not Romania's only concern. In private, many Romanians express their fears of being overrun by Russia. Memories of the U.S.S.R.'s annexation of Basarabia and Northern Bucovina (two regions within Moldavia province) still linger. The refusal of Russian-speaking Moldovans (from Basarbia—present-day Republic of Moldova) to accept a union with Romania has demolished the hopes of the ethnic Romanian majority of a unified, Romanian Republic of Moldova.

STATE OF AFFAIRS

The very good news is that, by many accounts, the Romanian economy is thriving. The embassy in Washington, D.C., reported in September 2006 that after several years of recession, Romania's gross domestic product has rebounded strongly in recent years. According to government figures, in 2004 it expanded by 8.3 percent. The World Bank's September 2006 report, *Doing Business 2007,* stated that Romania was the second "most active reformer" among 197 economies tested for "ease of doing business." Romania's finance ministers speeded up the drive toward a market economy as the country approached EU accession. On January 1, 2007, the day Romania joined, fireworks filled Bucharest's sky as the city threw its largest street party since the end of the 1989 revolution.

Issues that have plagued the nation are being addressed. Many badly run, state-owned companies have been sold off, corrupt orphanages have been closed down, a fledgling social security network is in place, and roads and railways are being improved to Western European standards.

No one, however, should underestimate the problems that still exist: Poverty is widespread, for instance, and many people are unhappy with a succession of governments they see as little more than communism under another name. But there are greatly encouraging signs. The Romanians have proven that they are incredibly resilient, adept at turning adversity into advantage. Young people in particular are showing that they want to see their country move ahead and can take charge. Right now they face huge, new challenges and uncertainties, but enormous opportunities as well. As the country moves forward into a new era, these are fascinating times, indeed. ∎

Food & drink

POFTĂ BUNĂ (BON APPETIT). ROMANIANS LOVE FOOD. THEY CAN SPEND hours choosing, preparing, and cooking it; and they adore sharing it with guests. A good meal is a source of pride. It is very important to be a good *gazdă* (hostess). Even when they have very little for themselves, Romanians will go out of their way to make sure that visitors have enough to eat and drink.

If you visit a Romanian's home, your host will offer you a glass of *ţuică* (plum brandy), to which you reply, "*Mulţumesc. Sănătate!*— Thanks. Cheers!" as you down it in one gulp. Even if the tuică, also known as *rachiu, palincă,* or *horincă,* has been properly distilled three times on a homebuilt copper boiler, it will feel as though your insides have been set on fire, so be warned. The writer Alan Ogden has coined the term "palinkered" for the state of stupefied merriment that a few glasses of tuică can induce. Wine, which is produced in many vineyards around Romania, is always flowing.

Romanians love to eat meat, and the meat is fat and flavorful. Many farmers keep livestock to provide their own food and to sell at local markets. Village farmers usually have a couple of cows, a few goats, a handful of sheep, a smattering of chickens and geese, and the indispensable pig. This last animal is fattened for Christmas, and every bit of the animal is used. The Romanians have a bewildering variety of sausages,

Bucharest's Piata Amzei hosts a lively and colorful open-air fruit and vegetable market.

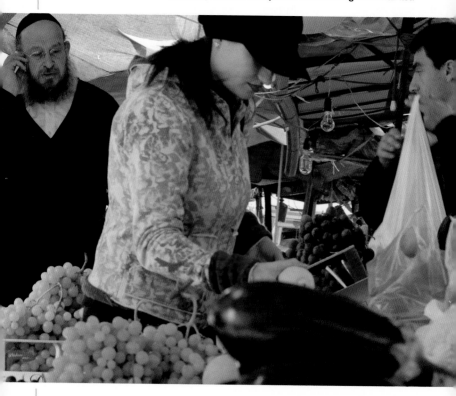

kremwursts, salamis, and black puddings. One of their favorite snacks is grilled *mititei,* skinless sausages made from a mixture of beef, pork, and mutton. Mititei are traditionally eaten with mustard and white bread and a glass of Romanian beer.

Women in country villages often make their own *pâine* (bread), pounding great masses of unleavened dough in broad wooden troughs. The term *harnică* (meaning a "sturdy, hardworking female") is regarded as a compliment. The old-fashioned communal ovens where villagers would take their bread to be baked have become a thing of the past, and the popularity of *pâine neagră* is on the rise; this black bread can either mean rye bread or whole wheat.

Romanians keep vegetable gardens or plots, and once the growing season is over they make pickles of *gogoșari* (red peppers) and *castraveți* (small cucumbers) to make sure they get vitamins during the winter. Most of the produce grown by smallholders is organic by default since few people can afford chemical fertilizers or pesticides. There have been enthusiastic moves to convert the large Romanian farms to organic production, but as yet they are few and far between.

Romanian open-air fruit and vegetable markets are marvelous places. Try buying your food from them as you travel around; it will be cheap, nutritious, and tasty. In late summer and autumn, the umbrella-shaded trestles will be piled high with fresh *mere* (apples), *pere* (pears), *struguri* (grapes), and *roșii* (tomatoes). The perimeter of the market will usually feature a *brutărie* (bakery) selling hot, fresh loaves; a *măcelărie* (butcher) for meats and sausages; and a little store for *apă minerală* (Romania has scores of different varieties of mineral water) or a *lăptărie* (dairy) for *lapte* (milk) and *cașcaval* (hard cheese).

At restaurants, you'll find traditional Romanian dishes such as *sarmale* (croquettes of pork and beef mince wrapped in cabbage leaves and cooked on a bed of chopped cabbage mixed with tomatoes); *salată de vinete* (baked eggplant pulp mixed with oil and masses of garlic);

tocană (a rich meat stew); and *ciorbă țărănească* (vegetable soup with sour cream and with or without meat). *Mămăliga,* regarded as Romania's national dish, is a delicious polenta made from bright yellow

Top: *Mămăligă, sarmale,* and sour cream. Bottom: Mititei, flavorful minced-meat rolls, are spiced with a variety of savory herbs before being grilled.

cornmeal that has been boiled slowly until it forms a mash and then turned out to set. It is usually served with sour cream and cheese or meat.

You can also enjoy the wild range of puddings and desserts; try a *papanași* (a warm doughnut drenched in jam and lashings of cream) or a Turkish-style baklava served with Turkish coffee and a glass of sherbet. ∎

Land & wildlife

ROMANIA BOASTS SOME OF THE FINEST LANDSCAPES IN EAST-CENTRAL AND southeastern Europe. They offer alpine heights, isolated plateaus, and crenellated karsts to rolling steppes, wide-open plains, and grand littoral, with many gradations in between. Most striking of all are the Carpathian Mountains and the Danube Delta, Europe's most extensive wetland. In the mountains, spring meadows bloom with magnificent displays of narcissi; as the year progresses, they unfold carpets of gentian, minute dianthus, and other flowers. With an abundance of mixed deciduous forests, the fall colors are splendid, too. Thanks to the relatively rural nature of the country and the difficulty of farming in the mountains, these landscapes support a wealth of wildlife.

Covering 91,700 square miles (237,499 sq km), Romania is roughly half the size of France. It has 140 miles (225 km) of coastline along the western edge of the Black Sea. Its southern border is defined by the Danube, which, along with the Siret and the Prut, drains the entire country. In the 1970s, a new dam near Drobeta Turnu Severin raised the river's height and made it easier for ships to navigate the Iron Gates gorges. The river provides the nation with an important source of hydroelectric power. Romania's other main rivers are the Mureș, which runs 477 miles (768 km) west from northeast Transylvania; the 457-mile-long (736 km) Olt, which cuts a wide valley in the southern Carpathians to the east of Sibiu before plunging south in a virtually straight line; the Siret, which runs southward in eastern Romania for 290 miles (470 km) before joining tha Danube; and the 445-mile-long (716 km) Prut, which forms Romania's border with Moldova and meets the Danube just west of the Danube Delta.

GEOLOGY

The Carpathian Mountains are Romania's most spectacular feature and cover a third of the country. They were created millions of years ago, a result of massive collisions between the two tectonic plates that folded the Earth's crust from the Himalayas to the Alps. The mountains once formed Europe's longest volcanic chain, but only one extinct crater remains; located north of Brașov, it holds the volcanic lake Lacul Sf. Ana.

With one end in the Czech Republic and the other in northern Serbia, the Carpathian range crosses Romania in a roughly U-shaped curve that runs from the northwest to the

southwest. The highest and broadest points lie in the center of the curve, in southeast Transylvania and northern Muntenia; they reveal that the rocks flowed away from the apex in both directions. Successive processes of sedimentation, further geological movements, and constant weathering have created dramatic skylines above densely forested slopes.

Although smaller than the European Alps, Romania's mountains are equally spectacular. Mount Moldoveanu stands the tallest at 8,346 feet (2,544 m). The Carpathians were glaciated; its Făgăraş and Retezat ranges are peppered with glacial lakes and rock massifs that were created when the ice melted about 10,000 years ago.

The geology of the Carpathians consists of three distinct layers. There is the outer, continuous flysch that binds them together, a central crystalline band, and an inner, volcanic ribbon. This rich blend of rocks has endowed the

Râşnov castle's scenic setting lies midway between Bran and Braşov in Transylvania.

mountains with supplies of ferrous and non-ferrous metals, delicately colored marble (found in the Apuseni Mountains), valuable building stone, and marvelous crystals. In many places the mountains are riddled with caves and underground streams.

The two-thirds of Romania not given over to the Carpathians is split equally between a series of hills and plateaus—which for centuries supported orchards and vineyards—and an eastern plain of rich, dark chernozem soil, which supports cereals, vegetables, herbs, and other crops. The easternmost area of Romania, Dobrogea, lies east of the Danube as it makes its final fling north to the Black Sea. Mainly low-lying steppe, Dobrogea contains a spine of hills called Munţii Măcinului. These mountains are the country's oldest, dating from between the Paleozoic and the Mezozoic periods, 543 million to 65 million years ago. Also known as the Hercynian Range, they have been designated a national nature reserve.

CLIMATE

Climatologists classify Romania's climate as temperate-continental; however, because of the varied geography, temperature and conditions can vary enormously from place to place. The warmest regions are in the south and on the coast. The seasons range between extremely hot summers and bitterly cold winters; temperatures as low as $-4°F$ ($-20°C$) are not unusual in mountain areas during the wintertime. There is usually a lot of snow from mid-December until the end of March. At the other end of the scale, the average summer temperature in the plains around Bucharest and near the Black Sea coast is between 75° and 86°F (24–30°C). These areas can be much hotter, especially Bucharest during July and August.

For most of Romania, spring begins in the middle of March, but in the mountains and the north it comes later. A lot of rain falls in the spring, especially in Transylvania and the Carpathian Mountains, averaging some 23 to 27 inches (600–700 mm). In summer, thunderstorms and heavy rain are common in the mountains. Autumn—a period of warm, balmy days—starts in September and lasts until late October. In 2002 and 2003, Romania suffered severe droughts, followed by devastating floods made worse by extensive deforestation.

THE CULTIVATED LANDSCAPE

Although the communists pursued an aggressive industrialization agenda, Romania escaped the industrial revolution that affected most of northern Europe and it is still extremely green, despite a recent acceleration in the deforestation rate.

About 41 percent of the country's total landmass is given over to arable farming. Once the collective and state farms had been broken up in the early 1990s, the small farms system returned with a vengeance. Owners of properties that had been requisitioned by the communists were granted up to 25 acres (10 ha) of agricultural terrain and 2.5 acres (1 ha) of forest, no matter how large their former holdings had been. As a result, many rural areas have been divided up into tiny parcels; the laws of partible inheritance have made some parcels even smaller. In some areas, like northeastern Moldavia, the countryside looks like a giant quilt. For mile upon rolling mile, the steppe is patterned with thousands of individual, unfenced strips lying parallel or at right angles to one another. This phenomenon is quite unlike what is seen in neighboring Bulgaria and Serbia, where large modern farms sprang up quite fast after the fall of communism.

In the dire economic conditions that prevailed after the fall of communism, these modest, private holdings helped to sustain many people who might otherwise have starved. After the property laws were relaxed, many country people started keeping a cow, a pig, and a clutch of chickens. In addition, many villages own common land where sheep, geese, and horses can often be seen milling about the sward. When the state farms and collectives disappeared, so too did a fair share of farming equipment. The sudden and mysterious disappearance of most of the country's tractors meant that smallholders had to revert to picturesque but time-consuming methods of tilling the soil and transporting their goods. Horse-, ox-, and donkey-drawn carts became a common sight since few people could afford a car. It was as though the Middle Ages had returned.

In mountain areas, where collectivization did not work, the landscape has been shaped by Romania's alternative to the industrial revolution: a revolution in wood technology. Necessity and creativity created rugged, handmade tools for gathering hay and cutting flax; water-powered mills for flour, oil, and wine presses; salt pestles; and outdoor whirlpools for washing clothes and fulling textiles. The most imposing of the rural wooden items are the very structures built to store these tools: Barns and sheds, as well as single-story homes and quirkily

with clusters of individualistic haystacks, all set against the sweep of Carpathian highlands, is an unforgettable experience.

WILDLIFE

Romania has a high level of biodiversity and ecological systems. They are largely dependent on the survival of the mountain forests and the Danube Delta. The forests support a full range of European fauna, including 60 percent and 40 percent, respectively, of the European

In spring millions of pelicans migrate thousands of miles from Siberia to the Danube Delta.

elegant churches. Many of these tools and buildings are still in use.

Sadly, many rural Romanians would prefer new housing because their timber houses remind them of the unhappy past. But to the visitor, these old-fashioned farm buildings make the country special. To survey whole villages of ground-hugging wooden houses with high-pitched roofs and formidable carved gates, panning out to orchards and closely mown fields dotted

brown bear and wolf populations, and part of Europe's only healthy population of wild lynx. Despite their numbers, these "big three" Carpathian carnivores are very difficult to spot (see pp. 142–43). Other mountainous, subendemic species include the red deer, chamois, and wild boar.

A huge range of birds can be seen in the mountains but the highest concentration of migrating species, including the rare white and pink pelican, are found in the delta. ■

Rounded bastions provided defense at Stephen the Great's 15th-century citadel in Suceava.

History of Romania

ON THE MAP ROMANIA LOOKS LIKE A SINGLE COUNTRY. BUT THE NATION-state is relatively young by European standards: It was founded in 1859 and incorporated Transylvania only in 1918. Before that, its lands were separated by political, religious, and geographical barriers. What links them is the language, a Latin tongue isolated amid Hungarian and Slavic speakers. As Romanians often say, "We are an island of Latinity in a sea of Slavs."

ROMANIA'S EARLY HISTORY

Many archaeologists believe that Romania has been inhabited continuously for at least 60,000 years. New evidence supporting this theory was found in 2002 when a 36,000-year-old skeleton discovered in the Peştera cu Oase cave in Oltenia. The oldest human remains ever found in Europe, the bones cast new light on the development between Neanderthal and early modern humans.

Romania was part of Old Europe, the southeastern area of the continent that developed faster than the west because of its proximity to the Fertile Crescent. Between 6000 and 4000 B.C., sophisticated neolithic peoples, including the cultures known as Ariuşd, Cucuteni, and Gumelniţa, inherited Near Eastern technology; glimpses of their skills can be found in superbly decorated,

modern-looking pottery and cult images made of stone and clay.

A scattering of words such as *balaur* (dragon), *doină* (lament), and *măgura* (hill) show that Thracians were among the Romanians' ancestors, too. These nomadic, horse-riding Indo-Europeans arrived in southeast Europe sometime after 2500 B.C. Fifteen hundred years later, the descendants of these brave and fair-minded people (to paraphrase the fifth-century B.C. Greek historian Herodotus) were still there. Some of their tribes occupied what are now Transylvania, Moldavia, and Wallachia. The Romans called them Dacians, while the Greek name for them was Getae. Under the dynamic Burebista (ca 82–44 B.C.), the Dacians' empire stretched from the Balkan Mountains (in Bulgaria) to Dobrogea in the south and from the Bug and Dniestr rivers in the east to the Danube River in Hungary and Moravia in the present-day Czech Republic.

The Romans wanted Dacia for its gold. During their 165-year occupation (A.D. 106–271), they extracted several billion dollars' worth of gold (at today's prices). They also built towns and cities, traded salt with the "free Dacians" of Crişana and Maramureş (which lay outside the Roman borders), cultivated vineyards, and intermarried with the indigenous population. In A.D. 271, menaced by Germanic and Asiatic tribes, Emperor Aurelian withdrew his legal protection of Dacia. After the army legions left, many Romans stayed behind to look after their estates.

During the next millennium, Asiatic and Caucasian tribes used Romania as a corridor to the west. As climate changes impoverished their grasslands, nomadic Cumans and Pechenegs (Turkic peoples) and many others traversed the Danube plains looking for better grazing and richer conditions.

ROMANIA AFTER THE ROMANS

Romania has rarely been absolutely free in the sense of a self-governing, sovereign state. Freedom has been fleeting and insecure. The four historic regions that constitute modern Romania—Dobrogea, Moldavia, Transylvania, and Wallachia—were dominated for most of their existence by Hungarians, Habsburgs, and Turks. Each region has its own unique history.

Dobrogea

Dobrogea—whose name is thought to come from a 14th-century ruler called Dobrotici or from a Turkic word for Bulgarians—comprises the lands between the Danube River and the Black Sea at the eastern end of Romania. Colonized by Greeks in the seventh century B.C., it was later ruled by Romans and then Byzantines. Between the 7th and 14th centuries, a succession of invading forces, including the Avars, Bulgarians, Genoese, Romanians, and Tatars, laid claim. In the early 15th century, the region became part of the Ottoman Empire. It remained in Turkey's hands until 1878, when Romania helped Russia to liberate the western fringes of the Black Sea. Although now unquestionably Romanian, Dobrogea remains a land apart.

Moldavia

In northeastern Romania, sandwiched between the Carpathian Mountains and the Prut River, Moldavia is all that remains of a medieval principality that once encompassed what are now southern Ukraine and the independent Republic of Moldova. Although partially conquered by Hungary, Moldavia came into Romanian hands when a Maramureş nobleman called Bogdan founded a principality there in 1359. Under the Romanians, Moldavia became predominantly Orthodox.

Moldavia had a Jewish presence as well. Some of the earliest records show that Jewish Khazars from the Caucasus settled in Basarabia, the eastern part of Moldavia, in the eighth century. Between the 15th and 17th centuries, many of the Jews who were expelled from Spain settled in northern Moldavia and Basarabia.

In 1453, Mehmet II's conquest of Constantinople, the center of Orthodox Christianity, sent shock waves throughout eastern Europe. By alternately fighting and paying a tribute, Moldavia's princes managed to keep the Turks at bay until the mid-16th century. Some of these leaders are celebrated as national heroes: Ştefan cel Mare (1437–1504) still raises a cheer for the 30-something battles he won against the Turks, and his son, Petru Rareş (R. 1504–1517), is admired for embellishing Moldavia's churches with stunning paintings. The only contemporary portrait we have of Ştefan (in a 15th-century Gospel book) shows a rubicund figure in an attitude of prayer. But Ştefan was a ruthless pragmatist who was known to impale his victims and deal in Gypsy slaves. Somehow, though, he has never provoked the opprobrium of his cousin, Vlad the Impaler, who resorted to the same methods.

Suleiman the Magnificent turned Moldavia into a suzerain state in 1526. He allowed the native princes to rule and worship as they wished provided they were compliant to him. Naturally, Moldavia's leaders continued to seek their freedom by forming secret alliances with other more powerful neighbors. This period ended in the early 18th century when Ahmed III imposed

Phanariot princes on Moldavia and Wallachia. These Greek-speaking rulers from the Phanar (European) district of Istanbul earned a reputation for outrageous corruption and extravagant behavior: One ruler made his horse a minister, while Nicolae Mavrogheni (*R.* 1786–89) used to ride through Bucharest in a carriage drawn by two stags. Despite what might be considered his eccentricities, Mavrogheni did introduce constructive reforms during his rule. In 1774, the Habsburgs annexed Bucovina (an area of northern Moldavia), which gave the Austrians a corridor to Transylvania.

Transylvania

Historic Transylvania comprises the Transylvania Plateau, which is enclosed within the deep curve of the Carpathian Mountains, and the regions of Banat, Crişana, and Maramureş, which lie west and north of the plateau. In the ninth century, Magyars (Hungarians) from the Don River began their thousand-year colonization of Transylvania.

In the 12th and 13th centuries, Hungary's kings invited northern Europeans to settle in Transylvania. In return for cultivating the land and protecting Transylvania's borders, they were given property and privileges. Although

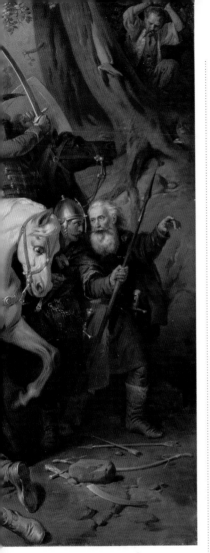

József Molnár's 1885 painting depicts the pivotal 1330 Battle of Posada.

troublesome Teutonic Knights. But the Saxons were not invincible. In 1241 and 1242, Mongolian horsemen from Batu Khan's army devastated Transylvania as well as neighboring Hungary, Moldavia, and Wallachia. The Mongols left thousands dead and the countryside was reduced to a smoldering ruin.

The Saxons lived in constant danger of Tatar and Turkish incursions. In response, the Saxons strengthened their cities and built scores of *kirchenbürgen*—fortified church complexes—to protect their rural communities. Their massive towers and walls still pepper the landscape.

Fascinating cultural crossovers occurred in Transylvania during Hungarian rule. For instance, a couple of decades after the Turkish conquest of 1526, some rapid horse-trading allowed Hungarian princes to rule the Transylvanian Plateau as a semi-independent state; a pasha installed Turkish baths in Banat's capital of Timişoara; and, farther east, Hungarian rulers introduced Renaissance architecture to Transylvania.

Under the Hungarian kings (who were Catholics), the mainly Orthodox Romanians existed on the margins. Most of them were serfs, peasants, and woodsmen. They were among the poorest, least privileged, and most despised members of society; they had little voice and their religion was barely tolerated. To prosper, ethnic Romanians needed to adopt Hungarian names (making it difficult today to tell how many actually lived in Transylvania). Pockets of "free Romanians" existed in several areas, including the Apuseni mountains, the Haţeg country, in Mărginimea Sibiului, around Făgăraş, and in Maramureş.

Outside of Transylvania, the Hungarians had their own run-ins with the Ottoman Turks. In 1683, the Turks besieged the city of Vienna for the second time; the Hungarians, along with the Polish, went to the aid of the Habsburgs. They successfully managed to push the Turkish army back across eastern Europe, but then the Habsburgs turned on the Hungarians. They captured Transylvania in 1687.

The Habsburgs saw themselves as enlightened and progressive. Social and

called Saxons because many of them came from Saxony in northern Germany, the settlers also came from the Mosel Valley and Lower Rhine, from Flanders, Wallonia, and Luxembourg, and from Bavaria and Hesse. Craftsmen and farmers, castellans (castle guardians) and priests, they brought technological know-how that they quickly put to use.

By the 14th century, the Saxons had established prosperous, self-reliant cities that resembled medieval German fortified towns. Industrious and determined, the Saxons proved reliable allies. In 1225, they helped King Endre II rid his country of the economic engineering went on apace. The Austrians were staunch Catholics and, thanks to the Great Schism of 1054, regarded Orthodoxy as anathema. Empress Maria Theresa ordered Orthodox churches to be burned and had their priests killed. Romanians were offered rewards if they converted to Greco-Catholicism, a halfway house between Orthodoxy and Catholicism, while army veterans from the empire's Czech, German, Italian, Serb, and Spanish territories were encouraged to develop the Romanian lands, which the Turks had neglected.

In 1848, Hungarians and Romanians joined forces in Transylvania against the increasingly hidebound Austrian reign. During the revolution, the Romanians switched sides, hoping that the Habsburgs would grant them more freedom. But Emperor Franz Joseph was terrified of losing control and brought in the Russian Army to crush the revolt. In the late 19th century, the ethnic Romanian majority (sustained despite 800 years of Hungarian, Austrian, and then again Hungarian colonization) increased its nationalist claims, but the newly formed Austro-Hungarian Empire—Hungary had submitted to Austrian rule, resulting in the creation of the empire in 1867—held firm, keeping Transylvania until 1918.

Wallachia

Containing the capital city of Bucharest, Wallachia is the most quintessentially Romanian of all the provinces. It lies in the south, between the Carpathian Mountains and the Danube River. Wallachia comprises two regions: Muntenia and Oltenia. Muntenia (known as Țara Românească, the Romanian Land) occupies the land between the Olt and Danube rivers. Oltenia, to the west of the Olt, was the Dacian heartland, and a distinct Roman province (Dacia Inferior and later Malvensis). In the 13th century, it had its own Romanian polity, which eventually merged with Muntenia to form Wallachia.

Wallachia's first independent Romanian ruler was Basarab I (ca 1310–1352)—his name probably comes from the fact that his family owned estates in Basarabia, the eastern part of Moldavia. Having thwarted the Hungarian king Carol Robert (Károly

A rare contemporary portrait of Dracula— brutal Prince Vlad III, known as the Impaler

Róbert) at the Battle of Posada in 1330, Basarab turned Wallachia into an Orthodox nation whose closest allies were the Bulgarians and Serbs.

As in Moldavia, Wallachia lay on the border between Christianity and Islam. Its princes fought ferociously to maintain their freedom, and they learned how to survive. In 1396, King Sigismund of Hungary asked Wallachia to help recapture the Bulgarian fortress of Nicopolis from Ottoman sultan Bajazet. Sigismund's crusade included French and English knights who were fired by a sense of chivalric idealism. In her telling account, *A Distant Mirror* (1978), Barbara Tuchman gives the Wallachian leader, Prince Mircea cel Bătrân (Mircea the Old, 1386–1418), credit for his greater military experience. But Sigismund regarded Mircea as an inferior "schismatic." Rejecting Mircea's advice, he charged headlong into a Turkish trap. The crusade was decimated, but Mircea lived to rule Dobrogea.

As a boy, Prince Vlad III Dracula (the Impaler) was held hostage from 1431 to 1436 in the sultan's court, where he learned Turkish methods of dealing with enemies, including impalement. Reigning three times between

1448 and 1476, Vlad frightened the sultan's army by impaling its advance guard on a forest of spikes. He meted cruel and summary justice to anyone who threatened his realm. His devilish reputation probably originates from 1460, when Vlad impaled 1,200 Saxons of Braşov in retribution for disobeying his trade laws. Woodcuts were circulated in Germany and Russia showing the ghoulish prince eating

Turkish sultans still their suzerain lords, Wallachia's princes were often caught in an impossible situation, preferring Western help but wary of provoking savage reprisals. A document of 1690 shows how Constantin Brâncoveanu (1654–1714) reacted to just such a dilemma. On hearing that a Habsburg general was on his way to Bucharest to ask for Romanian support against the Turks,

The Village Museum in the lakeside glades of Parcul Herăstrău, Bucharest

a meal beside the tortured townspeople. The prints set the seal on Dracula's reputation, and a whole industry was born. But even Vlad the Impaler could not stop the Ottoman flood. Eventually in the 1500s, the Wallachians had no option but to cede power to the Turks. An uncomfortable coexistence persisted for years, although some Turkish habits were embraced: The 17th-century traveler Paul of Aleppo tells us that Prince Constantin Şerban (R. 1654–58) kept a harem in Târgovişte.

After defeating the Turks at the 1683 Siege of Vienna, the rulers of Hungary, Poland, tsarist Russia, and the Habsburg Empire forced the Turks back across eastern Europe, where each country pursued its own agenda. With the

Brâncoveanu left town, leaving instructions that the Austrians were to be given all the supplies they needed. The general requested the prince return and talk. In response, Brâncoveanu called a council meeting to ask for advice. His ministers and nobles were divided: Some favored fighting the Turks, while others feared that fighting would provoke the nearby Tatars (the Turks' allies) to retaliate savagely and that the Austrians would not help. Faced with this quandary, the Wallachians went fishing, choosing to ignore the problem. Sadly such tactics did not save Brâncoveanu; in 1714 Sultan Ahmed III summoned him to Istanbul, where he was executed along with four of his sons.

A shrine to Ceauşescu lauds his communist ideals at the Museum of the Romanian Peasant.

As in Moldavia, a century of mixed Phanariot rule followed 200 years of Turkish suzerainty. Throughout the 17th and 18th centuries, Austria, Russia, and Turkey fought for control of the Danubian lands, frequently using Wallachia as their battleground. With their power beginning to erode, the Turks took their anger out on Romanians. While landowners protected themselves in fortified towers, the peasants of the plains literally dug themselves into the ground (you can see an example of a half-buried house in the Bucharest Village Museum).

Romanian princes were reinstated in 1821 after the Phanariots were thrown out, but Wallachia had to wait until 1878 before the Turkish veil was finally lifted. Nineteenth-century Wallachia experienced a cultural shift as reinstated Romanian princes looked to the West. France was a natural ally because of its language. Russia, which ruled Moldavia and Wallachia as a protectorate from 1829 and encouraged their union, also had a westernizing influence.

A UNIFIED ROMANIA

Following the first phase of unification in 1859, Romania experienced a few decades of prosper-

ity under the German-born King Carol I (*R.* 1866–1914). After the turn of the 20th century, the country regained Basarabia—the eastern part of Moldavia that lies between the Prut and Dniestr rivers and had been lost to tsarist Russia in 1812—in 1918, along with Bucovina (part of northern Moldavia) and southern Dobrogea. Romania's unification with Transylvania in 1918 brought great joy. Although Transylvania had been ruled by Hungary for more than a thousand years, Romanians see the region as part of their own even more ancient heritage. Over the centuries, Romanians had become Transylvania's majority population, validating Romania's claim to the region after the collapse of the Austro-Hungarian Empire and the end of World War I.

After the war, grain exports helped Romania become one of the richest countries in Europe. But fallout from World War I, the collapse of the Habsburg Empire, the rise of communism (which was widely attributed to Jews), and the resultant fascist retaliation spread fear and strife across young, volatile states.

During the interwar period, the government lived in fear of losing the territories it had gained, most especially the region of Basarabia. Anti-Semitism fanned by the fear of a Jewish-Soviet plot spawned the ultra-nationalist Legionary movement. To stem the growing unrest, King Carol II (R. 1930–1940) imposed a royal dictatorship, and hoping that the Germans would protect Basarabia in the event of a Soviet invasion, allied himself with Hitler. The Nazi leader then responded by giving part of northern and western Transylvania to the Hungarians (the Vienna Award, 1940–44). Also in 1940, Romania was forced to cede Basarabia to the Soviet Union (the Romanian peace treaty of 1947 confirmed the annexation of the land, which is now known as the Republic of Moldova).

That same year, King Carol fled the country with his Jewish mistress, leaving his 18-year-old son Michael behind as king and the right-wing Marshal Antonescu in charge. Under Antonescu, anti-Semitic pogroms took place in Bucharest and Iaşi, and thousands of Jews were deported to Transnistria across the Dniestr River. On Germany's request, Romania invaded the Soviet Union. In 1944, King Michael (R. 1940–47) made a secret deal with the Allies and Romania changed sides. But the country's fate was sealed at the Yalta Conference, which spelled disaster for Eastern Europe as a whole.

In the 1946 elections, Soviet agents claimed 80 percent of the vote. Widespread incidents of violence and fraud occurred, and opposition parties such as Iuliu Maniu's democratic Partidul Naţional Ţărănesc (National Peasants' Party) were pushed aside. In 1947, King Michael was forced to abdicate, leaving the communists completely in control. Forty years of brutal repression ensued, alleviated by a brief period of liberalization in the 1960s.

ROMANIA UNDER COMMUNISM

Romania's communist government was one of the most brutal regimes in Eastern Europe. By contrast with Poland, where dissidents were supported by the Catholic Church, no opposition was allowed in Romania and leaders of the Orthodox Church collaborated with the communists. The secret police, known as Securitatea, was split into several

The fighting that ended Ceauşescu's 24-year dictatorship left more than a thousand people dead.

Elation in Bucharest as Romania finally joins the European Union on January 1, 2007

different factions, each cruelly repressive and suspicious of the others. In the 1950s, under Gheorghe Gheorghiu-Dej's rule (1948–1965), "enemies of the people"—intellectuals, local priests, landowners, and anyone who opposed the authorities—were worked to death on the Black Sea canal project or sent to jails from which they never returned. Torture was commonplace. There were patches of resistance in the Făgăraş and Apuseni Mountains and here and there, now and then, people spoke out against the oppression. Gheorghiu-Dej and his successor, Nicolae Ceauşescu (R. 1965–1989), distanced Romania from the Soviet Union. In the first five years of Ceauşescu's rule, a liberating breeze blew through Romania, but delusions of grandeur soon went to his head; life for his people became increasingly dire, and he was widely but secretly viewed as a monster. Seemingly laudable attempts to pay off the national debt brought starvation, and thanks to the climate of suspicion, neighbor lived in fear of neighbor—sometimes families were even set against each other. Notoriously, women were forced to have children to increase the population; their unwanted babies were abandoned to Dickensian orphanages, where many became infected with HIV.

In 1987, factory workers in Braşov rebelled. Their uprising was crushed by the army. But the Iron Curtain was showing signs of wear. In March 1989, six prominent members of the Communist Party wrote an open letter to Ceauşescu criticizing his abuses

ideal solution, the world hoped that this would end the Romanians' terror and bring them happiness at last. It has been more complicated than that, but, for the moment at least, the Romanians are finding their way.

AFTER THE REVOLUTION

Economic conditions in Romania after the fall of communism were dire, with unemployment rampant. Thousands of Romanians became migrant workers abroad with the hope of sending money back to their families; sometimes they risked life and limb to get out of the country. The vast majority were respectable people determined to make an honest income, and they have not always been treated well. The Relief Fund for Romania reports that since the 1990s, the population has decreased by some two million people because so many have become migrant workers. The trend toward migrant work continues today, but construction opportunities in Romania are now better paid, enticing many Romanians to stay or return home.

In December 2006, President Traian Băsescu officially condemned the communist dictatorship. Speaking before the joint chambers of parliament in the presence of former Czech president Vaclav Havel, former Bulgarian president Jelio Jelev, and former Polish president and Nobel Peace Prize winner Lech Walesa, he called the regime "illegitimate and criminal." Bold in its language and stance, the speech named and blamed individuals who still held high office. But more important, Băsescu's statement was the first time the head of a former Eastern Bloc country spoke out about the past.

Faced with a terrible history—a seemingly endless onslaught of slavery and oppression, devastation and occupation—Romanians have coped with it in various ways: strong religious faith, resistance (frequent uprisings), compliance (bowing their heads to avoid decapitation), and escape (taking to the mountains). The Romanians used to say that music and laughter are the cure for all ills, and this lighter, more Mediterranean attitude still prevails. Another often repeated retort is *"Ce să facem?*—What can we do about it?" accompanied by a deep sigh and a wry smile. ■

of power and his economic policies. The letter was circulated in the West and read on Radio Free Europe. News that he had renewed his plan to "modernize"—destroy—thousands of Romania's rural villages also leaked out, causing an international outcry.

On December 14, 1989, the first Romanian outbreak against communism took place in Iaşi, the largest city in Moldova. It was quickly squashed, but just a few days later, László Tőkés, an ethnic Hungarian priest living in Timişoara, triggered the dictator's fall. This outspoken critic of the regime refused to accept dismissal and, for once, emboldened by events elsewhere, the people supported him. More than a thousand individuals were killed during the fighting that December and in ensuing months. But Ceauşescu had gone, shot after a kangaroo trial. Though not an

Romanian culture & art

TO MOST OUTSIDERS, THE THOUGHT OF ROMANIA CONJURES UP IMAGES OF Dracula and nothing else. The reality is much more interesting. Born from a group of neighboring countries, each of which looked in different directions, Romania has absorbed influences from practically every point of the compass. Thracian and Latin influences have merged with Asiatic and Germanic ones, French with Slavic, Greek with Hungarian, Jewish with Armenian. Romania's art, architecture, literature, and music all show signs of cultural crossovers.

Most of all, Romania's culture is expressed by its people. Museums can invent stratagems to engage your imagination, but the astonishing life of this country is to be found in the streets and villages, the mountainside sheepfolds, the pastures at haymaking time, the village celebrations, and the welcome you will find in people's homes. Fragile though they are, these traditions are what make Romania different. And even as they vanish, they have the capacity to gladden the heart.

Romania is in flux, struggling to reinvent itself culturally and economically as well as politically. From a Western, Christian perspective, Romania lies on the edge of Europe. Communism brought separation of a different kind: The Iron Curtain sealed the country more perfectly than the Turkish Empire did. Now that the curtain has risen, Romanian art and culture are changing dynamically.

The greatest impression on today's travelers to Romania is not so much the cultural interface between East and West but rather the differences between old and new. And in this context there are two versions of the new: Ceaușescu's wave of destructive urbanization and the post-1989 market explosion.

Right now, many individuals are cashing in by selling off property to foreign investors. As well as improvements in roads and telecommunications, the introduction of modern banking and Internet cafés, progress means shopping malls and masses of new building and an unregulated explosion of frantic advertising, garlanding anything that stands, including street lights, walls, and even trees.

In this tidal wave of consumerism and entrepreneurship, Romania's rural heritage stands out. As development takes place, the

Rehearsing the nightly folk dance performance at a restaurant on Strada Doamnei, Bucharest

amazing facets of Romania's country life may be the first to disappear. How do you save the charm of something that depends on isolation for its existence? Luckily, Romanians do not always share the pessimistic outlook of their Western friends.

VILLAGE LIFE

Romania's rural heritage is still alive, an invisible doorway into Europe's past. It incorporates all kinds of crafts, including spinning and weaving, woodcarving, metalwork, painting icons on glass, and painting gorgeous and intricate patterns on eggs. Specific customs relating to sheep rearing, house building, plowing, and hay making still exist, as well as such arcane rituals as celebrating the Green Man on St. George's Day, chasing the best farmer and baptizing him in the river, and welcoming spring with fertility dances.

Ironically, communism played a role in the survival of this heritage. Ceauşescu, no less, praised the Romanian ţărani (peasants) and the values of village life. During a 1974 visit to Maramureş, he implored his fellow country-

men to preserve their traditional customs and values. However, he completely reversed his position in 1988, planning to destroy all the country's old villages as part of a nationwide drive for industrialization and mechanization.

Yet some aspects of the traditional scenes the Maramureș land and the neglected plains is still remarkable. But even in the mountains, the communist regime discouraged large gatherings. They outlawed markets and even prevented people from taking their grain to be ground in the flour mills—in case the villagers

Images of the national poet, Mihai Eminescu, can be seen everywhere in Romania.

you see are actually steps backward in the progress. In the 1970s, Romania's roads and communications were in far better condition than they were in 1989. And after the 1989 revolution, much of the country's agricultural machinery disappeared. Tractors and combine harvesters were sold on the black market. Romania's smallholders had no option but to resort to ancestral methods: The remaining horses—in the 1960s, 600,000 of the best-quality animals had been slaughtered or sold from under their owners to signal industrialization was the future—as well as donkeys, oxen, and buffalo were pressed into service as draft animals to pull plows, carry hay, and transport people to town. The horse still has a special place in Romanian affections. Owners often decorate their driving bridles with red tassels; this tradition began as a means to frighten away evil spirits, but now it serves more to give the equipage a jaunty look.

In more inaccessible mountainous areas, traditional farming methods continued without disruption. The high pastures were not collectivized or turned into state farms. In the Maramureș, people continued to look after their smallholdings as they had always done. The difference in appearance between

should start discussing their grievances.

But the image of an ideal village life still persists, in Romanian minds as well as in the imaginations of foreign city-dwellers who long for a return to the land. It goes back to the spirit of national revival that pervaded Romanian culture in the late 18th and 19th centuries. As Romanians emerged from Turkish rule, and nationalist consciences emerged in Transylvania, they were inspired by the image of the Dacians as national heroes who symbolized courage, intelligence, and independence of spirit.

The rural influence on music & literature

Poets and composers began collecting vernacular words and recording country music, dances, and songs. Well-known writers and musicians such as Anton Pann (ca 1790–1854), Mihai Eminescu (1850–1889), Vasile Alecsandri (1821–1890), and Alecsandri's contemporary Alecu Russo (1819–1859) invested time and energy in researching Romania's cultural roots. Pann was a Roma poet and composer who wrote the music to *Deşteaptă-te, române!*, Romania's national anthem. Eminescu was an actor, polemical journalist, and ardent nationalist. But he is best known as Romania's national poet, the author of *Luceafărul (The Morning Star).* Acknowledged as his masterpiece, this deceptively simple poem of 98 rhyming verses is a deeply lyrical evocation of the world of the living and the dead; it was inspired by a Romanian fairy tale. Alecsandri and Russo researched folktales and legends and are credited with recording the *Miorița,* an oral poem that became an allegory for salvation through self-sacrifice.

Many of these writers found their individual voices thanks to Junimea (Youth), a movement founded by the influential critic Titu Maiorescu (1840–1917). Based in Iaşi, Maiorescu became one of Romania's leading Conservative politicians, but he is still remembered for his key role in promoting Romanian culture. After the 1829 Treaty of Adrianople, Turkey had to relinquish its monopoly of Romanian trade. This change opened the floodgates to Europe, offering a bewildering choice in cultural as well as material novelties. Maiorescu saw this influx as a threat. He wanted artists to forge identities from their own indigenous Romanian culture rather than slavishly copying Western European styles.

Junimea's literary progeny included the storyteller Ion Creangă (1839–1889), who charmed generations of children with his witty tales of peasant life, and the satirical playwright Ion Luca Caragiale (1852–1912). Strengthening the national tradition, Liviu Rebreanu (1885–1944) also concentrated on rural life in *Ion* (1920), a melodramatic story of love, jealousy, and betrayal. But Rebreanu's reputation rests more certainly on *Pădurea Spânzuraţilor (The Forest of the Hanged,* 1922). Based on his brother's life, this novel tells the World War I tragedy of Apostol Bologa, a man hanged for trying to escape from the Habsburg army so that he could join the Romanian side.

Mihail Sadoveanu (1880–1961) focused on the decency and uprightness of country people in his famous tale *Băltagul (The Hatchet).* By contrast, in the two-volume *Moromeţii,* Marin Preda (1922–1980) gave a searing picture of the miseries faced by peasant communities between the two world wars. The novel focuses

A villager in Oltenia spins yarn in front of a television decorated with a handwoven sampler.

on the narrowness and unsentimental practicality of their existence, but Preda's characters are brought to life by their stoicism and humor.

RELIGION

Romanians are very religious. Proud of their Christian ancestry, they say that they were "born believers." According to classical sources, St. Andrew preached to their ancestors, the Dacians, when he visited Scythia Minor (now Dobrogea).

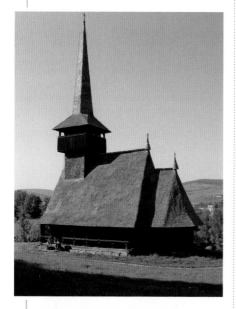

Ethnograhic Park in Cluj-Napoca, Transylvania

Today, more than 80 percent of the population belongs to the Romanian Orthodox Church. Officially recognized in 1885, it is one of 15 Eastern Orthodox churches that identify themselves with the original church founded by Christ. This pointed decision led to the famous Schism, a split over doctrine with the Roman Catholic Church that took place in 1054. As a result, no pope ever visited Romania until Pope John Paul II in 1999.

The level of churchgoing in Romania is remarkable, especially among older people in the countryside. In rural areas, the church still plays an important social role. On Sundays,

feast days, and especially at Orthodox Easter, worshipers pack the churches, often wearing their traditional clothes. Village women take pride in cleaning their churches and decorating them with colorfully embroidered *ştergari* (narrow cotton hangings).

Orthodox monasteries and convents

Orthodox monasteries also provide support for rural communities. During the communist regime, many religious foundations were closed or pressured to reduce their numbers, but the leaders of the Romanian Church collaborated with the Communist Party in order to maintain their positions. In the 1950s, the communists forced Greco-Catholics from Transylvania to convert to Orthodoxy. (The Greco-Catholic or Uniate Church combines Orthodox and Roman Catholic doctrines.) But while some members of the Orthodox clergy worked as police spies, many individual priests, monks, and nuns refused to give in to the oppressive regime and were persecuted as a result. The church that was so divided between support for the regime and resistance against it is working hard to regain the people's trust.

After the fall of communism, the lure of spiritual regeneration led some Romanians to take to the hills once more, where, like the first monks to follow St. Anthony into the desert, they became hermits. In contrast, large numbers of young people (particularly teenage girls) joined the monastic institutions. The reason for much of this influx stemmed from the belief that the monasteries provided the only hope of a decent life. As a result, in some areas the monasteries now number upward of 500 and 600 members.

Today there are nearly 400 Orthodox monasteries and convents in Romania, and just over 8,000 monks and nuns. They welcome pilgrims, and many provide accommodations for believers who are in search of rest and retreat. Monasteries generally have a positive attitude toward visitors, particularly if you want to admire their churches; however, even though some of them cater to tourists, monasteries are not hotels. You may attend services, but these can go on for hours and the congregation is

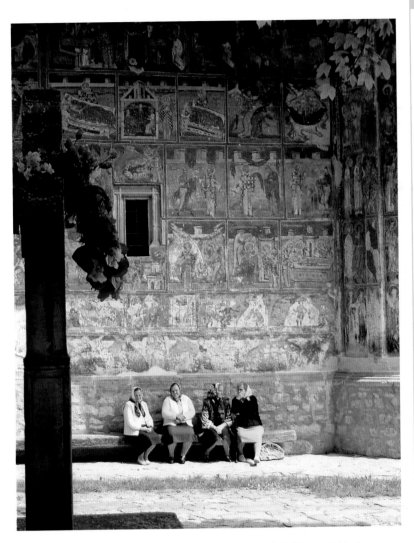

Sixteenth-century painted frescoes adorn the monastery walls in Humor, Moldavia.

expected to stand. Most Romanians drop in for just a few minutes, and it is perfectly all right for foreigners to do the same; people are always coming and going. There is constant activity as worshipers light candles for the living and the dead, pay for prayers, and kneel in silent communication, finding solace in the peaceful, incense-laden atmosphere. It is easy to see why people find this form of worship attractive: The electrifying chants, pungent smell of incense, and dark interiors glinting

with gold leaf make a powerful combination. Depending on the individual community, the monasteries are generally cheerful places. (Monasteries that are also historic monuments often charge for entry and for taking photographs.)

Orthodox churches

Some of Romania's greatest art can be found in its Orthodox churches. There are fantastic buildings in every region, from magnificent stone and brick cathedrals to humble country shrines made of logs. The most famous include the painted 15th- and 16th-century churches of Bucovina (northern Moldavia), a handful of ethereal constructions that are enveloped in frescoes. Unique for their quality and the extent of their coverage (much more than the painted shrines of Bulgaria and Macedonia), the paintings tell Christian stories that are based on Byzantine models but express an entirely local spirit. You can see the

Romanian opera star Angela Gheorghiu opening the 2006 Cannes Film Festival

most pressing political anxieties worked out in thinly veiled religious messages as the Moldavian princes fought for their independence from invading Turks. With their pointed, sweeping roofs, Gothic stonework, and Byzantine plans, the churches of Bucovina exemplify a unique type of architecture that is now known as the Moldavian style.

In rural areas, Romania's version of Orthodox Christianity is shot through with pre-Christian influences. Pagan beliefs and superstitions make their presence robustly felt as though they had been laid aside only yesterday. Among the many possibilities, look for images of signs of the zodiac in wall paintings and on the ceramic disks that were used to decorate church exteriors. In churches and monasteries, the congregation is often called to services by a *toacă*, a long wooden plank that is beaten with two hammers. Said to originate in the Middle Ages, the toacă was used to call people to arms. Another legend tells us that the plank symbolizes a piece of Noah's ark. The story of Noah permeates Romanian mythology since the Flood is thought to refer to a historical event when the Black Sea burst its banks. But there is another fascinating connection: Noah's ark is thought to have ended up on Mount Ararat, close to Armenia. Today, Armenian priests use an identical plank to call the faithful to prayer.

Judaism

At one time, Romania had a sizeable Jewish population; a notable influx occurred between the 15th and 17th centuries, when many of the Jews expelled from Spain arrived. They contributed hugely to the country's culture and economy, but until 1878 they were refused citizenship. Prejudices against them included the belief that they prevented the rise of a Romanian middle class. After World War I, antipathy and paranoia toward the Jews continued to rise. As a result, during World War II, 270,000 Jews were killed or deported to Transnistria, along with thousands of Roma. Today, some 8,000 Jews live in Romania—more than half of them in Bucharest—and there are approximately 800 functioning synagogues.

THE ARTS

Romania is famous for its theater, music, and, increasingly, films. Georges Enescu (1881–1955), the early 20th-century composer; opera star Angela Gheorghiu; and actress Maia Morgenstern need little introduction, while sisters Gabriela and Monica Irimia, better known as the Cheeky Girls, are fast making a name for themselves in the world of pop.

Theater, film, & literature

Since their introduction in the 19th century, Romania's theaters have usually been funded by the state—even today there are 52 government-financed playhouses and puppet theaters. They include Europe's only Yiddish theater, Teatrul Evreiesc de Stat, in Bucharest, which amazingly continued to function throughout the communist period.

Under communism, film and theater provided Romanians with a much needed release from oppression. Dissident playwrights could get their work past the censors by using allegory, and audiences would wait in lines for hours to get tickets for their plays. Some writers and directors did cross the invisible line, and having been banned, a few found fame abroad.

One of the 20th century's greatest playwrights, Eugen Ionescu, was born in Romania in 1909. Trapped in France by World War II, Ionescu chose to stay in Paris. There, known as Eugène Ionesco, he founded the theater of the absurd as a way of expressing the alienation of modern life but also as a reaction to ideological conformism. Ionescu had a particular horror of ideologies ever since the rise of Romania's ultra right-wing Iron Guard. His best known pieces include *Rhinocéros* (*Rhinoceros*), *La Cantatrice Chauve* (*The Bald Primadonna*), and *Les Chaises* (*The Chairs*).

The internationally known film director Lucian Pintilie (b. 1933), whose *Reconstituirea* (*Reconstruction*) caused a huge scandal for its implied criticism of Ceaușescu's Romania, was asked to leave in the 1970s. Widely acclaimed in the West, he has since returned home. Film and theater director Andrei Șerban (b. 1943) was refused work in Romania after a daring production of *Julius Caesar;* he emigrated to the United States in 1969 and has never looked back. More recently, Cristi Puiu's (b. 1967) black comedy *Moartea Domnului Lazarescu* (*The Death of Mr. Lazarescu*, 2005) has won numerous film awards.

Early in his dictatorship, Ceaușescu first relaxed traveling restrictions and allowed artists to go abroad. But after visiting North Korean leader Kim Il Sung in 1971, Ceaușescu became fixated on emulating him. From that time until his demise, Romania's official culture was forced to concentrate on one thing: boosting the leader's image as a "Great

Son of the Nation." In 1971, Ceaușescu initiated Cântarea României (The Praise of Romania), a sycophantic festival of song, poems, music, and dance directed at a single audience member. All Romanians were expected to collude in the fantasy, pretending that they lived in the best of all possible worlds when in fact it was one of the worst.

Outspoken critics of the communist regime included Marin Sorescu (1936–1996), a subversive poet whose best-known criticism of Ceaușescu's regime was his *House under*

One of Romania's most famous literary exiles, playwright Eugen Ionescu (1912–1994)

Surveillance, published after the fall of the communist regime, and Ana Blandiana (b. 1942), who started writing protest poems in 1980. Blandiana's poem, "Eu cred" ("I Believe," 1984), begins with these arresting lines:

> *Eu cred că suntem un popor vegetal,*
> *De unde altfel liniștea*
> *În care așteptăm desfrunzirea?*
> I believe we are a vegetable people,
> Why else are we so calm
> As we wait for the whirlwind to strip our
>   leaves?

Since the 1989 revolution, Blandiana has entered politics, campaigning for the secret files to be opened so that justice can be meted out to the persecutors of Ceaușescu's regime.

Postcommunist Romania has seen a

proliferation of newspapers and journals. Many are now suspected of having been muzzled by corrupt politicians, but some show independent streaks. Among these are the self-critical *Dilema*, the cultural and political review *22* (named after December 22, 1989, when Ceaușescu fled Bucharest in a helicopter), and the refreshingly satirical *Academia Cațavencu*, which is modeled on the French weekly *Le Canard Enchaîné* and the British *Private Eye*.

Above: Outspoken poet Ana Blandiana has become a leader of Romanian civil society. Opposite: Nicolae Grigorescu's 1881 "At the Seaside" can be seen at the Museum of Art Collections in Bucharest.

Visual arts

Romania's visual artists are generally less well known abroad, but one in particular stands out. Sculptor Constantin Brâncuși (1876–1957; see p. 91), known to the English-speaking world as Brancusi, was the creator of such innovative and sometimes controversial pieces as "Bird in Space," "Mlle Pogany," and "The Column of the Infinite." Like so many Romanian artists and intellectuals, Brâncuși made his home in France, where he emigrated in 1904. Brâncuși repudiated his homeland in the 1950s when its communist art historians condemned his work. But his sculptures radiate a love of natural forms

and sturdy peasant buildings that comes directly from his experience of childhood in rural Oltenia.

The best-known Romanian painter is the Impressionist Nicolae Grigorescu (1838–1907). In the 1860s, he studied in Paris before moving to the Barbizon Forest to paint alongside Corot and Millet. On his return home, Grigorescu turned his attention to depicting country life in Romania. Infused with brilliant light and an intimate understanding of his subjects, his rural paintings are epitomized by a series of canvases called "Care cu boi" ("Ox Carts"), but Grigorescu also painted some extremely moving portraits of soldiers who took part in the Romanian War of Independence (1877–78).

During the communist period, Romania's painters and sculptors often led dual lives. If they wanted to work, they were compelled to join the Artists' Union. Many survived by producing images that boosted the dictator's ego, while privately creating more thoughtful pieces. With the advantage of better communications with the West and relations across the border with Hungary, Transylvanian artists were often more progressive. In the 1980s, the group Mamu from Târgu Mureș staged secret art events in the countryside. They were photographed and distributed as antigovernment propaganda.

For many people who lived by their creative imagination, the end of communism spelled the end of security: However dull their work, artists and writers who toed the line were assured of an income. Now the safety nets have gone and each must succeed on his or her own talents. To counter this maelstrom across the collapsing East, Hungarian entrepreneur George Soros founded institutes that support innovative artists in all the countries of the former Soviet bloc. In Romania, the Soros Foundation funds exhibitions that, while looking to the future, explore pressing philosophical questions that encourage reflection on the painful past.

Several Romanian artists have confronted their nation's tortured past. Among them, Dan Perjovschi (b. 1961) has become a groundbreaker. Somewhere between a

Early morning silhouettes in Craiova's old town center

cartoonist and political activist, he uses drawing to highlight the anguish that many Romanians feel about their failure to stand up to persecution, and their willingness to accept perverted truths and corruption in high places. Uncomfortable, witty, but also strangely affectionate, his polemics are directed not only at Romanians but also to the world at large. Eastern Europe's relationship with the West is frequently called into question, along with the vexed issue of what role artists should play and how they should be rewarded. Perjovschi's sketches work as illustration, graffiti, and installation—sometimes covering whole walls like latter-day versions of the painted monasteries. He also publishes and illustrates the magazine *22* (see p. 44).

LANGUAGE

Romanian is closer to street Latin than any other living Romance tongue. Modern Romanian developed between the seventh and tenth centuries; Byzantine influences account for the high percentage of Slavonic words.

Exhibiting an extraordinary sense of insularity, especially in the face of the country's repeated occupations, the Romanian language remains one of the most homogenous in Europe.

Today, Romanian is also spoken in the Republic of Moldova, Ukraine, Hungary, Bulgaria, and the autonomous Serbian province of Vojvodina. Aromanian (which is similar to Romanian, but split from it sometime after the Roman conquest of the Balkans) is spoken in parts of five other countries of southeast Europe.

The Romance language connection helps explain why Romanians forged such close cultural links with France. French literature and philosophy were all the rage in 19th-century Romanian drawing rooms; Bucharest was redesigned on a Parisian model—and has an Arcul de Triumf, a traffic circle named after Charles de Gaulle, and a statue of the French leader. In 2006, Romania hosted the first Francophone festival ever to be held in Europe outside France.

All this and more is Romania—and we have not even touched on Dracula. ■

Bucharest, Romania's fascinatingly diverse capital, suffered mightily under Ceauşescu's rule. Luckily, while the race is on today to modernize the city as quickly as possible, something of its chaotic charm remains.

Bucharest

The *Memorialul Renaşterii* (the official 1989 Resurrection Memorial) at Piaţa Revoluţiei, Bucharest, is known jokingly as "the potato."

Traffic speeds along the main arteries of Bucharest, Romania's most modern metropolis.

Bucharest

ROUGHLY TWO MILLION PEOPLE LIVE IN BUCHAREST TODAY. VLAD THE Impaler, Prince of Wallachia, adopted the fortified settlement of Bucharest as his capital in 1459. Vlad III Dracula chose to settle his court here because it was farther from the Carpathian Mountains—and from Hungarian influence—than the previous two capitals. It also strategically lay on a trade route that connected southeast Europe with the north and west. The remains of Vlad's palace and church are still visible: They are the city's oldest standing buildings.

Directly southwest of Vlad's court lies the massive palace and boulevard that Ceauşescu commissioned in the wake of the 1977 earthquake. It now houses Romania's Parliament. The dictator bulldozed a fifth of the city, a far larger area than the quake destroyed, eradicating a great swath of perfectly sound, fine old buildings. This building phase was just one of many in Ceauşescu's planned systematization. In the 1960s, he had ranks of low-quality, high-rise flats built in the outskirts, extending the *mahalalele* (suburbs) where poorer people lived, while at the end of his rule, Ceauşescu began to demolish some of the surrounding villages.

Luckily, Ceauşescu did not destroy everything. A walk around the city's older areas

reveals some of the city's exuberant past, with several areas around Vlad's court still exhibiting an imaginative spirit. To the north, the area known as Lipscani is a collection of small streets where foreign traders used to congregate. To the east, across Bulevardul Brătianu, is a small area once inhabited by Armenian settlers, beyond which lies an oasis of eclectic villas and apartments—the old center of Bucharest.

To the west and northwest of Vlad's court lie the once fashionable length of Calea Victoriei, the elegant Cişmigiu Gardens, the splendid Medical Faculty building, Cotroceni Palace, the botanical gardens, and another parcel of once proud, private mansions. Finally, a fine reproduction of Paris's Arc de Triomphe stands amid peaceful, leafy streets of beautiful town houses and unusual museums north of Piaţa Victoriei.

Be aware when touring Bucharest that while the city is currently booming, it is also recovering from trauma. Conservationists and businesses have restored some of the capital's pretty town houses, but much remains to be done. ■

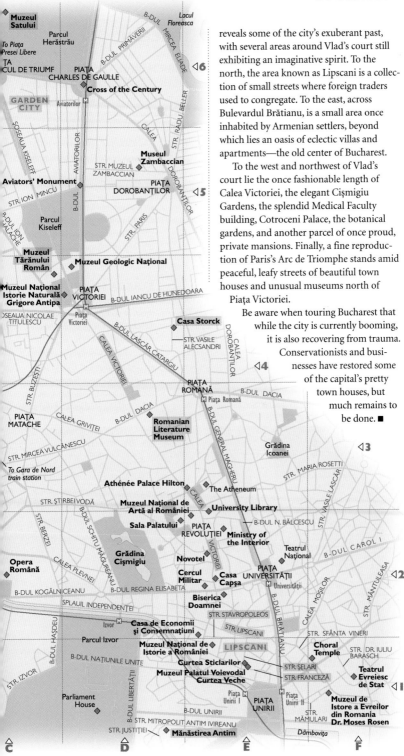

Lipscani

THE MEDIEVAL HEART OF BUCHAREST, LIPSCANI COVERS A small tangle of streets hemmed in by Calea Victoriei, Strada Doamnei, Bulevardul Brătianu, and Strada Halelor. It was a dynamic trading center before the city was born. The name Lipscani comes from the Romanian word for the Leipzig merchants who were the wealthiest and most innovative of the district's tradespeople. You can wander for hours and still find different corners, courtyards, and passageways that bring the district's history alive.

STRADA LIPSCANI

The district's main focal point is Strada Lipscani. Recently pedestrianized, it's a pleasant place to wander around; there are cafés and restaurants and funny old shops to browse. An archway at the eastern end of the street leads into an enclosed street: **Hanul cu Tei** (Lime Tree Inn). It was built in 1833 by two merchants, each of whom owned shops on either side of the passageway. The shops here now sell antiques and art materials. Nearby, the brick ruin of **Hanul Gabroveni** (*Str. Lipscani 86–88*), a former inn built in 1739, provides insight into its past architectural glory. Plans are to turn this building into an information center for the city.

STRADA ȘELARI

A significant stretch of Strada Șelari is occupied by **Curtea Sticlarilor,** the glassblowers' workshops. You can't miss the long, glazed, wooden balcony and arched windows of this 1716 building that once formed part of the royal court. You may visit the still-working studios and the shop.

A rare moment of privacy at Hanul lui Manuc (Manuc's Inn), one of Bucharest's most popular watering holes. The inn is undergoing restoration until 2009.

STRADA FRANCEZĂ

Strada Franceză, named after the French merchants who settled in this area, is home to the **Muzeul Palatul Voievodal Curtea Veche** (Palace Museum of the Old Royal Court), which was originally a 14th-century fortress built for Prince Mircea cel Bătrân (Mircea the Old). Prince Vlad III Dracula and a succession of later rulers added to or rebuilt the court several times, but the largest house, guardhouses, watchtower, and baths were built between 1690 and 1714 by Prince Constantin Brâncoveanu. His creations confirmed the city's status as the capital. In 1775, Prince Alexander Ipsilanti abandoned the palace for a New Court elsewhere in town. The court is open to visitors despite the ongoing restoration.

Next door stands Bucharest's oldest church, **Biserica Curții Vechi** (Church of the Old Court). Its alternating pattern of stone and brickwork is a typical Byzantine style. It was founded in the 1550s by Prince Mircea Ciobanul (Mircea the Shepherd). Several of Romania's medieval princes were crowned here. Destroyed several times over the centuries, the church was completely restored in the 20th century.

A few steps from the church is the entrance to **Hanul lui Manuc** (*Str. Franceză 64*). Named after the Armenian merchant who built it in 1808, Manuc's Inn is the only complete caravanserai left in Romania. Its huge, handsome courtyard was built to safeguard wagon trains on their journey across Europe. The inn is currently closed for renovations until early 2009.

STRADA STAVROPOLEOS

The diminutive but beautifully proportioned **Biserica Stavropoleos** (*Str. Stavropoleos 4*) sits at the corner of Strada Stavropoleos and Strada Poștei. Originally built as a

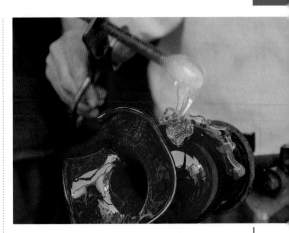

Goods & trade

In the 12th century, several small villages clustered near a crossroads linking the Silk Road with northern Europe, an area now known as Piața Unirii. Taking advantage of their strategic position, the villagers began to hold communal markets and annual fairs. This vigorous activity attracted others with similar ideas, including the country's rulers, who made their headquarters here. Street names show that at the height of its activity, Lipscani bustled with craftspeople and professionals: saddlers, knife grinders, hatters, bakers, furriers, quilters, and usurers, and their guilds. ∎

monastery in 1724 by Greek Orthodox monks, this church has several charming details, including the decorated stone pillars that support a row of pretty, Oriental-style arches and blind arcades that surround the building's side and rear walls. Many of the original neo-Byzantine wall paintings still hang in the incense-laden interior; there's also a superb, gilded icon screen and a delightful, creeper-covered cloister to one side. ∎

A glass blower at work in the medieval Curtea Sticlarilor, Lipscani

Curtea Sticlarilor
- 🗺 49 E1 & p. 53
- ✉ Str. Șelari 9–11
- ☎ 021 314 3228
- 🕐 Closed Sun. & Nov.–April
- Ⓜ Metro: Piața Unirii 1

Muzeul Palatul Voievodal Curtea Veche
- 🗺 49 E1 & p. 53
- ✉ Str. Franceză 25–31
- ☎ 021 314 0375
- 🕐 Closed Mon.
- 💲 $
- Ⓜ Metro: Piața Unirii 1

A walk through Old Bucharest

This walk brings you into another historic part of the capital, but one that is seldom traversed by tourists. An attractive jumble of streets that escaped the worst of Ceauşescu's depradations, this area shows the soft underbelly of this go-getting city.

The rear terrace bar at the House of the People of Science is a fine place for an outdoor meal.

Begin at the 1701 **Colţea Biserica** ❶ *(B-dul Brătianu 1)*, the first Brâncovenesque-style church in Bucharest. Its beautiful stonework and interior are worth seeing despite the on-going restoration work. Walk east along **Strada Colţei** to where Colţei gets lost in a muddle of other roads, a scene that epitomizes the description by essayist and physicist Horia-Roman Patapievici (b. 1957), who wrote that the street plan of the old city looks like "a heap of sheep's guts thrown in the dust."

Thread your way across Strada Ivo Andric and Bulevardul Hristo Botev, pass the entrance to Strada Sfinţilor, and enter **Strada Caimatei.** The building at **No. 20** was designed by Marcel Iancu, a founding member of the Dadaist movement who pioneered modernist architecture in interwar Romania.

Continue north up Strada Armenească then turn onto Bulevardul Carol I. A striking **Armenian church** ❷ *(B-dul Carol I 43, tel 021 313 9070 for appt.)* stands a little way down the street. Dating from 1915, it replicates the 17th-century Cathedral of St. Gregory the Illuminator in the old Armenian capital of Echmi-

adzin. A **museum** opposite the church contains embroideries and old books redolent of Armenia's beleaguered culture. According to some, Bucharest owes its name to an Armenian called Hapet Bukor. This church and Strada Armenească are virtually all that remain of Mahalaua Armenească, the Armenian quarter.

From the church, pass Strada Armenească and turn left into Strada Spătarului. The **Muzeul Theodor Pallady** is housed in the unobtrusive **Casa Melik** ❸ *(Str. Spătarului 22, tel 021 211 4979, closed Mon., $).* This 1760 house, built by an Armenian merchant for his family, is one of the oldest in Bucharest. The collection of paintings by the symbolist Theodor Pallady (1871–1953) is average, but the villa's rustic atmosphere is charming.

Walk to the north end of Spătarului, turn left into Strada Popa Petre, then right into **Strada Silvestru.** Oriental-looking houses from the Phanariot period, when this part of Romania was ruled by Greek-speaking rulers from Istanbul, line the street. A few houses exhibit the French influence that was the rage in the mid- and late 19th century, but it's hard to tell because the styles became wonderfully mixed. **No. 75,** however, is clearly another innovative 1930s Marcel Iancu building.

Backtrack slightly along Silvestru and turn right into Strada Salcîmilor. Turn left down Strada Toamnei, then right into Strada Maria Rosetti to reach the **Muzeul Vasile Grigore** ④ *(Str. Maria Rosetti 29, tel 021 211 54 09, closed Mon., $).* The excellent collection of fine and decorative art from Romania and abroad was donated by the painter Vasile Grigore (b. 1935), whose own engagingly breezy pictures can be found in museums around the country.

The magnificent facade of the **Şcoala Centrală** (Central Girls' School) ⑤ looms over the intersection of Icoanei and Calderon streets. This neo-Romanian masterpiece was designed by Ion Mincu (1852–1912). Close by, on the corner between Polona and Dumbrava Roşie streets, **Ioanid Gardens** ⑥ are a pleasant place to relax. From the

gardens, make your way right, to Piaţa Lahovari and the **Casa Oamenilor de Ştiinţa** (House of the People of Science; *Piaţa Lahovari 9)* ⑦. The rear terrace and rose garden of this former Phanariot palace (now a restaurant) are worth seeing. ∎

🗺	See area map p. 49
➤	Colţea Biserica
↔	2 miles (3.2 km)
⏱	I hour
➤	Casa Oamenilor de Ştiinţa

NOT TO BE MISSED

- Colţea Biserica
- Armenian church
- Muzeul Theodor Pallady
- Muzeul Vasile Grigore
- Casa Oamenilor de Ştiinţa

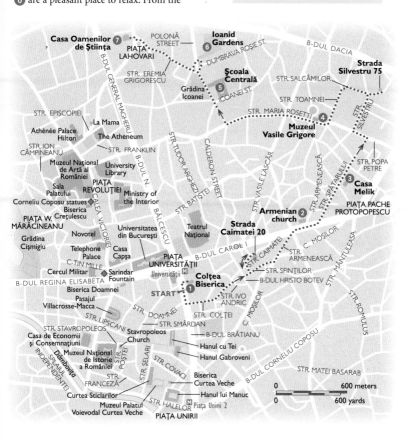

Calea Victoriei

The elegant Pasajul Villacrosse-Macca was modeled on 19th-century Western European shopping arcades.

BUCHAREST'S SMARTEST INTERWAR BOULEVARD, CALEA Victoriei (Victory Way) extends for about 2 miles (3 km) in gentle curves between Splaiul Independenţei and Piaţa Victoriei. Recent repairs and new buildings have started to restore its former glamour.

Muzeul Naţional de Istorie a României

🅰 49 E1

✉ Calea Victoriei 12

☎ 021 315 0782

🕐 Closed Mon.

💲 $

🚇 Metro: Piaţa Unirii 1

The street gets its name from the Romanian War of Independence of 1877–78 (also known as the Russo-Turkish War), when the country finally shed its Ottoman yoke. Most of the visitable sights are concentrated in the southern section, between Strada Lipscani and Piaţa Revoluţiei.

Beginning near the southern end, the imperial-looking **Muzeul Naţional de Istorie a României** (National History Museum of Romania) houses among its treasures the "Mother Hen and Her Chicks," 22 pieces of gold and gem-encrusted jewelry and vessels thought to have been buried by Ostrogoths in the fifth century A.D. The hoard includes four fibulas (clips) that resemble a hen with three chicks.

Next door, an extravagant 1897 building contains the **Casa de Economii şi Consemnaţiuni** *(Calea Victoriei 13)*, the country's main savings bank. Opposite the CEC are two entrances to the semicircular 19th-century shopping arcade **Pasajul Villacrosse-Macca.** A few steps farther north is a narrower opening; look inside and you'll find a 1683 church, **Biserica Doamnei** *(Calea Victoriei 28)*.

On the northern side of Bulevardul Regina Elisabeta stands another architectural showpiece, **Cercul Militar** (Military Club; *Str. Constantin Mille 1, tel 021 314 9551*). The Sarindar fountain in front of this early 20th-century building memorializes a church of the same name that stood here. The church, probably built by Prince Matei Basarab (R. 1632–1654), was felled by a 19th-century earthquake.

Opposite the club is one of downtown Bucharest's most famous sights, the 1886 **Casa Capşa** *(Calea Victoriei 36)*. Before the communists closed it down, Casa Capşa was the hotel of choice for European royalty; it was also a honeypot for artists and intellectuals. It reopened in 2003 (see p. 246).

The striking high-rise tower of the **Telephone Palace** *(Calea Victoriei 37)* contains the headquarters of the independent telecommunications company Romtelecom. The building's crisp 1930s lines and art deco features high up on the tower are hard to appreciate from the narrow street. Next door, the facade of Bucharest's brand new **Novotel** *(Calea Victoriei 37B)* is a copy of the old National Theater that stood here until it was destroyed in a bombing raid in 1944.

Farther north, the **Piaţa Revoluţiei** is dominated by King Carol I's (R. 1866–1914) former winter palace, now the **Muzeul Naţional de Artă al României.** With original pieces by the world-famous Romanian sculptor Constantin Brâncuşi and some fine medieval church art, this art museum is well worth visiting.

Piaţa Revoluţiei also contains (looking clockwise from the museum) the **Athénée Palace Hilton** (formerly the Athénée Palace; *Str. Episcopei 1–3; see p. 246*); **The Atheneum** *(Str. Franklin 1)*, a domed concert hall by Albert Galleron with a classical portico and beautiful interiors (1888); and the **university library,** whose collection was burned to a cinder in December 1989. Open-air concerts are often held in front of it. Past the library, beyond the shell of the former **Securitate archive building,** the **Ministry of the Interior** building was commissioned by King Carol II in 1938. The ministry has been damned for its associations with Ceauşescu, who made his last speech from the balcony. The low pyramid in front commemorates the people who died during the December 1989 revolution. To the right again are two bronze statues of

the liberal leader Corneliu Copusu, whose death in 1995 was mourned across the country, and the slim, redbrick, early 18th-century **Biserica Creţulescu** that was built by a royal steward near the city's gates.

After strolling the avenue, detour between the art museum and the Creţulescu Church to make a five-minute walk to the **Grădina Cişmiugiu.** Cross Strada Ion Câmpineanu and go straight into Piaţa Walter—the gardens lie on the opposite side of the square. With ornamental borders, hedge walks, specimen trees, a boating lake, and fountains—not to mention terrace cafés offering refreshments—this is the loveliest green space in the city center. ■

The Atheneum concert hall off Calea Victoriei was built by subscription.

Muzeul Naţional de Artă al României

◭ 49 E2

✉ Calea Victoriei 49–53

☎ 021 314 8119

⊕ Closed Mon.–Tues.

⑤ $

▦ Metro: Piaţa Universităţii

Cotroceni

THIS ATTRACTIVE RESIDENTIAL AREA WEST OF THE CITY center sits among parks and gardens. Containing the presidential palace and a wealth of picturesque if crumbling villas, it makes a pleasant alternative to the inner-city bustle.

Ash Tree Alley in the botanical gardens, Cotroceni district

The main focal point is **Palatul Cotroceni,** the Romanian president's official residence. It stands at the west end of Bulevardul Eroii Sanitari in extensive, walled grounds. Visitors may take a guided tour of parts of the palace and/or make an independent visit to the brick-vaulted kitchen areas, which are used for temporary exhibitions. The entrance to both is via a little gate in the side wall halfway along Şoseaua Cotroceni, opposite the botanical gardens.

Designed by Paul Gottereau for Crown Prince Ferdinand and completed in 1895, the main house stands on the site of a 17th-century monastery founded by a prince of Wallachia (this part of Romania), Şerban Cantacuzino. The monastery's church was dynamited on Ceauşescu's orders in 1984. The church has now been partially rebuilt on its original foundation.

In the 1920s, Ferdinand's wife, Queen Marie, employed architect Grigore Cerchez to extend and redesign the palace according to the neo-Romanian style pioneered by Ion Mincu.

The nearby **Grădina Botanică Dimitrie Brândză** was founded in 1860 by the famous Romanian physician Carol Davila. Originally located beside the Medical Faculty (see opposite), the botanical garden was moved to its present site in 1884 and was named in honor of the determined botanist Dimitrie Brândză (1846–1895), who campaigned for its survival. Covering about 42 acres (17 ha), it contains a museum, greenhouses *(limited visiting hours)*, formal and wild gardens, lakes, and ponds, as well as various buildings containing botanic research institutes. On a fine day, it's worth the extra effort to get here from the city center.

A STROLL TROUGH RESIDENTIAL COTROCENI

The picturesque residential streets of the Cotroceni district extend from the botanical gardens to the edge of the bleak area that surrounds the Parliament House. As a marked contrast to that building, the district is full of mansions, apartments, and churches that show how varied and colorful a city Bucharest once was. Every villa is different, with quirky details. Many of them are being restored, some by private owners and others by companies.

Threading your way from the botanical gardens to the Eroilor metro station, you pass the **Facultatea de Medicină** (Medical Faculty; *B-dul Eroii Sanitari 8*) on Bulevardul Eroii Sanitari, a majestic, classical building from 1903. A statue of its cofounder, Carol Davila, stands in the courtyard. The bronze is by another pioneer, Karl Storck (1826–1887; see p. 64), who established Romania's first fine arts academy.

Continue following Eroii Sanitari and then take a right into Strada Dr. Clunet. The next junction brings you to Strada Sfântu Elefterie. The pretty little Orthodox **church of Sf. Elefterie Vechi** stands on a traffic island *(Str. Sf. Elefterie 1)* in the intersection. Built in 1744 during the Phanariot period (see p. 33), it was isolated during Ceaușescu's systematization of Bucharest. The church and the neo-Byzantine paintings in its porch

---

Honoring the physicians

The streets in the Cotroceni area are named after doctors or scientists. A few carry well-known names like Lister and Pasteur, but others are named after more obscure people. Bulevardul Prof. Dr. Gheorghe Marinescu, for instance, honors a much-loved neurologist (1863–1938) who studied in Paris under the famous Charcot. Still others shine a light on 20th-century history. Strada Fr. Joliot-Curie memorializes French chemist Frédéric Joliot, who was the husband of Marie Curie's daughter, Irène. In 1935 they won the Nobel Prize in chemistry for the discovery of artificial radioactivity. Having helped prevent the Nazis from developing an atomic bomb, Joliot-Curie became a prominent communist. Stalin appointed him president of the Soviet-created World Peace Council; in 1959, Romania issued a stamp bearing his portrait. ■

---

have been restored and are well worth a visit.

Continue east along Strada Sf. Elefterie past the church and you'll find yourself in a place where many roads converge. Leave Strada Sf. Elefterie behind and cross the Dâmbovița Canal at Splaiul Independenței. Opposite, and set back from the street in its own green space, is the **Opera Română** *(B-dul Kogălniceanu 70–72, tel 021 314 6980)*. A relatively new building (it opened in 1954), the opera house is one of the liveliest music venues in the city. No visit to Bucharest is complete without taking in a performance of some kind here. ■

Palatul Cotroceni

🅰 48 A2

✉ B-dul Geniului 1 Șoseaua Cotroceni

☎ 021 317 3107

🕐 Closed Mon.; advance reservations required, same-day visit may be possible

💲 $$

🚇 Metro: Eroilor; Bus: 336; Trolleybus: 61 (ask for Grădina Botanica)

Grădina Botanică Dimitrie Brândză

🅰 48 A2-B2

✉ Șoseaua Cotroceni 32

☎ 021 410 9139

🕐 Closed Mon.

💲 $

🚇 Metro: Eroilor; Bus: 336; Trolleybus: 61 (ask for Grădina Botanica)

Sweet sounds

Rich in religious and folk traditions, and incorporating a wealth of different racial influences, music is a wonderfully colorful part of everyday Romanian life. An old Romanian saying avers that "music and laughter are the cure for all ills." Romania offers a huge range of transforming musical experiences, and music has become an essential part of every restaurant meal.

Inspired by such legends as the 13th-century Pied Piper who (according to Robert Browning) spirited the children of Hamelin's ungrateful burghers from Germany to Transylvania, ethnologists relish analyzing the components of Romanian folk music and dance: There are 18 registered ethnic minorities—not to mention a slew of regional variations in harmony, tempo, instruments and costume, as well as influences from neighboring countries, Turkey, and Western Europe. In short, Romanian folk music links the Balkans with Arabic, Hungarian, Jewish, and Turkish melodies and scales. But you'll probably be too busy dancing to worry about where it all comes from.

Romania has many kinds of folk dance; one of the most typical is a round dance called a *horă*. The word comes from the ancient Greek for a dance accompanied by singing, but the origins of the dance probably date much earlier. Figures of men and women arranged in circles have been discovered on prehistoric funerary urns in northeast Romania, and one of the most typical patterns on traditional Maramureș carpets shows men and women holding hands, apparently in a horă. Bulgaria and Israel have their own versions of the horă.

The most famous of all Romanian folk music is that created by the Roma (see pp. 204–205). Infectiously energetic, Roma music has helped to invigorate regional traditions across the country. The best-known Romanian Gypsy musicians are the all-male bands *(tarafe)* such as Taraf de Haiducs (The Bandits) and Fanfare Ciocărlia (The Skylark Band).

Folk music even has been incorporated into Romanian rock. When Ceaușescu strongly suppressed rock music because of its "subversive" nature, the band Phoenix introduced folk tunes into their repertoire, attempting to find an acceptable compromise. They were exiled regardless, but since 1989 Phoenix has risen again to popular acclaim. Today, groups such as Spitalul de Urgență also play a mixture of folk and rock music.

Within the classical tradition, the best-known Romanian composer is the violinist George Enescu (1881–1955). You can hear in his *Rapsodies* that Enescu was inspired by Romanian folk music. An international music

festival named for Enescu takes place in major Romanian towns and cities every September. One of its highlights is the open-air concerts held in Bucharest's Piața Revoluției. Less well-known abroad, Ciprian Porumbescu (1853–1883) comes a close second. Extremely patriotic, he has gone down in Romanian history as a great Romantic and a national hero.

Romanian opera and ballet are thriving, too. Opera was introduced here in the late 18th century, when groups of traveling players performed all over the country. A full opera company was launched in Bucharest in 1885. Its singers quickly won fame abroad, with the role of Tosca in Puccini's opera actually created for Haricleea Hartulary (known as Darclée); she sang at its premiere in 1900.

Stemming from the Byzantine period, Romania's Orthodox music can be bewitching. One of the magical experiences of traveling here is catching a live performance, whether it's by Madrigal, the Romanian national choir, or a couple of nuns intoning the liturgy by themselves in a small country monastery. ■

Traditional Romanian folk music is practiced and played in restaurants and other local venues across the country.

Garden City

IN THE EARLY 1900S, THE AREA BETWEEN PIAŢA VICTORIEI and Piaţa Presei Libere was meant to be part of a Garden City. Planned on English lines, and using the wide boulevards and round-abouts already redesigned by landscaped architects in the 19th century as a foundation, the idea was to make the capital greener and more pleasant for its growing population. This elegant part of town is worth exploring and has several inviting museums.

Face to face with Konrad Adenauer, one of several out-size busts depicting EU founders at Muzeul Satului

Muzeul Naţional de Istorie Naturală Grigore Antipa

🔺 49 D4

✉ Şoseaua Kiseleff 1

☎ 021 312 8826

🕐 Closed Mon.–Tues.

💲 $

🚇 Metro: Piaţa Victoriei;
Bus: 182, 300, 783,
784; Tram: 20, 24, 34,
46

Muzeul Geologic Naţional

🔺 49 D4

The northwest side of Piaţa Victo-riei, where Şoseaua Kiseleff begins, holds the **Muzeul Naţional de Istorie Naturală Grigore Antipa** (Grigore Antipa National Museum of Natural History). An-tipa was a respected naturalist who had this 1908 building custom-made for the museum, which he then managed for nearly 50 years. Arranged on three floors, its high-lights include a skeleton of a pre-historic herbivore, *Deinotherium gigantissimum,* which towers 13.5 feet (4.5 m) tall, and, for children, the chance to touch live reptiles (under supervision).

Two minutes north is the Muzeul Ţăranului Român (Mu-seum of the Romanian Peasant; see pp. 62–63) and opposite it, com-pleting the trio of museums at this end of Şoseaua Kiseleff, is the **Muzeul Geologic Naţional** (National Geological Museum). Victor Ştefănescu designed this light and spacious neo-Romanian building (1907) for the collection, and it's worth seeing for its interior alone. Even if you don't read Ro-manian, the displays are stimulat-ing enough to generate all kinds of cosmic questions.

A ten-minute walk north along Kiseleff takes you past a thickly wooded area and some of the grandest old houses in Bucharest, giving you a sense of a different age. At Strada Ion Mincu, turn right and walk to the street's intersection with Bulevardul Aviatorilor. The **Aviators' Memorial** (see sidebar) in the traffic circle makes a useful landmark. From here, turn onto Strada Muzeul Zambaccian.

The **Muzeul Zambaccian** at the far end of this street houses paintings and sculptures by some of the most famous artists of the late 19th and early 20th centuries, including Cézanne, Matisse, and Picasso, as well as the superlative Romanian Impressionist Nicolae Grigorescu. Krikor Zambaccian, an Armenian businessman, had the house designed specifically to show off his art collection. The Zambaccian family converted it into a museum in 1947 to keep the pieces together.

MUZEUL SATULUI

Sitting on the outskirts of the Garden City area (take a bus or taxi; it's a long walk), the Muzeul Satului (Village Museum) appeals to old and young alike. Allow half a day to do justice to the place. Laid out like a typical rural village, the open-air museum offers a network of tree-lined paths that lead to around 300 authentic rural buildings from every region of Romania. If you have no time to explore the Romanian countryside, be sure to come here. Village life has a special significance in Romanian culture because up until relatively recently most of the population led a rural existence. (If some of the buildings are closed, it is because the staff is on vacation.)

The museum, inspired by the Skansen open-air museum near Stockholm, opened in 1936 and covers several acres. To one side is one of the landscaped lakes that, like the museum, was an integral part of the Garden City plan.

The staff often organizes special events, such as craft fairs and dis-

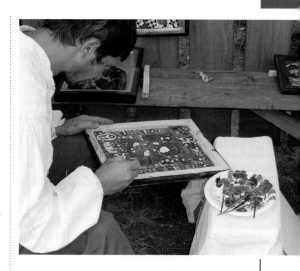

Craftsman at work at Muzeul Satului

plays of folk dancing. A souvenir shop sells traditional handicrafts such as rugs, pottery, and painted eggs, as well as a good selection of books and folk music. ∎

Art triangle

The Piața Charles de Gaulle circle holds the bronze **Cross of the Century.** Paul Neagu (1938–2004) designed the disk to form a triangle with the Aviators' Memorial to the south and the Arcul de Triumf to the west, establishing a continuous sense of movement between the three pieces. The **Aviators' Memorial** (located in middle of B-dul Aviatorilor) has as its centerpiece a muscular figure of a pilot modeled on the American boxer Joe Louis. The **Arcul de Triumf** (Triumphal Arch) commemorates the Romanians killed in World War I. The original wooden arch erected in 1922 was replaced with this concrete version in 1935. A stairway leads to the roof terrace, but at the time of writing it was not open to the public. ∎

Craftsman at work at Muzeul Satului

✉ Șoseaua Kiseleff 2
☎ 021 212 8952
🕐 Closed Mon.
💲 $
🚇 Metro: Piața Victoriei; Bus: 182, 300, 783, 784; Tram: 20, 24, 34, 46

Muzeul Zambaccian

🅰 49 D5
✉ Str. Muzeul Zambaccian 21A
☎ 021 230 1920
🕐 Closed Mon.–Tues.
💲 $
🚇 Metro: Piața Victoriei; Bus: 131, 331

Muzeul Satului

🅰 49 C6
✉ Șoseaua Kiseleff 28
☎ 021 317 9110
🕐 Closed Mon.
💲 $
🚇 Metro: Aviatorilor; Bus: 131, 331 to Herăstrău Park

Colorful costumes (above), vibrant painted eggs (below), and other traditional folk art make the Museum of the Romanian Peasant one of Bucharest's most popular attractions.

Museum of the Romanian Peasant

THE MUZEUL ȚĂRANULUI ROMÂN BEGAN AS A COLLEC-tion of traditional textiles in 1875 and has grown to become one of the most imaginative compilations of traditional folk art and design in Europe, let alone Romania. It should be at the top of your list of things to see in Bucharest.

Located at the lower end of Șoseaua Kiseleff in a 1930s neo-Romanian building that was made specially for it, the museum contains a huge collection of objects that shows the ingenuity and diversity of the country's rural heritage. It serves as a complement to the Village Museum (see p. 61). The spacious rooms and sensitive presentation put this institution in a class of its own, and each room has a simple guide written in several languages to help visitors find their way. On the ground floor, to the right of the entrance, there are displays of textiles, painted eggs, scores of small wooden table crosses, and other wooden items. In an amazing variety of shapes but usually no more than 5 inches (13 cm) high, these pieces epitomize the free and sturdy quality of Romanian folk design. Painted Easter eggs, wooden window frames, and dead tree branches used to hold cooking pots are just some of the objects that, while humble, are given the space to look extraordinary and marvelously resourceful.

At the end of this section is a group of large, decorated crosses that used to mark village boundaries. Pre-Christian signs, such as sun and moon motifs, are often intertwined with Christian symbolism, showing how Orthodox and pagan beliefs were interwoven in Romanian rural life. These crosses were often placed at crossroads to scare away the evil spirits said to traditionally haunt such places. The interconnecting rooms beyond this point exhibit icons painted on glass, a very characteristic form of Romanian folk art (see pp. 190–91).

To the left of the entrance are displays of regional dress and cult objects; a circular table that significantly places together items from many of Romania's ethnic minorities (issues of interracial hatred are dealt with extremely sensitively);

Şoseaua Kiseleff

The Russian-sounding Şoseaua Kiseleff is exactly that: The street was designed by and named after the energetic Russian general Pavel Dmitrievich Kiselyov (1788–1872). After the Treaty of Adrianople, Moldavia and Wallachia came temporarily into Russian hands. Kiselyov administered the Romanian principalities for Tsar Nicholas I from 1828 to 1834, and he introduced many beneficial economic and political reforms. "Kiseleff" is the French form of his name. ∎

Muzeul Ţăranu-lui Român

- 49 C4
- ✉ Şoseaua Kiseleff 3
- ☎ 021 317 9661
- 🕐 Closed Mon.
- 💲 $
- Metro: Piaţa Victoriei; Bus: 182, 300, 783, 784; Tram: 20, 24, 34, 46

and a complete (but nonfunctioning) fulling mill for strengthening newly woven blankets.

Upstairs, the tall interconnecting rooms and halls continue to present the country's rural heritage in simple but dynamic ways. There are cheese dollies, painted plates, drinking jugs in the shape of cockerels designed for newly married couples, decorated stove tiles, and beautiful carpets and rugs colored with vegetable dyes. There is also a timber house, complete with roof

and wooden porch; climb the set of stairs to see how joints of meat were hung above the ceiling so they would cure in the smoke.

Before you leave, head to the underground room to the right of the main entrance to visit the small **Museum of Communist Iconography,** which offers a thoughtful presentation of posters and bric-a-brac from a difficult period in Romania's history.

The museum has a modest café and a souvenir shop. ∎

The old guard: defaced busts of Marx, Engels, and Lenin outside the Museum of the Romanian Peasant

More places to visit in Bucharest

CASA STORCK

Located in an attractive residential area left untouched by Ceauşescu, this small museum, the former home of two Romanian artists, sculptor Frederic Storck (1872–1942) and his wife, sculptor, painter, and muralist Cecilia Cuţescu (1879–1969), is well worth a visit.

Storck was a contemporary of the world-famous Romanian sculptor Constantin Brâncuşi; some of his expressive sculptures show the same love of simple outlines prevalent among innovative artists of the time. Cuţescu was the first female in Europe to graduate from a state-run arts academy. Trained in Munich and Paris, in 1916 she exhibited in the French capital alongside Brâncuşi, Fernand Léger, Max Jacob, and Oskar Kokoschka.

The intricate murals in the hall and dining room were inspired by Cuţescu's love of Anatolian carpets. The diptych at the end of the dining room shows "Love of the Earth" and "Love of the Spirit." Other rooms contain lively sketches from Cuţescu's travels in Italy and Portugal. There are also carvings by Frederic's father, Karl (1827–1887), who immigrated to Romania from Germany in 1849. His sculptures adorn the front of the university building on Bulevardul Regina Elisabeta and the Palace of Justice. Frederic's brother, Carol (1854–1926), completes the original family firm.

🅰 49 D4 ✉ Str. Vasile Alecsandri 16 ☎ 021 317 3889 🕐 Closed Mon. 💲 $ 🚇 Metro: Piaţa Romană

JEWISH SIGHTS IN BUCHAREST

A cluster of sights near the northeast corner of Piaţa Unirii bears witness to an extraordinary survival. Housed in what was once Bucharest's main synagogue, the **Muzeul de Istorie a Evreilor din Romania Dr. Moses Rosen** (*Str. Mămulari 3, tel 021 311 0870, closed Tues. & Fri.–Sun.*) charts the history of Jews on Romanian territory from the second century A.D. It contains a wealth of material, including books, models, and superb paintings by many of the country's leading artists.

The nearby **Choral Temple** (*Str. Sf. Vineri 9, tel 021 312 2196*) stands as a moving memorial to the hundreds of thousands of Romanian Jews murdered during the Holocaust, while a few yards away is Europe's only Yiddish theater, **Teatrul Evreiesc de Stat** (*Str. Iuliu Barasch 15, tel 021 323 3970*). Founded by Avram Goldfaden in Iaşi, the theater was adopted by the state in 1948, and in 2006 it celebrated 130 years of uninterrupted activity. Enjoying an international repertoire, the theater counts Maia Morgenstern as one of its regular performers.

🅰 49 F1 🚇 Metro: Piaţa Unirii 1

MĂNĂSTIREA ANTIM

Close to the Parliament House, tucked near the southwest end of Bulevardul Unirii near the intersection with Strada Justiţiei, Antim Monastery survived Ceauşescu's regime relatively unscathed. The beautifully proportioned Brâncovenesque church inside contrasts dramatically with the architecture outside.

The great Georgian scholar and theologian Antim Ivireanu (Anthim the Iberian, 1650–1716) founded the monastery in 1715. He first came to Romania about 1690 at the invitation of Constantin Brâncoveanu. Antim also ran Romania's first printing press and became metropolitan (or archbishop) of Wallachia in 1708. It's said that Antim himself sculpted the stone icon screen and the ornate church doors. A staunch anti-Phanariot, he was assassinated on the way to exile on Mount Sinai. He was canonized in 1992.

During the 1980s, the Palace of the Holy Synod that stands in the courtyard was moved 82 feet (25 m) from its original position and swiveled by 13 degrees. Antim still functions as a monastery; the monks' living quarters are built into the perimeter walls.

🅰 49 D1 ✉ Str. Mitropolit Antim Ivireanu 29 ☎ 🕐 💲 🚇 Metro: Piaţa Unirii; Izvoral

MUZEUL LITERATURII ROMÂNE

On the southeast corner of Calea Victoriei and Bulevardul Dacia, the Romanian Literature Museum (the former Union of Writers building) is reinventing itself as an interactive study center, shop, and library. It is a book lover's paradise.

🅰 49 D3 ✉ B-dul Dacia 12 ☎ 021 212 9654 🕐 Closed Mon. 💲 $ 🚇 Metro: Piaţa Romană; Bus: 131, 133, 186, 266, 286, 300, 331; Trolleybus: 79, 86 ■

Containing areas of startling natural beauty, Muntenia is one of the historic principalities that gave birth to modern Romania. The capital, Bucharest, lies at its heart, so visitors can get the best of both worlds.

Muntenia

Domes on an early 20th-century church, Curtea de Argeş

Muntenia

ROMANIANS HAVE SEVERAL NAMES FOR THE AREA EAST OF THE OLT RIVER that exudes a rare natural beauty: Muntenia, Țara Românească (literally "the Romanian Land"), and Wallachia (from *vlach,* a German word for people who inherited Roman culture and education). Strictly speaking, Muntenia is smaller than the other two areas.

In the Făgăraș Range that forms Muntenia's northwestern rim, Romania's tallest peak, Mount Moldoveanu, rises to 8,346 feet (2,544 m). Mountain slopes give way to gently undulating foothills or steep, narrow gorges, while farther south the well-tended fields and

orchards of small, family-run farms vanish into the tumble-down of abandoned land. Beyond them, on the edge of the Danube River basin, lie the vineyards of Dealul Mare. Some of Romania's best wine is produced here.

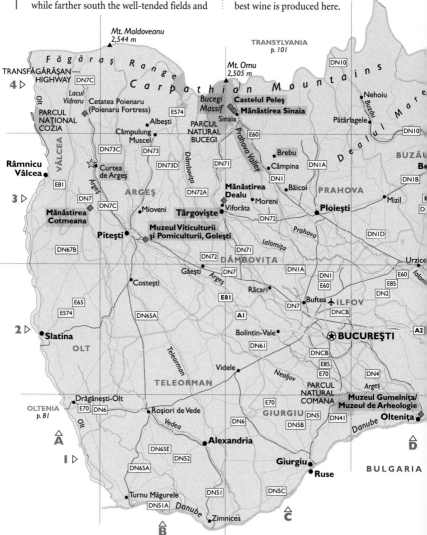

The nodding donkeys nearby mark the northern edge of the Ploieşti oil fields. Dating back to the 1850s, these fields are some of the oldest in Europe. They were considered so important during World War II that the Allies chose to bomb Ploieşti rather than allow the oil fields to fall into the hands of the advancing German Army.

Today, huge tracts of land in central Muntenia are being snapped up for the development of agribusinesses, while at the same time unrestricted commercial and private building creeps ever farther into the countryside.

East of the Carpathians, Muntenia reaches into the notorious Bărăgan Plains. In the 1950s, communist leader Gheorghe Gheorghiu-Dej banished thousands of Germans and Roma to this bleak area. Their only crime was their industriousness and their race. Ironically, the Bărăgan is famous for its *chernozem* (from a Polish word for "dark, fertile soil"). During the 1930s, the Bărăgan produced much of the grain that made Romania one of Europe's richest nations of the time.

In Muntenia's southern extremes, the broad expanses of flat, riverine land often look depressingly neglected. They are neither as picturesque nor as tourist oriented as the mountains, but for that very reason they hold some interest. Thanks to their proximity to the Danube River and the remnants of their precommunist prosperity, the riverside towns have a curious charm. An added attraction in this area is the old-fashioned car ferry that you can take across the Danube from Calaraşi to Silistra. It's at this point that the river starts to turn north, separating Muntenia from the easternmost region of neighboring Dobrogea.

People who want to delve deeper into Romania's history and architecture may well enjoy the historic towns of Câmpulung Muscel, Curtea de Argeş, and Târgovişte—all of which once enjoyed the status of capital of Muntenia. There are frontier castles and well-furbished manor houses. Unsurprisingly for such a religious country, there is also a wealth of old churches and monasteries in Muntenia. They range from humble *sketes* (small monasteries) and hermitages to imposing royal foundations. Some of Muntenia's roads follow medieval trade routes that once linked Muntenia with Asia and northern Europe. Others, such as the switchbacking Transfăgărăşan Highway, are impressive feats of engineering. Not to mention that, as you travel the latter over the pass into Transylvania, the sight of the aerie-like Cetatea Poienaru (Poienaru Fortress) of Vlad Ţepeş (also known as Dracula) towering high above you is sure to send chills down your spine. ∎

MUNTENIA

Bucharest

Area of map detail

Curtea de Argeş

Curtea de Argeş

🅰 66 A3

Visitor information

✉ Primăria, Str. Basarabilor 99

☎ 0248 721 033

THE FORMER MUNTENIAN CAPITAL OF CURTEA DE ARGEŞ (Court of Argeş) lies beside the Argeş River surrounded by the Carpathian foothills. In historic terms, Curtea de Argeş is one of the most important places in Muntenia, and since the 1990s, the city has been enjoying a revitalization, attracting tourists to its two famous churches and medieval court.

The 16th-century church within the Curtea de Argeş Monastery complex was rebuilt in the 1870s after it had fallen into disrepair.

As its name suggests, Curtea de Argeş was a royal town. The **Municipal Museum,** north of the market beside the main road to the county town of Piteşti, oversees the **Curtea Domnească** *(enter via gateway at back of Municipal Museum's parking area),* the first princely citadel of independent Muntenia. It was built in 1330 soon after the Battle of Posada, when Prince Basarab I fought off a Hungarian invasion attempt. The victory gave Muntenian rulers the impetus they needed to create an independent principality. What is left of the court stands in a walled enclosure.

The court contains the ruins of the 13th-century church, **Biserica Sf. Nicoara,** but the most complete building in the complex is the chunky Byzantine-style church of **Sf. Niculae** (St. Nicholas). Dating from the mid-to late 14th century, this church is one of the oldest Orthodox shrines in Muntenia and has been designated a World Heritage site. Its founder was Vlaicu Voda (R. 1364–1377), who moved the Muntenian capital from Câmpulung Muscel to Curtea de Argeş in 1369. The church is modeled on a Greek design, with a single, central tower over a cross-in-square ground plan. The exterior is attractively decorated with a pattern that alternates bricks and river stones. Most of the interior frescoes are original and date from the reign of Vlad I (1395–97). The frescoes are lively and fun and reveal the confidence of a newly independent state. The painters drew inspiration from local folk styles and early Renaissance naturalism as well as formulaic Byzantine art.

Drive north along Bulevardul Basarabilor to see **Mănăstirea Curtea de Argeş** and the

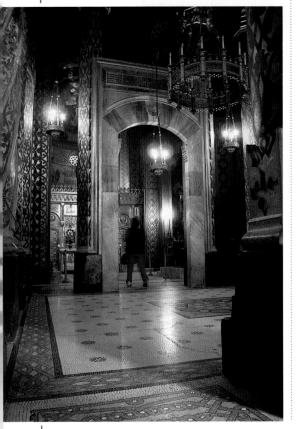

Episcopal Church (*B-dul Basarabilor 1, tel 0248 721 735*). The monastery was founded in 1517 and the church is a marvelous confection of delicate stonework. Ornamental rosettes and squares, tracery, and miniature figures make the church look like a giant *chivot*, or reliquary case, which some art historians believe might have provided the inspiration.

Prince Neagoe Basarab (*R. 1512–1521*) hired a mason from Nicosia called Manole to design the church. The result is a blend of Romanian, Oriental, Byzantine, Caucasian, Balkan, and Western styles. One of its striking features is the slanting design of the cylinders that support the two cupolas at the west end of the church. The design makes the cylinders appear as though they are leaning to one side. Basarab supervised the church's construction himself, hoping it would be "a piece of God's heaven." The exterior walls are made from the same creamy, Albeşti limestone as Mănăstirea Dealu (see p. 69).

The church became an archbishop's residence in 1739 and later the resting place for united Romania's first two royal couples, King Carol I (*R. 1866–1914*) and Queen Elizabeth and King Ferdinand (*R. 1914–1927*) and Queen Marie. Most of the superb 16th-century frescoes, by one Dobromir of Târgovişte, have been lost, but a few fragments can be seen in the National Museum of Fine Art in Bucharest.

To gain a sense of what Curtea de Argeş was like before the communist period, explore the area around **Piaţa Centrală** (Central Square). Most of the houses in this district were built between the late 18th and early 20th centuries. **Casa Goangă,** an inn on Strada

Manole's legend

A famous legend relates that Manole immured his wife between the outer stone and inner brick walls of the Episcopal Church to make sure he would be able to complete it. Once it was finished, Manole's patron stranded him on the roof, because he wanted to make sure that no one else would have a finer church. The desperate builder is said to have made himself a pair of wings and crashed to earth beside the church, whereupon a spring of pure water burst forth beneath him.

Viorelelor, is one of the oldest.

Market day (*Thurs.*) is a good time to visit. After browsing among stalls in Piaţa Centrală, try a glass of Romanian beer with scrumptious *mititei* (little grilled rolls made with a mixture of beef, mutton, and pork and served with fresh white bread and mustard) at **Mrs. Mitrofan's terrace restaurant** housed in a former Phanariot mansion opposite the entrance to the market building. In the back of the building, you can see an authentic interior and painted ceilings from 1821. ■

Municipal Museum
✉ Str. Negru Vodă 2
☎ 0248 721 446
🕑 Closed Mon.
💲 $

Tasty *covrigi* (pretzels) for sale in Curtea de Argeş

A 15th-century *Brădet skete* (wooden church), north of Curtea de Argeş

A drive in the Iezer Hills

The deeply folded mountains to the north of Curtea de Argeş offer breathtaking views and shelter secluded villages and lonely monasteries. This area lay on the border between Muntenia and Transylvania from the 14th to the early 20th centuries.

Before you set off, be aware that signposting in most of Romania's rural areas is often nonexistent. If in doubt of a direction, always ask. Begin at the Royal Court in the center of Curtea de Argeş and take the right turn for Câmpulung Muscel along the DN73C. Drive through Valea Iaşului and in 9 miles (14 km), you will reach Robaia and Muşăteşti, where a signpost points left for Brădet. Turn onto the small, poorly maintained country road and drive through the villages of Galeşu and Brăduleţ until you reach **Brădet** ❶ (sometimes called Brădetu), 17 miles (28 km) total from Curtea de Argeş.

Brădet means "fir forest." Commanding some wonderful views, the town is bordered by dense, mixed-leaf woodlands. It is a very popular spot with Romanian walkers. Some people come here to collect water from sulfurous springs that can be found near the village. If you wish to stay overnight, Brădet has several guesthouses—try Casa Cristina

(contact Mrs. Cristina Popescu, tel 0744 993 860), for example, where the founders of the Făgăraş anticommunist resistance met for the first time.

In the center of the village, beside the mill and a group of fir trees, turn left up a rough hillside track. In about 1 mile (2 km) you will reach a charming 15th-century wooden **skete** (small Orthodox monastery). The building is a copy of Mănăstirea Cozia (see p. 90). Close by is an 18th-century bell tower. Another forest track leaves the village and follows the **Vâlsan River** to the north, winding through the Keys (Gorges) of Vâlsan. Part of the river is home to a prehistoric fish, *Romanichthys valsanicola,* called *asprete* in Romanian.

Return to the main DN73C at Muşăteşti and turn left. In the next village, **Domneşti,** cross the bridge and take another country road to the left. The surface has one or two 50-yard breaks in it but is generally not bad. The road follows the Doamnei River and goes through Stănești and Corbșori (5.5 miles/9 km from Domnești), but ask for directions if you're in doubt. Continue until you reach **Corbi** ❷ (another 2 miles/3 km from Corbșori).

The village's full name (Corbii de Piatra) means "the stone ravens." It was founded in the mid-18th century by shepherds from the Transylvanian village of Jina (see p. 133) who were fleeing from Austrian rule. Once settled here, they kept to themselves. Muntenians say that you can still tell people from Corbi apart from the rest of the region's people.

In the center of Corbi, turn right, drive over the bridge, and follow the road to the right for approximately half a mile (1 km). This route brings you to the rock-cut **monastery church of Sts. Peter and Paul** (*for entrance after 4 p.m., ask at the house that stands opposite the cliff*). The church has been carved into the bottom of a massive gritstone cliff. The monastery was founded by a group of nuns in the 14th century. At times of trouble during Muntenia's history, the church has been a

favorite sanctuary and hiding place for the principality's leaders.

The church contains some of the purest Byzantine-style frescoes (also 14th century) ever found in Romania. Its stone icon screen was painted in 1804, probably by a local master called Ștefan Zugravu (Stephen the Painter). Although services are still held here, the

---

✚ See area map p. 66
▶ Curtea de Argeș
↔ 57 miles (91 km). Parts of the main road (DN 73C) between these two towns are often washed away by snowmelt. A 4WD is recommended.
🕐 4 hours
▶ Nămăești Monastery

NOT TO BE MISSED
- Brădet
- Corbii de Piatra
- Nucșoara
- Câmpulung Muscel

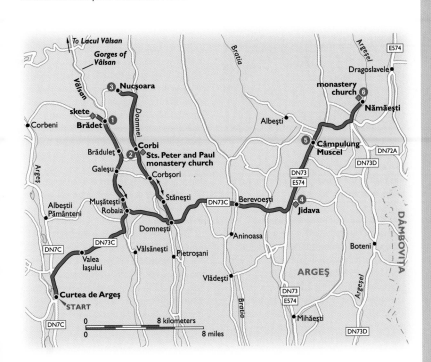

interior is in a very fragile state. Tree roots are forcing the walls apart, which is allowing water to damage the frescoes. Please do not touch the walls. Beside the church is another man-made hollow. Known as the **Tribunal,** it was used by Prince Neagoe Basarab in his role as judge.

From Corbi, drive about 6 miles (10 km) north to the village of **Nucşoara** ③. During

The unique monastery church in Nămăeşti was built in the 16th century into the stone of the cave around it.

the 1950s, Elizabeta Rizea, who was imprisoned and tortured for supporting the anticommunist movement (see pp. 78–79), lived here. Her cottage still exists and is being looked after by her daughter. Ask for directions when you reach the village.

Return to the main road and drive east to the junction with the DN73, then turn left. Down a grassy track on the right, about half a mile (1 km) past the junction, lie the

remains of a little Roman fortress called **Jidava** ④, which stood on the *limes transalutanus* (the Olt frontier that protected the Bran Pass, farther north, in the second and third centuries A.D.).

In 4 miles (7 km) you will reach the lovely old town of **Câmpulung Muscel** ⑤. Standing on one of the main medieval roads linking Muntenia with Transylvania, Câmpulung (whose name means "long field") was founded by northern European traders, probably in the first half of the 13th century.

Drive into town and park near the 17th-century **monastery of Negru Vodă** *(Str. Negru Vodă 64, tel 0248 510 750)*. The working monastery stands below the road on the right-hand side, just beyond the left turn into Strada Elena Doamna. Made of handsome local limestone blocks, it stands on the former site of Basarab I's court.

Walk toward the historic center and take the left-hand fork into Strada Republicii. The **Ethnographic Museum** *(Str. Republicii 5, tel 0248 510 465; closed Mon., $)* stands on the left in a splendidly rustic villa from 1735. The building needs some restoration work, but for a concentrated look at ingenious and often beautiful handmade artifacts, it is well worth a browse.

Either walk or drive farther north (in the car your right of way will be along Str. Negru Vodă) to the **Primăria** (Town Hall). Walk to the left up the hill past Town Hall, cross Strada Lascar Catargiu, and continue up Strada Soldat Golescu. After a short, stiff climb you will reach **Casa Golescu** *(Str. Soldat Golescu 3, tel 0248 512 481)* on the left. This beautiful 1910 house has been restored to its neo-Romanian glory with funds raised by the charity Pro Patrimonio. The house and gardens will open as a cultural center, with accommodations for visitors, in June 2007.

Drive out of town east on the DN73. A couple of miles (3 km) from Câmpulung, turn left into **Nămăeşti** village. Here, up a short, steep driveway on your left (west), is another fascinating little rock-cut **monastery church** ⑥. Legend has it that two shepherds carved the church out of a cave where they found a mysterious icon showing the Virgin and Child. ∎

Prahova Valley

SHROUDED IN MIXED-LEAF FORESTS AND CROWNED BY spectacular crags, the Prahova Valley beckons romantic souls and hardy explorers. A main road linking Bucharest and Transylvania courses through the valley, providing numerous access points to the mountains and tributary valleys.

The hills of Valea Dorului near Sinaia provide some of the best skiing in Romania.

SINAIA

Most action in the valley revolves around the resort of Sinaia. Also known as the Carpathian Pearl, the town is a harmonious mix of picturesque 19th-century villas and modern, high-rise hotels. Sinaia clings to the lower slopes of the towering Bucegi Massif, some 75 miles (120 km) northwest of Bucharest.

Sinaia developed as a spa after King Carol I (a member of the Hohenzollern family) built his summer palace, or castle, here. Carol began **Castelul Peleş** in 1866 after he acceded to the throne. The final touches were made in 1914, two years before he died. Peleş is a fantastical mixture of German neo-Renaissance and neo-Gothic architecture. Its interior contains heavy, Germanic wood carvings, a colonial-style display of weapons, and a series of rooms devoted to typical interiors from different parts of the world—styles include Venetian, Moorish, and Turkish. While the ground-floor rooms are spectacular, if you have a chance, try to visit the castle on a day when the first-floor rooms are open to the public; it happens only a few times during the year (call for dates). The castle draws many visitors, so be prepared for lines.

The grounds of the castle also hold two other palaces, Pelişor and Foişor. **Pelişor,** the larger of the two, is open to the public. Its half-timbered, chalet-style exterior was designed by a Czech architect in 1902. Queen Marie of Romania

(1875–1938) decorated the hall and apartments using art nouveau themes. By comparison with Peleş, the interior of Pelişor is pleasantly warm and airy. **Foişor** *(closed to the public)* was built by Ceauşescu and stands higher up the hillside, symbolically allowing him to look down on the royal family.

Sinaia's royal connections date back to a much earlier time. The town gets its name from the 17th-century **Mănăstirea Sinaia** that stands halfway up the winding road to the castle. The monastery was founded by Muntenian prince Mihai Cantacuzino after he made a pilgrimage to St. Catherine's Monastery on Mount Sinai. (Legend has it that Romanians helped to build the monastery during the reign of the Byzantine emperor Justinian.)

The larger of the monastery's two churches dates from the late

Prahova Valley

[Map] 66 C3–C4

[Mail] Centrul de Informare şi Promovare Turistică Sinaia, B-dul Carol I 47

[Phone] 0244 315 656

[Car] By car: The DN71 from Sinaia to Târgovişte is a pretty alternate to the main Ploieşti route. The DN1 (Bucharest-Sinaia-Braşov) can be extremely congested on summer weekends. By train and bus: From Bucharest and Braşov to Sinaia.

Castelul Peleş

- ⓜ 66 C4
- ✉ Str. Pelişului 2
- ☎ 0244 310 918
- ⏱ Closed Mon. Apr.–Sept.; Mon.–Tues. Oct. & Dec.–Mar.; all Nov.
- 💲 $$

Mănăstirea Sinaia

- ⓜ 66 C4
- ✉ Str. Mănăstirii 2
- ☎ 0244 314 917
- ⏱ Closed Mon. & Tue.
- 💲 $
- 🚌 DN1/E60 highway; train or bus from Bucharest and Braşov

Bucegi Massif

- ⓜ 66 B4

Brebu

- ⓜ 66 C3
- 🚌 Take the DN1 to Comarnic then take a local road 8 miles (13 km) to Brebu. A minibus runs from the Câmpina bus station

Opposite: Peleş Castle, Sinaia: King Carol I's eclectic extravaganza is now a state museum.

19th and early 20th centuries and copies the Brâncovenesque style. Cantacuzino's more modest (and in many ways more attractive) shrine stands in a second courtyard. It dates from 1695.

The **monastery museum** contains a copy of the first Bible to be printed in Romanian (albeit in Cyrillic letters); the publication was sponsored by Mihai Cantacuzino's brother, Şerban, in 1688.

BUCEGI MASSIF

Towering vertically above Sinaia is the Bucegi Massif. These peaks are among the highest in the Carpathian Mountains—Mount Omu at 8,219 feet (2,505 m) is the tallest in the vicinity. Some curious rock formations have been given names such as the Babele (Old Women) and the Sfinxul (Sphinx).

You can easily gain some elevation in the massif by taking a **cable car ride** (contact Centru de Informare Turistica Sinaia, B-dul Carol I 47, tel 0244 315 656, $$) from the center of Sinaia to the peak Vârful cu Dor. The town terminus is located behind Hotel Montana on Strada Teodor Aman. There are two stations, or stops—

Striking stones

Strewn with great chunks of limestone rock that resemble human and animal figures, Corbi and the area around it have inspired many legends. Ion Andreescu, a local teacher, spent his life studying evidence of ancient cults that he found preserved in the stone. His finds include prehistoric altars, similar inscriptions to the Sanskrit alphabet, and sculpted faces. His finds came to light when the weekly Romanian magazine, *Formula AS*, published an article about him in August 2002. ∎

the highest, Cota 2000, sits at 6,560 feet (2,000 m). You may elect to walk back to Sinaia via the marked path; the descent from Cota 2000 takes about two hours.

Cabins with hostel-style rooms are available for people who wish to spend more time on the mountain. They include **Cabana Valea cu Brazi** (contact Gheorghe Mocanu, tel 0723 249 844) at 4,500 feet (1,372 m) and **Cabana Mioriţa** (tel 0244 312 2999, reserve at least 1 week in advance) at 6,560 feet (2,000 m). There is also the 3-star **Hotel Cota 1400** (tel 0244 314 990).

The terrain is rugged and the weather on top can change rapidly without warning—this is not a place for a casual stroll. Winter sports programs are also offered in the nearby resorts of **Azuga, Busteni** (which has a cable car as well), and **Predeal.**

BREBU

The village of Brebu, some 27.5 miles (44 km) from Sinaia, has one of the most well-preserved 17th-century manor houses in Wallachia. The imposing **Casa Domnească de la Brebu** (Palace of Breb; tel 0244 357 731, closed Mon., $) in the center of town was started in 1650 by Prince Matei Basarab and completed by the energetic Prince Constantin Brâncoveanu about 40 years later. Serving the dual purpose of family home and barracks, the building complex boasts a massive protective wall with lookout towers. The entrance alone is a 80-foot-high (27 m), four-story building. Brâncoveanu also added summer houses and a monastery to the palace. To make room for the new buildings, he razed many cottages, displacing many villagers and incurring their long-lasting wrath. In Brebu, his name is still mud. ∎

Aurel Vlad's 1997 sculpture "Cortegiul Sacrificatilor" (Cortege of the Sacrificed) is a poignant reminder of Romania's past at the Memorialul Victimelor Comunismului și al Rezistenței in Sighetu Marmației.

Resistance fighters

Romania had one of the nastiest communist regimes in Europe. The authorities used mass murder, starvation, and torture to eradicate their opponents and intimidate the population at large. Unlike those in Poland, Romania's rulers allowed no opposition of any kind. As a result, resistance was very limited. As the years went by, a kind of moral apathy seemed to have siezed the country by the throat.

Exceptions did occur, however; throughout the 40 years of communist rule (1947–1989), isolated individuals and groups fought for an end to the oppression. In days of old, Romania's refugees and outlaws took to the mountains during Turkish attacks, Tatar raids, and other invasions; they did so as well during the communist period. In the 1950s, resistance fighters formed spontaneous groups in the Apuseni range, in Obcinele Bucovinei (Bucovina), on both sides of the Făgăraș range, in the Vrancea Mountains, and elsewhere in the Carpathians. Another group made its base in the Babadag forests of Dobrogea. The resistance groups contained people of both sexes, all ages, and all conditions.

The most famous resistance fighters in the Făgăraș Mountains were the Haiducii Muscelului, the Muscel Outlaws (so named because they came from areas near Câmpulung Muscel). The group's leaders included Col. Gheorghe Arsenescu and the brothers Toma and Petru Arnăuțiou. They and their supporters came from the village of Corbi (see pp. 72–73), Nucșoara, the Doamnei River Valley, and the Iezer Mountains. From 1949 to 1958 they and their successors formed what became the first and longest-lasting defiance of any communist government in Europe.

In 1949, four members of Haiducii were surprised by the Securitate. They shot two secret service officers in self-defense. The group then retreated higher into the mountains. Soon other villagers came to join them. The partisans lived in the wild year-round, sometimes camping in a network of underground grottoes. Their wives and

the partisans' families and anyone suspected of helping them. One such person was Elizabeta Rizea (1912–2003), a farmer from Nucșoara (see p. 73). She and her husband had joined the guerrilla movement because she was opposed to collectivization. When captured in 1949, Mrs. Rizea refused to give information about the other partisans' whereabouts and was sentenced to death as "an enemy of the people." Her sentence was commuted to seven years, during which she was tortured in the notorious Jilava prison. She subsequently was sentenced to another 25 years in jail. She was released in a general amnesty in 1964 and survived to tell her tale after the fall of the communist regime.

The **Sighetu Marmației** memorial includes **"Femei în închisoare" (Women in Prison)**, which documents bitter details of the country's autocratic communist regime.

daughters supplied them with food while they waited for the day when Romanians as a whole would rise against the communist dictatorship. They practiced a policy of nonviolence, and their victims were few and far between. Arsenescu managed to evade the secret service until 1960, when he was caught and killed. Toma Arnăuțiou then led the partisans for ten years, but he eventually was killed in the mountains, too.

In retaliation against the resistance fighters' acts, the secret service persecuted

The Romanian satirical weekly magazine *Academia Cațavencu* is hoping to raise funds for a statue of Mrs. Rizea to stand proudly and defiantly in front of Casa Scânteii in Bucharest, a spot occupied until 1990 by a figure of Joseph Stalin. Other monuments that memorialize the courage and deeds of the resistance fighters already exist around the country, such as the Memorial of the Victims of Communism and the Resistance in Sighetu Marmației (see p. 186). They serve as a poignant and visible reminder of a harrowing time. ∎

More places to visit in Muntenia

MĂNĂSTIREA COTMEANA

Looking more like a fortress than a church, the little monastery of Cotmeana stands in a walled enclosure surrounded by open fields. It's a charming place that makes a welcome respite from the road. You can reach it from the main DN7/E81 highway between Piteşti (28 miles/43 km) and Râmnicu Vâlcea (15.5 miles/25 km). Turn left at the sign for Cotmeana and follow the road around a dogleg bend into the village, then turn left again, so that you are heading out into open country. You've arrived when you see an ornamental wooden lych-gate on the left-hand side.

Cotmeana is Muntenia's oldest monastery. It was originally built for Radu I, a grandson of the principality's founder, who ruled between 1377 and 1383. His sons, Dan I (R. 1383–86) and Mircea cel Bătrân (Mircea the Wise, R. 1386–1418), adopted the church after their father's death. Radu was an energetic constructor of churches, counting Tismana and Cozia monasteries as well as the Royal Church at Curtea de Argeş among his 12 foundations. Some of them were Catholic rather than Orthodox, showing how the sands of religious influence were constantly shifting even in this area, which is usually thought of as a bastion of Eastern Christianity.

As was so often the case in the Middle Ages, the building fulfilled the role of strategic defense point as well as religious sanctuary. Thanks to subsequent alterations, Cotmeana looks as though it's been created from two separate buildings, one Byzantine with characteristic Balkan zigzag brickwork and ceramic disks, the other modeled on the Saxon hall churches of nearby Transylvania. Inside are the remains of 14th-century frescoes. The separate bell tower (the bells date from before 1386) acted as a lookout post, since the monastery was built to defend this area from Tatars and Turks. Constantin Brâncoveanu also cared for Cotmeana; under his rule, the window frames and nave door were replaced, the narthex was enlarged, and a new porch was added on the north side. The monastery is run by a handful of monks who came here after the church was reopened in 1991. Its *stareţ* (abbot), Parintele Ioasaf, has won a reputation for supposedly exorcising evil spirits, and on Fridays the church is full to bursting with believers who are looking for his help.

▲ 66 A3 **Visitor information** ✉ Episcopia Argeşului şi Muscelului, B-dul Basarabilor 23, Curtea de Argeş ☎ 0248 722 410

MUZEUL GUMELNIŢA (MUZEUL DE ARHEOLOGIE)

At the southern end of Muntenia, on the banks of the Danube River, the Muzeul Gumelniţa (archaeology museum) in Olteniţa has one of the best prehistoric pottery collections in Romania. The objects include tiny, lifelike figures of people and animals, ceramic altars, model houses and furniture, beautiful bowls, shamans' masks, fat-thighed goddesses, and zoomorphic jars and jugs. They give fascinating insights into little-known cultures such as the Dudeşti, Boian, and Gumelniţa that flourished on both banks of the river from the fifth millennium B.C. to the Iron Age Thracian period in the first century B.C. It's an hour or so drive from Bucharest, but the pieces on display are especially rewarding.

▲ 66 D1 ✉ Str. Argeşului 101, Olteniţa (39 miles/62 km on DN4 from southeast Bucharest and through Budeşti) ☎ 0242 511 174 🕒 Closed Mon. 🚌 Minibus from Piaţa Sudului in Bucharest

MUZEUL VITICULTURII ŞI POMICULTURII, GOLEŞTI

Since it opened in 1939, this delightful 17th-century manor house near the industrial center of Piteşti has combined the functions of a working winery and fruit farm with a fascinating museum of village life. The museum consists of an entire village of wooden buildings with traditional interiors. The manor has preserved the interior of the Golescu family home.

▲ 66 B3 ✉ Str. Banu Radu Golescu, Goleşti (9 miles/15 km E of Piteşti on DN7) ☎ 0248 266 364 🕒 Closed Mon. 🚏 $ 🚌 Minibus from Piteşti to Goleşti ■

W ith its wild crags, thickly wooded glens, and secluded clifftop monasteries, this region exudes a haunting quality. The Oltenians themselves are partly responsible: They have a reputation for maintaining their *obiceiuri vechi* (old customs).

Oltenia

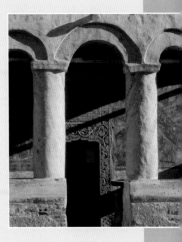

Orthodox church, Oltenia

Oltenia

COVERING A DIVERSITY OF LANDSCAPES FROM THE DANUBIAN PLAINS TO the southern Carpathian Mountains, Oltenia can look like a rural idyll—one made all the more welcoming by its hospitable inhabitants.

The Bujoreni open-air museum in its pastoral setting

At Oltenia's western extremity, where the mountains and river meet, the plant life is noticeably more Mediterranean than in other areas of Romania. This area is famous for its biodiversity, of which a portion lies protected in the nature reserve at Domogled, near Băile Herculane. Great forests of fir and deciduous trees blanket the mountains, and the higher outcrops support isolated pockets of striking *pina nigra,* the Romanian black pine. In autumn, swathes of beech trees create glorious displays of yellow and red-gold leaves. Where the Carpathian foothills merge with the plains, contented-looking cows graze in fields of velvety grass; apple, cherry, and pear orchards thrive; and stands of mature and stately trees grow thick.

Under communism, life was generally harder in the plains than in the mountains: For logistical and economic reasons, mountain dwellers usually escaped the harshest forms of collective and state farming. Oltenia was no exception, and as a result there is a marked contrast between its northern and southern halves. In the southern half, thanks to Ceauşescu's attempt to industrialize at any cost, dead or dying factory buildings and sterile quarry waste have left ugly gashes in the countryside and in the outskirts of towns. Unemployment is rampant, much of it resulting from the late 1990s government shutdown of the bituminous and lignite coal industries concentrated in the Jiu Valley, which employed tens of thousands of people. Flooding caused by indiscriminate logging and the wanton destruction of hillside orchards has devastated homes and blocked watercourses. Often it seems that little has been done to clear up the damage or prevent it from happening again.

Such conditions have left a pall of sadness hanging over the area; however, things are not bad for everyone, and there are hopeful signs of a regeneration, one that is growing on the back of a nascent tourism industry. Oltenia has the advantage of picturesque, alpine landscapes and its famous hospitality to lure visitors to the area. Oltenians, like Romanians in general, have a subversive sense of humor, and they are nothing if not enterprising.

Oltenia is for those travelers who enjoy life off the beaten path. The area between the Jiu and Cerna valleys contains some spectacular mountain scenery and affords visitors a chance to see true Romanian rural life. Several of Romania's most historic and beautiful monasteries stand in the northern half of the region, often sited in breathtaking places. The cities of Târgu Jiu and Caracal reveal architectural vestiges of a precommunist past. The southern Carpathians and the Danube River Basin sustained prehistoric communities, whose creative genius continues to inspire artists and thinkers to this day; remnants of the later Roman occupation are visible in Drobeta-Turnu Severin and Corabia. ■

**Built by
Muntenia's Golden
Prince, Constantin
Brâncoveanu,
Hurezi Monastery
is one of
Romania's finest
religious buildings.
Beautifully
restored, it draws
pilgrims and
tourists alike.**

**Mănăstirea
Govora**

- ⛰ 83 D3
- ✉ Băile Govora
- ☎ 0250 770 342
- 🚗 By car: 9 miles
  (15 km) S of
  Râmnicu Vâlcea
  via DN67, then
  follow signs

Oltenia's monasteries

OLTENIA IS FAMOUS FOR ITS ORTHODOX MONASTERIES,
which form a distinct architectural group of their own. Several were
built under the creative patronage of Wallachia's "Golden Prince,"
Constantin Brâncoveanu (*R.* 1688–1714), but other earlier foundations also played a crucial part in forging Romania's cultural identity.

Balancing precariously between
neighboring Hungary, his suzerain
lords in Turkey, and the Habsburg
Empire that was increasing its
power in east-central Europe,
Brâncoveanu was one of the
outstanding figures in Wallachia's
history. His support for the arts,
and learning in general, helped
rekindle a sense of pride in
Romanian identity, which is as
true now as it was then.

The word *mănăstire* refers to
both monasteries and convents.
Today Romania has about 400
monastic foundations, served by
3,500 monks and 5,000 nuns. As
in most of Romania's religious
foundations, you are welcome to

look around as long as you respect
their regime. Five of Oltenia's most
striking and historic monasteries,
and a few others, lie on or near
the DN67 between Râmnicu
Vâlcea (see p. 100) and Târgu Jiu
(see pp. 92–93).

MĂNĂSTIREA GOVORA

The strongly fortified, 15th-
century Govora Monastery stands
on a steep slope outside the town
of Băile Govora. Inside the fortress
walls, a row of handsome ancillary
buildings huddles next to the
Orthodox church. A few nuns
manage the place today and the
atmosphere is devout but relaxed.
Govora's founder, Prince Radu cel

Frumos (Radu the Handsome, R. 1495–1508) attracted many scholars to Govora, and you can see the appeal of the place: The strength of the complex provides a sense of security, and the views from the hill are spectacular. Decades later, Brâncoveanu reconstructed the church and brought several artists from Hurezi Monastery (see below) to paint its charming frescoes.

Clinging to the sides and bottom of a steep valley, **Băile Govora** (Govora Spa) has a protected feel. Old-fashioned, timber-fronted villas and hotels with wide wooden balconies give it an air of solidity and permanence. There has been some investment in new hotels, and the town is starting to thrive.

MĂNĂSTIREA HUREZI

The most glorious of Oltenia's religious foundations stands some 25 miles (39 km) west of Râmnicu Vâlcea on a low hill surrounded by wooded valleys. The working monastery of Hurezi (pronounced without the final "i" and sometimes spelled Horezu) is fortified, and from a distance it gives the impression of being a castle; however, its awe-inspiring sense dissipates the moment you walk inside. This building was one of the crowning achievements in Brâncoveanu's life; it has recently been restored and designated a UNESCO World Heritage site.

The 1690 **church** is one of the great examples of the so-called Brâncovenesque style. Byzantine, Islamic, and Palladian features combine in such a way that the entire complex sits together in perfect proportion and nothing is allowed to upset its overall serenity and balance. The style is displayed in full flight: round-headed arches that form a wide arcade along the

entire west entrance of the church; tall, helmeted towers; open-work balustrades of limestone carved into curling fronds and zoomorphic heraldic motifs.

An open-sided canopy stands in front of the main steps that lead into the arcaded porch, a feature found in traditional peasant homes. The canopy's cornice is decorated with religious images and whimsical landscapes containing birds and animals. The landscape panels have a Western sense of perspective; they are a common feature in many of Brâncoveanu's churches. Inside the porch is the largest "Last Judgment" scene in Wallachia. Balancing heavenly virtues against the damnations of hell, this graphic theme became very popular with Romania's medieval Orthodox leaders. The most beautiful version is at Voroneţ (see pp. 203 and 206). In happy proximity to the Paradise

Mănăstirea Hurezi

🗺 83 D3

✉ Str. Mănăstirii, Hurezu

☎ 0250 860 071

🚗 By car: 25 miles (39 km) W of Râmnicu Vâlcea via DN67, then follow signs

🏨 Basic accommodations are available, but preference is given to church officials.

Cule

The Wallachian countryside is dotted with towerlike *cule*, a name derived from a Turkish word for "tower." These 18th- and 19th-century manor houses were built by the country's lesser nobles and landowners who refused to abandon their estates during savage raids by Ottoman soldiers. As solid as rocks, they are surprisingly elegant. Their designs vary, but a typical *culă* has two stories, thick, tapering walls, and a steeply pitched roof. The ground-floor cellar-storage area cum barn could be isolated to prevent intruders from reaching the family above. The top floor usually has an arcaded balcony open on two sides that allowed its occupants to see any approaching enemy. ∎

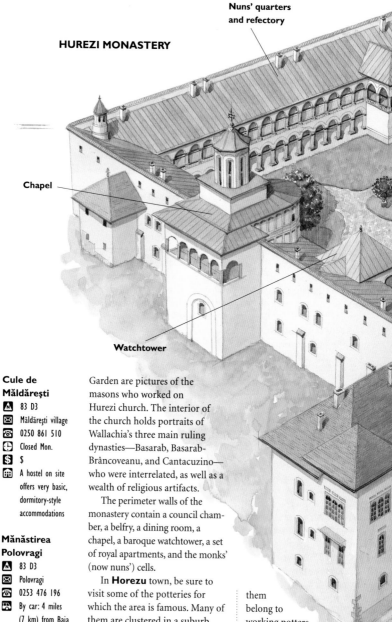

Nuns' quarters
and refectory

HUREZI MONASTERY

Chapel

Watchtower

**Cule de
Măldăreşti**

🏚 83 D3
✉ Măldăreşti village
☎ 0250 861 510
🕐 Closed Mon.
💲 $
🏨 A hostel on site
offers very basic,
dormitory-style
accommodations

**Mănăstirea
Polovragi**

🏚 83 D3
✉ Polovragi
☎ 0253 476 196
🚗 By car: 4 miles
(7 km) from Baia
de Fier

Garden are pictures of the
masons who worked on
Hurezi church. The interior of
the church holds portraits of
Wallachia's three main ruling
dynasties—Basarab, Basarab-
Brâncoveanu, and Cantacuzino—
who were interrelated, as well as a
wealth of religious artifacts.

The perimeter walls of the
monastery contain a council chamber, a belfry, a dining room, a
chapel, a baroque watchtower, a set
of royal apartments, and the monks'
(now nuns') cells.

In **Horezu** town, be sure to
visit some of the potteries for
which the area is famous. Many of
them are clustered in a suburb
about 3 miles (5 km) from town
called **Satul Olari** (guided tours
available, ask at Town Hall, tel
0250 860 190). Visit any of the
houses that display colorful plates
in their front gardens: Most of

them
belong to
working potters
who will be happy to
show you around their
studios or direct you to their
neighbors. The potters of Olari
make a range of traditional and
modern wares. Some of their

Main church

Bell tower

Inner courtyard entrance

designs are modeled on the prehistoric ceramic styles for which southern Romania is rightly renowned. The nearby village of **Măldăreşti,** about 2 miles (3 km) south of the town of Horezu, has two towerlike ***cule*** (see sidebar p. 85) that are well worth visiting. They are decorated with attractive

stucco reliefs and contain a fascinating collection of icons.

MĂNĂSTIREA POLOVRAGI

The 17th-century monastery of Polovragi stands sheltered under the spectacular karstic outcrops of Cheile Oltețului, about 9 miles (14 km) northwest of Măldăreşti.

Mănăstirea Lainici

🅰 83 C4

✉ Lainici

☎ 0253 463 333

🚗 By car: 20 miles (32 km) from Târgu Jiu

🏨 Accommodations may be available

Folk architecture

Many of Romania's 41 counties have a publicly funded museum of vernacular architecture. Oltenia's Gorj County **Muzeul Arhitecturii Populare din Curţisoara** (Curţisoara Folk Architecture Museum; *Str. Bumbeşti-Jiu, Bumbeşti-Jiu, tel 0253 223 890, closed Mon., $*) opened in 1975 after Ceauşescu adjured the people to preserve their rural heritage. The timber cottages, barns, and ornamented gateways here lie around like slumbering dinosaurs in a park dotted with walnut trees. There is also an example of a fortified *cula* here. The museum often holds workshops and exhibitions that encourage visitors to try their hands at traditional skills. ■

It is named after *polovraga*, a medicinal herb that the Dacians used more than 2,000 years ago. The monastery's secluded location set against a backdrop of the tree-strewn Olteţ Gorges makes it a striking place to visit, even if you do not enter the monastery precinct.

Inside, an early 18th-century neo-Byzantine painting of Mount Athos in Greece covers the entire west wall. Protected from the rain by a glassed-in porch, the fresco is a delightfully schematic and patterned view of the holy mountain. Romania's medieval princes often endowed Athonite foundations with gifts and land because it helped sustain their connections with the Orthodox Church after the Byzantine Empire was crushed.

The surrounding countryside holds a couple of interesting sights. In the gorges, there is a spot where the **Olteţ River** shoots through a tiny channel between the Parâng and Căpăţânii ranges of the southern Carpathians. At only 6 feet wide (2 m), it is claimed to be the narrowest gap between two mountains in the world. The nearby 6.3-mile-long (10.2 km), lime-encrusted **Peştera Pahomie (or Polovragi)** (Pahomie's, or Polovragi's, Cave; *closed Mon., $*) is named after a monk from Polovragi who painted images on the walls. Bones of prehistoric cave bears and neolithic pottery have been found here. The cave is believed to have connections with the Dacians' god-priest, Zalmoxis. It is not very cold inside and has been partially lit by electricity. A lovely ancient forest of sweet chestnuts and a narcissus meadow lie about 2.5 miles (4 km) south of the gorges.

MĂNĂSTIREA LAINICI

Standing some 20 miles (32 km) from Târgu Jiu, Lainici Monastery is reached by sweeping through narrow, winding beech-lined gorges. The monastery is relatively young. The older of its two arcaded churches, dating from 1812–1817, has paintings of saints around the exterior. The newer church was founded in 1990 and it would seem that no expense has been spared on its neo-Brâncovenesque lines.

Lainici's main claim to fame is that the 14th-century Balkan monk Nicodim once lived here. Nicodim spent his formative years cloistered on Mount Athos in Greece. He was a hesychast, a person who practiced an extremely ascetic form of devotion. He came to Wallachia in 1369 at the invitation of his distant cousin, Prince Vlaicu Vodă, and was responsible for building Wallachia's first Orthodox monasteries.

Aided by some devoted followers, Nicodim built a wooden **skete** (small monastery) on the site where Lainici Monastery stands

today. For centuries, it was regarded as a spiritual frontier post of the Orthodox faith. Befitting his modest lifestyle, Nicodim himself lived in a cave (it is near the Lainici railway station).

The monastery has experienced its share of hardships and drama. In the mid-18th century, Empress Maria Theresa of Austria commanded her soldiers to burn Nicodim's old church. In the 19th century, the Romanian revolutionary Tudor Vladimirescu hid in the monastery disguised as a monk to evade the Turks. During World War I, German soldiers stabled their horses in the church and burned its precious archives. And in 1961, the communists closed the monastery.

Since 1989, the monastery has risen from the ashes like a bejeweled phoenix. Seen against the thickly forested mountainsides with the sound of waterfalls nearby, the two churches encourage reflection and repose.

Explore the monastery's beautiful surroundings. A 3-mile (4.5 km) hike winds up a steep forest track to Mount Gropu and the modest but charming **monastery of Locurele.** Founded in 1850 by two priests from Târgu Jiu, it was abandoned in World War I and reopened only in 1957. The paintings date from 1897. Today Locurele is run by just two monks and is officially attached to Lainici. The views across the mountains are worth the climb.

MĂNĂSTIREA DINTR-UN LEMN

The monastery of Dintr-un Lemn (literally, "from one wood") lies farther off the beaten track, southwest of Râmnicu Vâlcea. Surrounded by pasture fields, the monastery stands on a sloping hillside beside the Otăsău River on the south side of the little village of Dezrobiți (before the bridge if you approach from Frâncești). The beauty of the countryside is as much a reason to visit the monastery as the buildings themselves.

Legend says that the original church was built by a shepherd from one gigantic oak trunk, but it has long since disappeared. Walk

A detail of a painting inside Mănăstirea Dintr-un Lemn. According to local tradition, the church is built on the site of a much older building that was constructed from the wood of a single oak tree.

Mănăstirea Dintr-un Lemn

🗺 83 D3

✉ Dezrobiți

☎ 0250 762 756

🚗 By car: 15 miles (24 km) W of Râmnicu Vâlcea via DN64

Mănăstirea Cozia

⚑ 83 D4

✉ Călimănești

☎ 0250 750 852

Mănăstirea Turnu

⚑ 83 D4

✉ off the DN7/E81

☎ 0250 750 851

Mănăstirea Frasinei

⚑ 83 D4

✉ Muereasca

up the steps into the second quadrangle and you'll find the main church. Founded in the 1630s, it has been altered, added to, and restored at least nine times, but it pales in comparison to its attractive secluded garden setting. At the back, standing in its own enclosure above a group of majestic oak trees, is a small timber church (not the one that gives the monastery its name). The monastery also manages a working farm and maintains several rooms available as accommodations.

MĂNĂSTIREA COZIA

The fascinating 14th-century Cozia Monastery stands a couple of miles (3 km) north of Călimănești

Above: The Orthodox church near the two Măldărești cule

Opposite: Constantin Brâncuși sitting on a forerunner of the "Table of Silence" in his Parisian studio (1932)

(and unfortunately close to a trucking route). The main church dates back to 1390; masons from the Morava Valley in Serbia came to work here for Prince Mircea cel Bătrân. Cozia's architecture is a wonderful blend of styles. The Byzantine influence shows most clearly in the flat-helmeted cupola, the round-headed walls, the ocular windows high up in the walls, and the trefoil apses at the east end. The typically Brâncovenesque arcaded porch and the icon screen are 17th-

century additions. The earliest paintings date from the 1300s; they line the *pronaos* (the westernmost chamber of the church).

Across the road is another part of the monastery and a slender 1542 brick church called a *bolniţa,* where monks could worship when they were sick. Cozia gets its name from the mountain that overlooks it from the northeast.

In the 15th century, some monks retreated from the Cozia Monastery and founded the **Mănăstirea Turnu,** which lies somewhat off the beaten track, farther north and on the eastern side of the Olt River. The monastery is named after a Roman observation tower that stood nearby.

MĂNĂSTIREA FRASINEI

Frasinei Monastery, some 20 miles (32 km) northwest of Râmnicu Vâlcea, is the only one in the region to maintain a strictly Athonite monastic regime. The monastery has two churches. The upper church, dating from 1863, stands surrounded by gorgeous ash glades (hence the monastery's name) at the upper end of an unstable mountain track. Visitors need a 4WD or a good pair of legs.

Dedicated to the Dormition of the Virgin, this church is forbidden to women, and the monks eat no meat. Women have been barred from the upper church since 1867 when a visiting abbot caught the monks having an orgy. Legend has it that when a shepherdess broke the no-females rule, she was struck down with epilepsy, and ever since, this event has been referred to as the Curse of Frasinei. The monastery's other church, about a mile (1.5 km) lower down the hill, is open to females and provides accommodations for them, too. ∎

Constantin Brâncuşi

The world-famous Oltenian sculptor Constantin Brâncuşi (pronounced Brn-COOSH) helped to liberate three-dimensional art from the pictorial style of the 19th century. Known for his "direct cutting" techniques (carving stone without making preparatory sketches), he took his ideas from a huge range of sources, including antiquity and contemporary technology.

Although Brâncuşi (1876–1957) spent most of his life in France, he was born in the village of Hobiţa, which lies to the west of Târgu Jiu (see pp. 92–93). His father was a landowner and his mother an artist-weaver. Brâncuşi showed talent as a carver from an early age. He studied furniture-making and design before moving to Bucharest, where he concentrated on his new love, sculpture, at the Fine Arts Academy.

Keen to broaden his artistic horizons, Brâncuşi set out for Paris in 1904. He took nearly a year to complete the journey, often traveling on foot. He rubbed shoulders with innovators like Picasso, Braque, Derain, and Modigliani, and as a result, his revolutionary sculptures were inspired by the ferment of political radicalism and artistic experimen-

tation. Like many of his contemporaries, he became aware of the beauties of non-European art and philosophy and of prehistoric art. Having graduated from the Bucharest academy as a brilliant naturalist, Brâncuşi realized that the simpler, and in some ways cruder, forms of woodcarving that he grew up with at home in Oltenia had something powerful to offer.

Brâncuşi broke new ground in 1907 with a carving called "The Prayer." Made to commemorate a Romanian businessman, it stood in a graveyard in the town of Buzău, in eastern Romania. He often worked in series. Key works such as "The Kiss" (of which he made many versions), the magic bird called "Maiastră," the astonishing marble and bronze figures of "Bird in Space," and the wooden three-dimensional zigzag form "Endless Columns" are just a few of the pieces that show his quest for the essence of human and animal forms.

Although Brâncuşi maintained that he was never an abstract artist, he was no stranger to controversy. In 1913, he was one of the first progressive European artists to exhibit in the United States. Following his New York debut, the American lawyer and collector John Quinn bought several of his works. In 1922, one of his bronzes, "Mademoiselle Pogany," was withdrawn from a Parisian show because one of the selectors thought it was pornographic. In 1926, two curators at the Metropolitan Museum in New York objected to a sleek bronze cast of "Bird in Space." They persuaded a customs officer to refuse it entry as artwork; he classified the piece as "kitchen utensils and hospital supplies" instead. The ensuing court case ruled that the bronze bird was in fact a work of art. This case proved to be a watershed in the future status of progressive art in the United States.

Brâncuşi was exhilarated by the United States and went on to show regularly there. Before he died, he made sketches for a Chicago high-rise building modeled on his "Endless Columns." The warmth and humor in his work makes it accessible to many who might otherwise steer clear of it. ∎

Târgu Jiu

TÂRGU JIU IS BEAUTIFULLY SITUATED BESIDE THE JIU RIVER, in sight of the southern Carpathian Mountains. Although the systematization of the 1960s wreaked havoc on the town's historic nature, its association with the world-famous sculptor Constantin Brâncuşi (see p. 91) has helped give it a new lease on life.

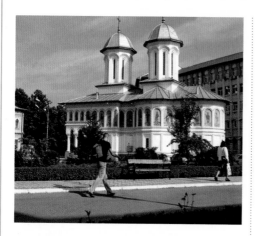

The attractive Biserica Sf. Voievozi (Holy Princes' Church) lies on a pedestrian-only section of Calea Victoriei in downtown Târgu Jiu.

Târgu Jiu
🔼 83 C3
Visitor information
✉ Centrul de
Informare Turistică,
Str. Victoriei 7A
☎ 0253 222 555

Târgu Jiu was the site of a devastating World War I defeat. In the days between November 11 and 17, 1916, the German Ninth Army advanced toward Bucharest from the mountain passes to the north. The ensuing battles, which included a heroic defense of the town's river bridge, claimed some 8,500 Romanian soldiers.

Brâncuşi commemorated the tragedy in a group of three monumental sculptures that lie about a mile (1.5 km) apart on an east-west axis that runs straight through the town. Sculpted out of stone, the 15-foot-tall (5 m) **"Poarta Sărutului"** ("Gate of the Kiss") and the low **"Masa Tăcerii"** ("Table of Silence") stand within sight of each other in Parcul Central (Central Park) between the Jiu River and Bulevardul Constantin Brâncuşi. The two pieces are linked by **Aleea Scaunelor** ("Alley of the Seats"), so-called because Brâncuşi designed 30 square stones to stand on either side of the pathway.

At the far end of the axis, the 100-foot-high (33 m) **"Coloana fără Sfârşit"** ("Column of the Infinite") consists of 15 brass-coated cast iron rhomboids slotted onto a steel shaft. The sculpture occupies a triangular space on the east side of town (between Calea Bucureşti, Strada Gheorghe Tătărascu, and Strada Tudor Vladimirescu). Brâncuşi was committed to finding the essence of being. He often drew inspiration from his own native folk art as well as from ancient sources such as Egyptian, Iberian, and pre-Columbian carvings: In the column you can see the affinity between the iron "beads" and the decorated wooden poles that support the verandas of old village houses. (The artist's birthplace is just such a house, see p. 94.)

Between the three sculptures, and lying on the same axis, is the Orthodox church of **Sf. Apostoli Petru şi Pavel** *(Calea Eroilor & Str. 16 Februarie).* The church is an integral part of the ensemble. Revitalization of the town center will enhance Brâncuşi's artistic placement of the sculptures. Town planners have begun clearing the line of sight along the axis and are turning the town center into a leafy, pedestrian area.

Close to the center, the old prefecture building houses the **Muzeul de Istorie** *(Str. Geneva 8, tel 0253 212 044, closed for restoration until 2008, $).* This history museum contains a Celtic grave and colorful examples of Oltenian folk art. A little north of Calea Eroilor, near **Biserica Sf. Voievozi** (Holy Princes' Church), you'll find the sarcophagus-shaped **memorial dedicated to Ecaterina Teodoroiu.** A well-known Romanian heroine from World War I, she disguised herself as a man so she could fight alongside her fellow Romanians; she was killed on the eastern front near Mărășești in 1917. The reliefs were sculpted by the Moldovan artist Milița Petrașcu (1892–1976), who studied under Brâncuși in Paris. Teodoroiu's story is told at the **Casa Memorială Ecaterina Teodoroiu** (*B-dul Ecaterina Teodoroiu 270, closed Mon.–Tues., $*), a museum dedicated to her memory.

The area around the Teodoroiu memorial holds a few buildings of architectural interest. The hardy-looking, *cula*-style (see sidebar p. 85) **house and church of Cornea Brăiloiu,** a 17th-century Ban (governor) of Oltenia, stand near the memorial. Another outstanding building is the 18th-century **Casa Gănescu** (*Piața Revolutiei 2*) near the Sf. Voievozi church; Brâncuși stayed here while he was overseeing the installation of his sculptures.

For an entertaining half-hour, visit **Topi New Glass Design** (*Str. Unirii 92C, tel 0253 219 179, call for appt.*), the workshop and showroom of glass artist Mihai Țopescu (b. 1956). Sporting a Brâncuși-like beard, Țopescu creates wacky objects out of colored glass, which he and his assistants blow on the premises. Some of his products are for conventional household use, such as bowls and vases, but other designs are pure whimsy. You can walk to the studio from Brâncuși's "Column of the Infinite" or take a taxi from the center.

Târgu Jiu's open-air **fruit and vegetable market** *(located in the town center; ask for directions)* is a wonderful cacophony of activity and people. You can enjoy haggling over the price of fresh produce, rub shoulders with the locals from the surrounding countryside, and maybe find some bargain traditional handicrafts, too. ∎

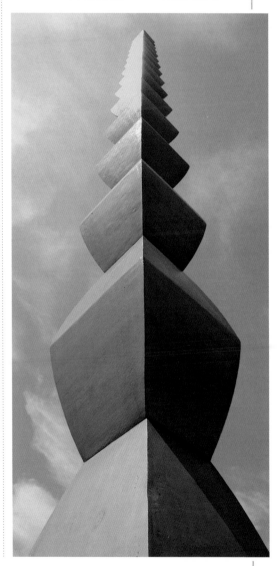

Brâncuși's "Coloana fără Sfârșit" ("Column of the Infinite") is a tribute to Romanians who died fighting Germany in World War I.

The Cerna River's springs burst out of the ground beside the valley road.

Driving to the Cerna Valley

Winding through impressive mountains and a breathtaking countryside that tourists rarely see, this drive from Târgu Jiu to the Cerna Valley affords an opportunity to see how people live in remoter areas. It makes a stunning and adventurous excursion.

Begin by heading west out of Târgu Jiu via the DN67D. In 14 miles (22 km), you'll reach the village of Pestişani; turn left here for the suburb of **Hobiţa** ①, the birthplace of sculptor Constantin Brâncuşi (see p. 91). He lived at the **timber house** *(village center, closed Mon., $; large groups contact the art museum in Târgu Jiu in advance, tel 0253 218 550)* with roughly carved gates and veranda posts in the center of town until he went to art school in Craiova (see p. 98). The house now bears his name.

Return to the main road in Pestişani and continue west. Turn right after 5 miles (8 km) onto another country road signposted to Tismana. Drive through the town until you reach **Mănăstirea Tismana** ② *(tel 0253 374 317, $).* Enjoying a stunning mountaintop setting, the 14th-century monastery was founded by Nicodim (see p. 88), who is buried here. The monastery was rebuilt and restored in the 16th century, and painted by Dobromir of Târgovişte in 1564 (some of his original work can be seen in the antechamber that precedes the main body of the church). The monastery's museum contains Nicodim's handwritten gospels. The monastery's crafts shop sells handmade rugs and icons painted on glass, and

overnight, hostel-style accommodations are available on the monastery premises.

Return to the DN67D and head west roughly 9 miles (14 km) through the pretty, wooded tablelands of **Plaiul Cloşani** to the town of **Baia de Aramă** ③, whose name means "copper mine." People have extracted Baia de Aramă's copper for more than 2,000 years. In modern times the mines thrived, but today roughly half of the town's 6,000 inhabitants are unemployed; however, the charm of this town, one of the most rural of Romania's country towns, has not been lost. More than half of the population lives in one of eight outlying villages.

On leaving Baia de Aramă, turn left onto a country road that makes a sharp, right-hand bend and leads to the hamlet of Ponoarele. Roughly 2 miles (3 km) farther along this road brings you to the forest reserve called **Ponoare Lilac.** On the first Sunday in May, the villagers of Ponoarele don traditional, embroidered costume and celebrate the spring blossoms with folk music, crafts stalls, and traditional fare, including *mici* (meatballs). Three miles (5 km) later, you'll reach a massive, natural **stone bridge** ④. It's known as God's Bridge because several cars have slipped off the roadway, and yet, fortunately, nobody has died. Nearby, between the bridge and Lake Zaton (due south) is an impressive field of calcareous rocks.

Make your way back to the DN67D and continue heading west. After passing through the villages of Brebina, Titerleşti, and Mărăşeşti, the highway climbs steeply to the 3,150-foot (1,050 m) pass that separates Oltenia from the Banat (see pp. 156–57). Along the way, the road makes a series of tight serpentine loops through a bucolic countryside strewn with scattered houses, orchards, hayfields, and one or two other villages, including Obârşia-Cloşani. One of the tallest ridges in the vicinity, 5,199-foot-high (1,733 m) **Vlaşcul Mic,** rises to the northwest. At the pass, leave your car and take a blazed footpath west through beech woods and meadows to the **Mehedinţi Plateau** ⑤. The plateau is ringed with spectacular karstic outcroppings that sport isolated specimens of the hardy *pina nigra* (black pine).

The countryside in this region has been used since antiquity for sheep grazing, and working sheepfolds still dot the area. Bucolic as they are, be careful of the *ciobăneşti carpatici:* these big, tough Carpathian sheepdogs take their guard duties seriously. If they approach you, stand still until the shepherd calls them off. Also be on the lookout for the nose-horned viper. Although the snake is rarely aggressive, its bite is potentially fatal. Its name derives from the spike that sticks up from the front of its

mouth. It favors dry, sunny rocks and lives in western Oltenia, the Banat, and Dobrogea. Larger fauna can be found in the northern half of the **Valea Cernei** (Cerna Valley) ⑥, which lies beyond the pass; it's one of the few places in Europe where brown bear and lynx live relatively undisturbed.

Drive south along the Cerna Valley with the river on your right until you reach the spa town of **Băile Herculane,** where the Romans eased their aches in the revitalizing waters. Popular with Romania's prewar gentry and present-day hikers, planned and much-needed restorations should soon improve the town's appearance. ∎

✚ See area map p. 83
► Târgu Jiu
⇄ 70 miles (110 km) The DN67D may be closed during winter due to heavy snowfall. In spring and summer, repairs are not always carried out, and the surface may be very rough.
🕐 2 hours—more with stops
► Băile Herculane

NOT TO BE MISSED
- Hobiţa
- Mănăstirea Tismana
- Cerna Valley

The shores of Serbia lie across the Danube from Drobeta-Turnu Severin.

Drobeta-Turnu Severin

DROBETA-TURNU SEVERIN IS A LIVELY PLACE DESPITE THE fact that its shipyard is in a state of advanced torpor. Laid out in the 19th century with mathematical precision, the center is a jumble of handsome old and trashy new buildings. This recipe works surprisingly well, mainly because the city has a grandstand view of the Danube River.

Drobeta-Turnu Severin
🅜 83 B3
Visitor information
✉ Primăria Municipiului Drobeta-Turnu Severin, Str. Maresal Averescu 2
☎ 0252 314 379

Muzeul de Artă
✉ Str. Rahovei 3
☎ 0252 317 377
🕐 Closed Mon.
💲 $

The city was founded in 1833 as Turnu Severin (Severin's Tower) after an international agreement allowed free navigation along the full length of the Danube. Although little-populated before that time, this area became a historically strategically important site, most famously fought over by the Dacians and Romans; the Byzantines and Hungarians; and, at different times and in different combinations of all five, the Habsburgs, Hungarians, Romanians, Serbs, and Turks. Turnu Severin stands on the site of a Roman fort called **Drobeta,** which probably comes from a Dacian word. The communist authorities added the fort's name to the town's name to emphasize the city's Latin heritage, but most people leave it out. The name Severin is believed to honor Emperor Septimus Severus, who raised the town's status to a *colonia,* which gave its people the same rights as Roman citizens.

Laid out by Pavel Kiseliov (see sidebar p. 63) and the Wallachian prince Alexandru Ghica, the city's street plan follows an orderly grid pattern. Its main street, Bulevardul Carol I, contains some imposing edifices such as the **city library** and **cultural center** *(No. 4).* Thanks to some frenetic new building, finding your way around Turnu Severin is not easy; you'll probably need to ask for directions.

The **Muzeul de Artă** on Strada Rahovei specializes in early

20th-century Romanian post-Impressionists, such as Theodor Pallady and Nicolae Tonitza, but it also has a lively collection of modern Romanian art. The 1890 house itself is a joy to see; it has a magnificent neobaroque facade with elongated windows and an elegant spiral staircase.

Set on the banks of the Danube, the **Muzeul Regiunii Porţilor de Fier** (Iron Gates' Regional Museum) is divided into three sections: history and archaeology, natural science, and ethnography and folk art. The highlights held in this impressive, three-story 1926 building include the 8,000-year-old remains of a human body, an aquarium containing species from the Danube, and traditional buildings from the nearby Mehedinţi Mountains.

The museum's grounds contain the lackluster ruins of a fort, and you also can see a remnant of the A.D. 103–105 **Roman bridge** that was flung across the Danube so that Trajan could invade Dacia more easily. Only a broken pillar of this massive 20-pillared, 56-foot-high (19 m), 44-foot-wide (14.5 m) engineering feat remains. The man who designed it was Apollodorus of Damascus, the future creator of Trajan's Column, which celebrates Rome's conquest of Dacia. (The bridge's wooden superstructure was destroyed in the third century when Hadrian withdrew his troops from the province.)

As the Danube courses through this area, it is just over half a mile (1 km) wide. To harness its power, the communist government built a hydroelectric dam 8 miles (13 km) west of the city in the 1960s. It is called **Porţile de Fier** (Iron Gates) after the gorges that can be found 35 miles (55 km) to the west. Large traffic can now ply the

Danube's upper waters, but the view is no longer as spectacular. You can walk onto the dam, and a small **visitor center/museum** (*closed Mon, $*) contains several archaeological finds.

A spur of northern Serbia is easily visible across the river. Immediately to the east, more or less in midstream, is the island of **Şimian.** The island is home to a half-reconstructed Turkish settlement that used to stand on a

Cruising the Danube

Three- to four-hour boat trips along the Danube are available from Băile Herculane and Orşova *(contact S. C. Hercules, tel 0255 560 454),* and from Turnu Severin *(contact S. C. Axxa International, tel 0252 327 253).* Other European companies run cruise ships along the river from Budapest to the Danube Delta. For a small fee, you can sail privately owned vessels along the Romanian section of the Danube. Private boats are subject to a technical inspection, and there are border checking points at Orşova and Drobeta-Turnu Severin. For more information on cruising the river, contact the Orşova Danube River Authority *(tel 0252 361 295)* or the Drobeta-Turnu Severin Danube River Authority *(tel 0252 316 493).* ■

neighboring island, Ada Kaleh, which was submerged following the dam's construction. Consisting of a fort and a mosque that were somehow forgotten when the Ottoman Empire withdrew from Romania, the settlement survived as a territorial curiosity until World War I. ■

Muzeul Regiunii Porţilor de Fier
✉ Str. Independenţei 2
☎ 0252 312 177
🕐 Closed Mon.
💲 $

Craiova

OLTENIA'S CAPITAL CITY IS BEGINNING TO SHOW SIGNS OF recovery from the systematization that befell it in the 1960s. During that period, whole streets were demolished in the name of progress; however, today there is an air of expectation about the place, and visitors will find some unexpected treasures among the fragmented architecture of the city.

Craiova's art museum is one of a handful of magnificent buildings that survived Ceaușescu's "restructuring" in the city.

Craiova

🗺 83 C2

Visitor information

✉ Primăria Municipiului Craiova, Str. A. I. Cuza 7

☎ 0251 416 235

Muzeul de Artă

✉ Calea Unirii 15

☎ 0251 412 342

🕓 Closed Mon.

💲 $

Muzeul Olteniei

✉ Str. Madona Dudu 44

☎ 0251 418 631

🕓 Closed Mon.

💲 $

The city's crown jewels are seven **original sculptures by Constantin Brâncuși.** They include the first, surprisingly tender version of his ground-breaking carving, "The Kiss" (1908), in which the two human heads are seen as one block of stone articulated by a few simple, well-chosen cuts. Brâncuși's "studio" has been recreated in the **Muzeul de Artă,** which also displays a range of interesting Romanian and European art. The art museum is housed in the Palatul Jean Mihail, a sumptuous neobaroque palace designed by French architect Paul Gottereau, who also built the CEC building in Bucharest (see p. 54). Before it became a museum, the mansion had a lively political past, including playing host to the exiled Polish government in 1939.

A visit to the **Muzeul Olteniei** (Olteniei Museum) reveals the area's fascinating history; ask for an English-speaking guide to explain the exhibits to you. Over the last 7,000 years, southern Romania has experienced scores of different ethnic influences with some mind-stretching examples of cultural exchange, such as an Egyptian amulet that was found in a Celtic tomb. The prehistoric pottery collection also contains some diverting objects.

The bright and cheerful **Secţia de Etnografie** (Ethnographic Section; *Str. Matei Basarab 14, tel 0251 417 756*) of the Olteniei Museum is closed for restoration until further notice, but the building's exterior gives a sense of how Craiova used to look. It is a former Ban's (ruler's) house and dates back to the 15th century. ∎

Southeast Oltenia

THE PLAINS OF SOUTHEAST OLTENIA REVEAL FASCINATING insights into the life of a border zone. Although economically depressed, the area's towns contain vestiges of a prosperity that grew during the 18th and 19th centuries as the Habsburgs tried to integrate Romania into their empire, while at the same time the Turkish-run Phanariot regime attempted to impose Enlightenment values.

Brâncoveni
🅰 83 D2

Caracal
🅰 83 D2

Corabia
🅰 83 D1

A few sights in the region shine in the riverine landscape, notably the Brâncoveni monastery and the towns of Caracal and Corabia.

BRÂNCOVENI

The village of Brâncoveni lies a little east of Craiova (see opposite) and is notable for its lovely, late 17th-century **monastery** *(look for signpost, tel 0249 413 243)*. In the summertime, the monastery's white paint job gives it a Mediterranean flavor. The monastery still functions as a religious foundation.

CARACAL

The impoverished town of Caracal (pop. 30,000), 15 miles (24 km) south of Brâncoveni, has dozens of magnificent but run-down 19th- and early 20th-century mansions. They show how Oriental and Western tastes merged in this area. Stroll **Strada Iancu Jianu** for a sense of the town's once proud appearance.

Southeastern Oltenia has a rich but sparsely illustrated past dating back to neolithic times. The **Muzeul Romanaţiului** *(Str. Iancu Jianu 26, tel 0249 511 344, $)* contains pottery from the neolithic Vădastra culture that once flourished nearby. (The museum's website, *www.museum. com,* also provides local tourist information.) From a purely touristic point of view, Caracal is a sad place, and one can only hope that the town will find the funds to rebuild itself soon. For now, a handful of dedicated staff mans the museum, switching the dim lights on and off to save electricity as you pass from one room to another. The collection is not nearly as good as the one in Craiova, but as an example of the Romanians' sheer resilience in the face of long odds, these enthusiasts surely deserve encouragement!

CORABIA

The once thriving river port of Corabia lies almost directly south of Caracal on the Bulgarian border. Corabia means "ship," and legend has it that the old town was built from the remains of a wrecked Genoese galley. In A.D. 328, the Romans built a bridge across the Danube to Oescus (modern Gigen, in Bulgaria). The woeful remains of this extraordinary 2-mile-long (3 km) structure can be seen on a tributary riverbank in the western suburb of **Celei** *(follow signs for "podul")*. Half a mile (1 km) away, a little mound supports the ruins and secret well of **Sucidava** *(tel 0249 561 364, closed Mon., $)*, which was built by the Dacians and adopted by the Romans who held this area until the start of the seventh century. Since those times, the river has retreated a mile or so to the south. The secret well was recently flooded and, at the time of writing, the little stone stairwell is wet and impassable. The area needs a lot of loving care to improve its appearance, and the riverbanks have sadly become a local trash dump. For now, come here if you're passing and enjoy the distant view of the glistening Danube. On a bright day, it can lift the saddest heart. ◾

More places to visit in Oltenia

BALŞ

The town of Balş is home to the **Colecţia de Ceramica Tradiţională de pe Valea Olteţului** (*Str. Popă Şapcă 10*). This collection of traditional ceramics from three different Oltet Valley communities is a must-see for pottery enthusiasts.

🅰 83 D2 ✉ 15 miles (25 km) E of Craiova via E574/E65

DANUBE RIVER CAR TOUR

As an unusual alternative to the main tourist routes, follow the Danube River across southern Romania from Drobeta-Turnu Severin to Corabia. The road surface can be rough, and few services exist along the way; as a result, this road is really only enjoyable as an adventure in late spring or early autumn.

At the town of **Calafat,** you can catch a ferry to Vidin in Bulgaria and explore that side of the Danube. From Calafat to Corabia on the Romanian side, the larger DN55A takes over and you can hop from one reasonable highway to another for more or less the river's full length. Continue the journey east to **Giurgiu** (home of Romania's largest community of Roma musicians; see map p. 66), where you can detour across a bridge to the Bulgarian city of Ruse; to Olteniţa (see p. 80); and on to Calaraşi, where the river turns north into Romania. A car ferry (*$*) will carry you to Silistra on the Bulgarian side. From there, it's a short distance to the beautiful and largely unknown Roman archaeological site of **Adamclisi** (see p. 222).

🅰 83 B3-D1

VALEA LOTRULUI

Still relatively unspoiled, the Valea Lotrului (Robber's Valley) is an ideal area for intrepid hikers who want to explore the Carpathians' southern slopes. A road through the valley connects **Brezoi** (20 miles/32 km north of Râmnicu Vâlcea) to the mining town of **Petroşani.** You can follow the tracks of shepherds on their annual transhumance and immerse yourself in authentic, rural culture. There are plenty of modest guesthouse accommodations in villages along the valley and by staying here you will be helping local people, who badly need the extra income.

🅰 83 D4

RÂMNICU VÂLCEA

Râmnicu Vâlcea stands on the banks of the Olt River at the southern end of the widest pass through the Carpathian Mountains. Its name can be variously interpreted as "backwater glen," or more prosaically, "fishpond dale," but today it is a lively town of just more than 100,000 people. With plenty of hotels, guesthouses, and restaurants on offer, the town makes a good base for exploring northern Oltenia and a couple of nearby attractions.

In Râmnicu Vâlcea itself, the **Muzeul de Artă Casa Simian** (*Str. Carol I 25, tel 0250 738 121, closed Mon.–Tues., $*) is housed in a pretty Italianate villa that was the former home of 20th-century industrialists from Mărginimea Sibiului (see pp. 132–134). It exhibits a small but engaging collection of 19th- and 20th-century Romanian paintings and sculptures, including some works by Nicolae Grigorescu, who captured Wallachian country life with rare brilliance.

Located 3 miles (5 km) outside town, the fascinating **Muzeul Satului Vâlcean** (*Calea lui Traian 302, Bujoreni, tel 0250 746 869, closed Mon., $*), occupies a hillside orchard overlooking Râmnicu Vâlcea. The views from here alone are worth the trip. This museum offers architectural treasures from Vâlcea County's deeply rural past. You'll find country farmhouses; technological items, such as a watermill and an ingenious homemade system for drying fruit; an inn; a village school; a cula (see sidebar p. 85); a magnificent shepherd's cottage known as a *stână* (sheepfold), which though accurate hardly does this splendid building justice; and much more. The turnoff for the museum is easy to miss. Heading north from Râmnicu Vâlcea, keep a close lookout for a narrow, unmarked side road on the left-hand side of the DN7/E81. The tall, wooden gateway into the museum is a few yards along it on the right-hand side.

🅰 83 D3 **Visitor information** ✉ Centrul de Informaţii Turistice Vâlcea, Str. General Gheorghe Magheru 18 ☎ 0250 734 307 ■

Embraced by the Carpathian Mountains and breathtakingly beautiful, Transylvania is one of the jewels in Romania's crown. Its multilayered culture and glorious open landscapes offer stimulus to the mind and senses.

Transylvania

Unashamed kitsch: souvenirs at Bran Castle

Transylvania

WILD AND MYSTERIOUS TRANSYLVANIA IS A LAND OF COMPLEX HISTORY IN which, despite horrific conflicts and suffering, Eastern and Western cultures have become interwoven in extraordinary ways. The still largely pristine countryside offers myriad wonderful places to explore on foot, by bicycle, or on horseback.

Transylvania is bounded on three sides by the Carpathian Mountains; on its western edge rise the smaller Apuseni Mountains. Romanians have always regarded Transylvania (particularly the southwestern portion) as their own heartlands, since it was here that their Iron Age ancestors, the Dacians, had their most famous strongholds. For most of the past thousand years, however, this region formed part of the Hungarian kingdom and later Austro-Hungarian Empire, and as such, its history and people reflect a strong Hungarian influence. The German

influence is almost as strong, because the Hungarian kings invited settlers from German-speaking lands in the 12th and 13th centuries. Known more popularly as Saxons, they have left

The view from the belfry of the Evangelical Church, Piaţa Huet, in Sibiu

magnificent buildings in their wake, most notably the medieval citadel churches— *Kirchenbürgen*—that pepper southern Transylvania. Hungarian castles, manor houses, palaces, and churches also abound in the region's many fascinating towns. Among the most interesting are Braşov, Cluj-Napoca, Alba Iulia, Sighişoara, and the old Saxon city of Sibiu (voted one of Europe's two Cities of Culture for 2007).

Western Transylvania is dominated by the Apuseni Mountains. Here the people call themselves the Moţi. Tracing their history back over thousands rather than merely hundreds of years, these farmers and miners are proud of their origins and are fighting to save their beautiful mountains from being destroyed.

To the south, the German influence survives in the shape of wonderfully sturdy buildings. The Saxons themselves have all but vanished. Since the Romanian communist government signed an agreement with West Germany in the 1970s, the ethnic Germans have left Romania in droves. Apart from their fairy-tale architecture, their legacy has been one of self-reliance, hard work, and order.

The eastern end of the province has the highest concentrations of ethnic Hungarians in Transylvania. Their language (many are bilingual) and features are different, and you will see subtle differences in building style and traditional dress.

Benefiting from a subalpine climate, Transylvania's breathtaking countryside is spectacular at any time of the year, but in springtime its wealth of wildflowers and flowering trees come into their own. ■

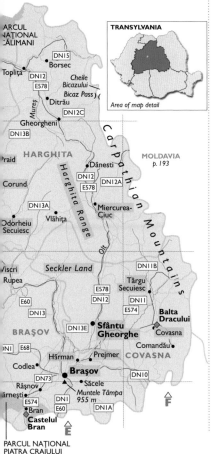

A statue of the
18th-century
Romanian
democratic
revolutionary
Avram Iancu
graces the
square outside
Cluj-Napoca's
Orthodox
cathedral.

Cluj-Napoca

SURROUNDED BY SEVEN HILLS, CLUJ-NAPOCA IS THE
cultural and economic hub of Transylvania. Its lively historic center is
small enough to walk around in an hour or so, but so much is concentrated here that you may want to linger for several days.

Cluj-Napoca
🗺 102 B4
**Visitor
information**
✉ Primăria Cluj,
Piața Unirii 1
☎ 0264 592 301 or
0264 596 030

The early Saxon settlers gave Cluj
its original Latin name of
Castrum Clus (Closed Camp).
This was a direct reference to its
sheltered and inaccessible
location. The name has stuck in
various forms: to Hungarians it
became Kolozsvár, and later
Saxons called it Klausenburg.
Today, the city's proper Romanian
name is Cluj-Napoca, from the
Roman *colonia* of Napoca that
existed here in the second century
A.D. Most people just call it Cluj.

Cluj is modernizing rapidly,
but because it escaped systematization under the communists, it
still exudes an air of quiet
grandeur thanks to a range of
period architecture. In the city
center, medieval town houses with

massive walls and wide courtyards
rub shoulders with Hungarian
and Habsburg buildings. Most of
the worthwhile sights lie within a
large square area created by Piața
Avram Iancu and Piața Ștefan cel
Mare to the east, Strada Petru
Maior to the west, the Someș
River to the north, and Strada
Avram Iancu to the south.

Cluj's Austro-Hungarian
buildings cluster around **Piața
Unirii** (Union Square), the city's
main square, which makes a good
landmark to organize seeing
Cluj's sights. One of the most
atmospheric is the neobaroque
Hotel Continental (*Str. Napoca
1;* see sidebar p. 106), set between
two roads that meet at the
southwest corner of the square. A

favorite haunt of the Hungarian nobility between the World Wars, the hotel retains the decor from that period.

The square itself holds the great Gothic **St. Michael Church** and the much photographed **statue of Corvin Mátyás** (Matei Corvin in Romanian, R. 1458–1490) on his charger. Corvin was one of Hungary's greatest Renaissance kings, and he was born in Cluj in 1443. His birthplace at Strada Matei Corvin No. 4 (just off the square's northwest corner) looks every inch the part, but is now an **art school** (also known as Casa Bocskay). The building has been listed as a historic monument; you may walk inside the entrance hall to the inner courtyard.

Cluj was the favorite haunt of the Bánffys, one of Transylvania's leading families. One of their many superb palaces stands on Piața Unirii. It now houses the **Muzeul Național de Artă al Transilvaniei** (Piața Unirii 30, tel 0254 596 953, closed Mon.–Tues., $), which contains the region's largest holdings of Romanian fine and decorative art from the 15th to the 20th centuries. The art museum often stages challenging temporary exhibits. There is a café bar in the courtyard.

Walk east along Strada Iuliu Maniu, which radiates off the square's east side, and you'll notice that the houses on either side of the road are mirror images of each other. Iuliu Maniu dead-ends into Piața Avram Iancu, which holds a modern Orthodox cathedral; to the right, in another square, is the **Teatrul Național Lucian Blaga** (Lucian Blaga National Theater; Piața Ștefan cel Mare 24, tel 0264 595 363). Formerly the Hungarian State Theatre (which now occupies a building near the central park), it was designed by the celebrated

It's very Continental

The Hotel Continental achieved immortality in Patrick Leigh Fermor's 1986 Between the Woods and the Water. This engaging book describes a journey the author made on foot from the Hook of Holland to Constantinople in the mid-1920s. He spent many happy days in Transylvania, some of them in the company of a beautiful, young Hungarian woman who had run away from her husband. Together with another friend, they visited the Hotel New York (today the Continental). Leigh Fermor noted the sumptuous "Regency neo-Roman décor," which he and his companions enjoyed with "misgiving and delight like naughty children," while sipping cocktails invented by a "demon-barman." ■

firm of Fellner and Helmer. The theater has an excellent international program.

Two museums each lie about a five-minute walk from the square's northwest corner. The history museum, **Muzeul Național de Istorie a Transilvaniei** (Str. Constantin Daicoviciu 2, tel 0264 595 677, closed Mon., $) displays fascinating old maps of the city and some of the vast collection of Bronze Age tools for which Transylvania is famous.

The **Muzeul de Etnografie al Transilvaniei** (Ethnography Museum of Transylvania) is housed in a former 16th-century palace. Walk in through the wide carriage entrance. The museum has just been restored, giving a much-needed lift to the curious tools, furnishings, and cult objects that half a century ago were considered quite ordinary. Highlights include the dugout

Muzeul de Etnografie al Transilvaniei

✉ Str. Memorandumului 21
☎ 0264 592 344
🕑 Closed Mon.
💲 $

Parcul Etnografic Romulus Vuia

✉ Str. Tăietura Turcului
☎ 0264 586 776
🕑 Closed Mon.
💲 $
🚍 Bus: 27 (from railway station), 28 (from Piața Mihai Viteazul), or 30 (from opposite Ethnographic Museum), then get off at Piața 14 Iulie and walk; Car: From city center, cross river and head west along Str. Drăgălina and Str. Eremia Grigorescu. Turn right on Str. Tăietura Turcului.

boats and a gorgeously decorative hobbyhorse, which was used in one of Romania's most arcane pagan fertility dances, the Căluş.

The ethnographic museum's counterpart, the open-air village museum **Parcul Etnografic Romulus Vuia** (Romulus Vuia Ethnographic Park), dates from 1932 and is the oldest of its kind in Romania. Spread out across a

Slice of life: In line for the bus in Cluj-Napoca

hilltop meadow that overlooks the city, the museum's treasures include an ingenious timber contraption for making windows. Coming here helps you to understand that Romania had its own industrial revolution, supported by wood technology rather than iron or steel.

The area just south of Piața Unirii hosts Romania's largest university, **Babeş-Bolyai.** It was named after two scientists, one Romanian and the other Hungarian, to emphasize its bilingual status. The university is one of the oldest in the country, claiming links with a college founded here in 1581. Its departments are scattered around the city, but its oldest buildings can be found on Universității and Kogălniceanu streets near Piața Unirii. When the students are in

town, the whole place comes alive, swelling the city's 300,000 full-time residents by a third.

Near the east end of Strada Kogălniceanu stands the handsome but gloomy Hungarian **Biserica Reformată** (a Presbyterian church) from 1436. The atmosphere inside is charged with references to the city's Hungarian ancestry, and there are splendid devotional carvings on the choir stalls. Outside, you will see a reproduction of a lively bronze statue of **St. George and the Dragon.** The original, made in 1272 by Márton and György Kolozsvári, two brothers who were born in Cluj, can be seen in the cathedral precincts of Prague Castle in the Czech Republic.

Close by, on Strada Baba Novac, a section of the medieval **Saxon citadel wall** incorporates the restored 15th-century **Tailor's Bastion.** At some point in the future, the bastion will be open to visitors, but until then you'll have to be content with looking at the exterior.

Cluj's superb **Grădina Botanică** (Botanical Gardens; *Str. Gheorghe Bilaşcu 42, tel 0264 592 152, $*), south of the university area, feature a lovely Japanese garden laid out in the traditional *gyo-no-niwa* style. Another section presents species in their respective families, orders, and classes, arranged as if in an open book.

Far north of the gardens, the hill **Cetăţuia** looms over the northern bank of the Someşul Mic River, which roughly divides Cluj in two. A number of footpaths lead to the top, where you may be able to detect the scant remains of a Habsburg-period, early 18th-century citadel, but the impressive views of Cluj are truly why you should make the climb. (A hotel now occupies the summit.) ∎

Bistriţa

THE NORTHERNMOST OF TRANSYLVANIA'S SEVEN FORTIFIED Saxon towns, Bistriţa makes a great stepping-off point for exploring the eastern Carpathians. Surrounded by villages where ancient customs and crafts still thrive, the town has a modest but charming center that invites you to walk back in time.

Bistriţa
102 D4
Visitor information
Primăria Bistriţa, Piaţa Centrală 6
0263 223 923

Bistriţa's first settlers were Saxons who received land, mines, and privileges in return for protecting Transylvania's borders. The majority of Bistriţa's historic buildings center around **Piaţa Centrală**. Looking at this sleepy square, it's hard to believe that Bistriţa was once a thriving marketplace that had to protect itself from repeated enemy attacks. The tall Gothic tower dominating the scene belongs to the **Biserica Reformată** (Reformed Church; *Sun. services in German; in summer at 10 a.m.*). Built originally for Franciscan Minorite monks, it is a jumble of styles: 13th-century Romanesque, 14th- and 15th-century Gothic, and 16th-century Renaissance.

A row of 13 arcaded houses called **Sirul Sugălete** (The Cornmarket) runs along the north side of Piaţa Centrală. These late 14th-century, fortress-like homes-cum-craftshops housed guildsmen. They were the first two-story dwellings in Bistriţa; they are still in use, although the original interiors and long rear courtyards have been lost. At the right-hand end of the row, you can see the carriage entrance to the 1480 *casa parohiala*, or parish house.

To the east, the patrician, 16th-century **Casa Argintarului** (Silversmith's House; *Str. Dornei 5*) now houses a school of art. The Italian mason Petrus da Lugano who worked on the

Reformed Church also may have carved the stonework here.

The imposing U-shaped, two-story **Muzeul Judeţean Bistriţa-Năsăud** (Bistriţa-Năsăud County Museum; *Str. General Grigore Bălan 19, tel 0263 211 063, closed Mon., $*) is a short walk from the town center. Its displays detail the area's history, ethnography, and natural history, and it also has some art. The building is a former Austrian Army barracks. Under Empress Maria Theresa (*R. 1740–1780*), the Habsburgs established border garrisons across northern Transylvania to guard against attacks by Tatars, Russians, and Poles. Bistriţa was one of the key strongholds.

AROUND BISTRIŢA

The northern part of the Transylvanian Plateau is much quieter than the south. Time seems to pass at a more leisurely pace. The main road (DN17/E576) runs between Dej and the Tihuţa (Borgo) Pass; the eastern section is remarkably pretty.

The village of **Cristur-Şieu** lies some 14 miles (22 km) west of Bistriţa. The inhabitants celebrate Pentecost (June 14) with a pre-Christian custom called **Înstruţatul Boului** (Garlanding the Ox). They deck the village's most handsome ox with flowers, embroidered cloths, and plaited loaves and then parade the main street, followed by feasting and partying. Other villages in this area as well as in neighboring Maramureş carry out similar traditions, which are a throwback to ancient fertility rituals.

Three and a half miles (6 km) east of Bistriţa, the village of **Livezile** has an authentic Saxon farmhouse, **Casa Sasească** *(Str. Dorolei, tel 0263 270 109, closed Mon.–Tues., $)*. Its colorful, painted furniture is specific to this region.

Another 3.5 miles (6 km) east brings you to a string of villages with the suffix "Bârgăului," meaning they are near the Bârgău River. **Mijlocenii Bârgăului** has two traditional potters *(olari),* Ştefan Gănău and Ştefan Gâţa, who use foot-powered wheels *(ask*

in village or contact ethnography department of the Muzeul Judeţean Bistriţa-Năsăud; see p. 107)

Beyond this village, and before you cross over the Tihuţa Pass into Bucovina, a side road travels past Bistriţa Bârgăului to **Lacul Colibiţa.** The woodlands setting and mountain backdrop have made this attractive town popular with vacationing Romanians.

SOMEŞ VALLEY

From Năsăud to Şanţ, the Someş Valley offers breathtaking scenery. Thanks to its sheltered position, the valley often has the lowest recorded winter temperatures in Romania, and spring always arrives later here than elsewhere.

Haystacks dot an open field south of Bistriţa.

East of Năsăud, a small country road turns off the main D17 road at Poderei and winds north 10.5 miles (17 km) to **Parva.** This is the kind of place where people will invite you into their homes and generously offer you a glass of the local firewater (*țuica*).

East of Poderei, the mineral waters of **Sângeorz-Băi** have made the town a popular Romanian vacation spot. At the **Muzeul de Artă Comparată** (*Str. Republicii 68, tel 0263 370 219, appt. required for groups, $*), created by artist Maxim Dumitraș, modern art and traditional handmade tools interact in a traditional cottage setting. The museum represents

Bram Stoker's *Dracula*

Bram Stoker set his 1897 novel *Dracula* in and around the valleys surrounding Bistrița. Stoker drew elements of his fictional work from both folklore and history, but his accurate mapping of Transylvania truly added a layer of authenticity to the tale. For instance, the "hero," Jonathan Harker, spends a night in Bistritz (Bistrița) in transit to Dracula's castle on the Borgo Pass. (Stoker used the Hungarian name for the Tihuța Pass.) He stays at the Golden Krone inn, which is today's Hotel Corona de Aur (*Piața Petru Rareș 4*); you can eat a "robber steak" here just as Harker does in the novel. ■

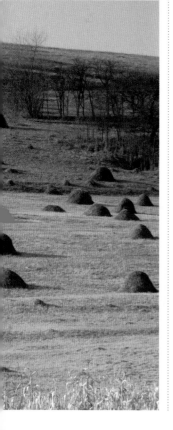

the work of more than a hundred living Romanian artists.

At the town of **Maieru,** farther east along the D17 road toward Șanț, you can visit **Cuibul Visurilor** (Nest of Dreams Museum; *No. 200, tel 0263 372 031, call in advance, $*). Founded in 1959, the museum's collection now contains more than 3,000 objects relating to rural life and other subject matters. One section is devoted to Liviu Rebreanu, author of some of Romania's most searing historical novels; he spent six happy childhood years in Maieru.

An easy and fun way to enjoy the valley's fantastic scenery is to board the train in Năsăud that runs along the valley and through the mountains to Gura Humorului in Bucovina. Little-known and underused, it is one of the most scenic rail journeys in the country. ■

Romanian myths

Blessed with a resilient rural heritage, Romania still has deep wells of mythology. Even during the communist period, Romanians continued to believe in a panoply of supernatural beings. They included fairies, witches, sprites, and vampires. These beliefs have been traced back to antiquity. They were often linked with the need for good weather to grow crops, but also to a fear of the unknown, and more pragmatically with a need to keep communities together. Many of these beliefs have been absorbed into mainstream Christian Orthodoxy (for example, you can see pagan symbols of the sun and moon and signs of the zodiac in many churches). Pre-Christian mythology survived independently, too. Shamanism, which was practiced in Romania as long ago as the fifth millennium B.C., did not die out until the mid-20th century.

In Maramureş and the northern mountains of Transylvania, there is the myth of Fata Pădurii (Girl of the Forest). Irresistably attractive, Fata Pădurii lures lonely shepherds into her arms. As soon as they succumb, she subjects them to a savage attack. In some extreme cases the shepherds may lose a limb or die. This is a thinly veiled warning to make sure the men never stray from their duty (the flocks belong to the entire village). Another belief holds that it is dangerous to allow the sheepfold's fire to go out: It must stay continuously lit from April to October. In some areas, Omul Nopţii (Man of the Night) acts as a counterweight to Fata Pădurii: He will punish bad women and restricts some of Fata Pădurii's excesses.

Miorița is one of the best-known Romanian myths. This story, too, involves shepherds. The countless variations of the myth build on a basic outline: Two jealous shepherds plot to murder their friend and steal his sheep. One of the victim's ewe lambs (miorița) overhears them and, in the poem, she warns her master of the danger so that he can escape. Rather than resist or run away, the shepherd replies that he would rather die than avoid death. The folk epic was passed down orally through the generations until the 1860s, when a written version was published. It has been taken as an allegory for Romania's early adoption of Christianity.

From a Western perspective, the most famous myth about Romania concerns the Transylvanian Count Dracula. This fictional vampire was modeled on a widespread East European belief that tormented souls could rise from their graves and survive on blood that they sucked from living people. Stories about vampires were well known in Romania and in neighboring Bulgaria and Serbia.

Ever since Bram Stoker's 1897 novel, Dracula, was turned into a film, Romania has become synonymous with the fictional character of Dracula. However, Stoker's Dracula—a Székely (Hungarian) aristocrat—is neither the one of Romanian myth nor the one of history. The historical Dracula was a Muntenian prince. Vlad III Dracula, also called Ţepeş (Impaler), is said to have been born in the Transylvanian town of Sighişoara. His soubriquet actually means "son of Dracul" or "the Dragon." The name comes from a title that Sigismund of Luxembourg gave to his father, Vlad II, when he went to ask for the Holy Roman emperor's assistance in gaining the Muntenian throne.

Romanians are generally philosophical about the misconception Stoker's Dracula has engendered, and with tongue firmly in cheek have turned the cliché into a lucrative part of their tourist industry. ∎

Left: Romanians make light of their best-known export. Above: A detail of the Dacian Wars from Trajan's Column in Rome. Some Dacian pre-Christian beliefs carried over into Romanian culture. Below: The Sea Goddess rides a pair of dolphins in a religious mural at Bucovina's Voroneţ monastery. The Church sought to appeal to a people brought up on pagan beliefs.

Turda

Turda

🗺 102 C3

Visitor information

✉ Centrul de Informare Turistică, Piaţa 1 Decembrie 1918 1

☎ 0264 314 611

NESTLED AT THE FOOT OF THE APUSENI MOUNTAINS, ON the main road between Cluj and Alba Iulia, the often overlooked town of Turda has a storied history and offers a range of sights in its medieval center and in the outskirts, too.

In the 16th century, Turda was the seat of the Dieta (a parliament consisting only of nobles) of Transylvania. In 1568, the Diet proclaimed the Edict of Turda, which forbade anyone to intimidate, imprison, or expel others because of their faith. This was an unusually liberal move, and a century later it was overridden by the Habsburgs' intolerance of the Orthodox faith.

exhibits, among other displays, artifacts found at the nearby third-century A.D. Roman *castrum* (military town), which existed to the southwest of what is now Turda. For something completely different, visit the gigantic, bell-shaped chambers of the **salt mines** (*Str. Salinelor 54B, tel 0264 311 690, $*) that are located east of the main Cluj–Turda road on the northern edge of town.

An endangered species? A Romanian shepherd with his flock

Turda's medieval center comprises several handsome baroque and Magyar buildings, all within easy walking distance of each other. Among them are the **Primăria** (Town Hall; *Piaţa 1 Decembrie 1918 28*) and the **Muzeul de Istorie** (*Str. B. P. Haşdeu 2, tel 0264 311 826, currently closed for restoration*). The latter, the History Museum, is housed in a rugged, square, two-story, 16th-century palace that was built for the influential Báthory family. The museum

The Romans exploited Turda's salt long before the Saxons developed the deposits in the 12th century, and over the ensuing centuries they became some of the most important mines in Transylvania, generating enormous wealth for Turda. The commercial operation closed down in the 1930s, but the salt mines have been turned into a visitor attraction. Dress warmly (the caves are a constant 50–54°F/ 10–12°C) and bring a flashlight to see the less well-lit areas. ■

Aiud

THE CHARMING TOWN OF AIUD LIES IN THE FOOTHILLS OF the Apuseni Mountains. It is noted for its 14th-century citadel and the nearby Râmet Monastery.

The robust **Cetatea** (Citadel) occupies most of the central square, Piața Cuza Vodă. Its thick, castellated walls are unusually wide for the building's small girth. In the early 17th century, the castle belonged to Prince Gábor (Gabriel) Bethlen (1580–1629), one of Transylvania's most cultured and enlightened rulers. You can climb the defense towers *(ask at the museum)*. The Citadel houses the **Muzeul de Istorie** *(Piața Consiliul Europei 24, tel 0258 865 459, closed Mon., $)*. In addition to Romanian antiquities, the History Museum contains objects from Papua New Guinea collected in the 19th century by explorer Samuel Fenichel.

The **Aiud Museum of Natural Sciences** *(Str. Gábor Bethlen 1, tel 0258 862 569, closed Mon., $)*, is located in the nearby 1796 Gabriel Bethlen College. The collection of stuffed animals and birds shelters under glorious but decaying baroque ceilings.

The premiere attraction near Aiud is the **Mănăstirea Râmet,** some 17 miles (27 km) from Aiud via the town of Teiuș. Take care on the country road from Teiuș, because the surface may be dreadful—road crews rarely get this far. The monastery, founded in 1377, is named after the *eremiți* (hermits) who isolated themselves here long beforehand. It commands an impressive position on a wooded hillside, with the tremendous, bare rock faces of the Râmeț gorges towering behind like a gigantic wall. A 1980s, Moldavian-style church sits near the top, while a simple, late 14th-century basilica with a thick, square tower and diminutive body occupies a lower position on the hill. The latter's interior features fragments of some of the earliest known frescoes in Romania, from circa 1300. The **monastery museum** *(open on request)* shows local tools and textiles. ∎

Aiud
- 102 C3

Mănăstirea Râmet
- 102 B3
- ✉ Râmet
- ☎ 0258 880 111
- $ $

Arieş Valley

Arieş Valley
⚠ 102 B3

FAMED FOR ITS NATURAL BEAUTY, THE ARIEŞ VALLEY BRINGS you into the heart of the Apuseni Mountains. The asphalted DN75 road between Turda and Câmpeni follows the river along most of its course. Every turn reveals new vistas, the only constant being green pastures punctuated by haystacks, dense woodland, and rocky peaks.

Heading west from Turda, drive about 4.5 miles (7 km) through the suburb of Mihai Viteazul to the turnoff for the **Cheile Turzii** (Turda Gorges). This country road brings you over the Arieş River through a village called Cheia (Gorge, literally "The Key"); the gorges lie to the northwest. Inhabited by the Dacians circa 500 B.C., the 1.5-mile-long (2.5 km) canyon is now a nature reserve. Wander the various trails to see waterfalls that cascade down vertiginous rock walls and to explore the network of caves, hollowed out of calcareous rock that formed during the Jurassic period. Eagles sometimes soar overhead.

From the gorges, an easy, 5-mile (8 km) detour south takes you to the amazingly picturesque village of **Rimetea.** The village originally was founded by Hungarians, but it truly developed only when the Saxons colonized the area in the 14th century to exploit the region's iron ore. Today, thanks to a dynamic mayor and some assistance from the city of Budapest, nearly half of the village's 315 Saxon homesteads have been restored. The effort won Rimetea the Europa Nostra prize for conservation in 1999. During the summer season, thousands of visitors pour in. Visit the **Muzeul Satului** (*Rimetea No. 34, 0258 768 001, closed Mon., $*), a small village-life museum, for a vivid picture of the area's history and culture.

Dwarfing Rimetea to the east is the striking outline of **Piatra Secuiului** (Seckler's Rock). At 3,400 feet (1,129 m), reaching the summit involves a stiff two-hour climb, but the view justifies the effort.

West of Buru on the DN75, numerous villages on and just off the road, such as **Vidolm** (famous for its larch forests), **Ocoliş,** and **Lunca Arieşului,** offer visitors more opportunities to linger and explore. Away from the main road, life continues as it has for hundreds of years. Backbreaking as it may be for the villagers, the rural life is astonishingly picturesque for those who merely observe.

South of **Sălciua,** you'll find the 1.25-mile-long (2 km) cave of **Huda lui Păpară** (*ask for directions in village; trail from road crosses railway line and river*). All over the surrounding area, little mountain churches dot the hillsides. The **wooden church** at **Sartaşu,** a village at the eastern end of Baia de Arieş, was built in 1780 and stands on a hilltop to the north of the main road. Its interior features a wonderful cycle of naive frescoes showing Christian stories (*for entrance, ask for key holder in village*). A historic monument, the church has services only once or twice a year. The pagan custom of placing a fir sapling on a child's grave is still practiced here.

In **Lupşa,** the **Muzeul Etnografic Pamfil Albu**

(phone village hall, tel 0258 769 225, or ask for key holder in village, $) provides an excellent look at local rural life. The museum is housed in a two-story, 19th-century, stone-and-wood house in the village center on the north side of the main road. The collection was founded in 1938 by a teacher who collected more than 8,000 items of local history and traditional household tools. The exhibits include such curiosities as a hedgehog-skin comb, homemade shelves, and musical instruments. At the western end of Lupşa is a working Orthodox **monastery.** It dates back to the 14th century. Most of the buildings are modern except for the wooden church, which is said to be the oldest in

Derailed

A narrow-gauge railway track roughly parallels the DN75 (sometimes it even runs on the road); it was built by the Austro-Hungarians for a steam train popularly called the Mocăniţa (Little Shepherdess). The train used to call at every halt along the valley from the mining area of Abrud to Turda, but it stopped running in 1913. Efforts to revive the line have been unsuccessful to date. ∎

Transylvania. The church was founded by the Cândea, a Romanian noble family; the recently repainted murals are charming. ∎

Against the impressive backdrop of Piatra Secuiului (Seckler's Rock), Rimetea's youngsters enact Înmormântarea Farsangului. As in the Anglo-Saxon rite featuring the Lord of Misrule, all normal rules are suspended for the day while the village heralds the spring.

Apuseni Mountains

Apuseni Mountains
🅰 102 A4–B2

THE HISTORY OF THE APUSENIS HAS BEEN ONE OF GREAT prosperity mixed with appalling deprivation. The mountains are home to the Moţi, who trace their ancestry back more than 4,000 years. Farmers and miners by long tradition, the Moţi cling to some of Romania's most magically serene landscapes.

Near Gârda de Sus: One of the many beautiful valleys in the Apuseni Mountains

NORTHERN APUSENI MOUNTAINS

Rising to an elevation little more than 4,200 feet (1,400 m) on the western edge of the Transylvanian Plateau, the northern Apuseni Mountains offer a chance to get away from it all. They are much more sparsely populated than the southern mountains; the wildness of the landscape allows some of Romania's surviving carnivores—

such as lynx and wolves—to live in relative peace. Most of the few human settlements are strung along the valley roads between Turda and Ştei, and beside the highway that heads north from Ştei to Oradea. In the high reaches of the mountains, hamlets of scattered homesteads cling to the hillsides. They are among the first villages in Romania and are thought to be thousands of years

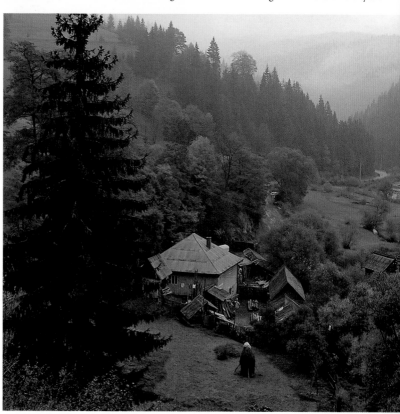

old. Apart from them, the largest centers of habitation on the higher slopes are the sheepfolds.

The area between **Huedin** and the village of **Albac** exemplifies the area's awe-inspiring peacefulness. Be warned: The roads that link the two communities may be very poor in places, especially south of Beliş and the nearby lake, Lacul Fântenele. At the lake, the main road doubles back to the east, but a smaller, partly cemented track heads southwest via Poiana Horea, the Ursoi Pass, and through Horea; the road surface improves outside Albac.

The most famous natural attractions in the northern Apusenis are the karstic ice caves. Of these, the best-known is

Gheţarul Scărişoara, which contains a glacier. The cave is about 4 miles (6 km) north of **Gârda de Sus,** a town on the DN75 west of Câmpeni *(once in Gârda, follow signs, $)*. Scărişoara Cave has two chambers at the bottom of a 144-foot (48 m) shaft. Both are filled with ice, but the largest one is the most impressive: It covers an area of 120,000 square yards (100,000 sq m) and bristles with stalagmites and stalactites. The cave maintains a steady, year-round temperature of around 30°F (−1°C), which preserves the ice even when the thermostat outside soars in summer to 104°F (40°C). Dress warmly and beware of slippery walking surfaces.

Another interesting cave lies near the village of **Chişcău.** The village itself, half a mile (1 km) south of Pietroasa, is home to the quirky, privately run folk museum **La Fluturi** *(No. 86, tel 0259 329 085, open on request)*. The collection, named for its founder, Aurel Flutur, focuses on the village and nearby surroundings. It displays several examples of embroidered clothing, including the traditional men's *sumane* (felted wool coat).

A newly completed visitor's center greets tourists to the nearby **Pestera Urşilor** (Cave of the Bears, *closed Mon., $*). Although this is not one of the largest caves open to the public, it has the most fascinating rock formations. Its name honors the huge cave bears that were trapped here after a rockfall some 15,000 years ago. Some 140 of their skeletons were found when workers from the marble quarry in Chiscău discovered the cave after blasting it open by mistake in 1983. You can still see some of the skeletons.

Mining Romania's ore

Romania's mountains contain a wealth of metals, rock, and minerals that have attracted people for millennia. Bronze Age people were extracting gold some 5,000 years ago. Evidence of Apuseni gold has been found in Egyptian pharoahs' and Mycenean tombs. Later, the Dacians extracted iron, silver, gold, and salt. The Romans built a bridge across the Danube in order to reach the gold in the Apuseni Mountains. The event was so important that they recorded it on Trajan's Column.

The western Carpathians were the Romans' El Dorado. Chronicles describe an unbroken train of ore-laden wagons stretching from Alburnus Maior (Roşia Montana) and Ampellum (Zlatna) to Rome. Romania's gold was so plentiful that it allowed the authorities to waive taxes.

Roşia Montana has yielded considerable evidence of its mining past. In the 18th century, archaeologists discovered waxed tablets that turned out to be handwritten contracts between the mine owners and laborers, some of whom came from as far as Dalmatia. Carbon dating has shown that the Dacians worked the Roşia Montana mines before the Romans. A network of clean-cut galleries up to 5 miles (8 km) long and some remarkable tombs and other extraordinary vestiges highlight the Romans' presence. After the Romans left Dacia in A.D. 271, the local population and later the Hungarians and the Habsburgs exploited this area.

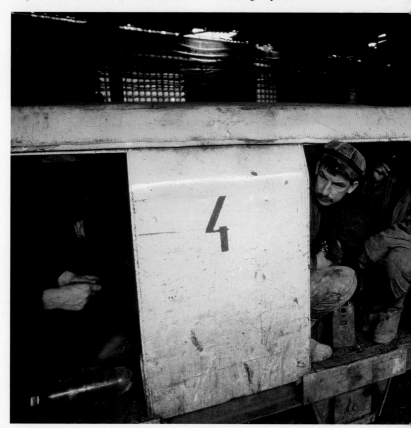

Throughout these periods of changing rule, the indigenous Moți mined their own personal gold veins. The country people's mines became the source of legend and song. Some panned for it in the mountain rivers. Others used the "fire and water" technique. Mentioned in the Bible, this method involved lighting fires against the rock face to make it so hot that the rock would explode. Then water was poured onto the surface so that the broken pieces could be removed more quickly. In the 19th and early 20th centuries, these miners would exchange their gleanings for money at the twice-yearly gold market in Brad. In Bucium Poieni, families became so wealthy that they decorated their clothes with gold thread.

Today, a multinational mining company called Gabriel Resources wants to exploit Roșia Montana's scattered gold desposits. To

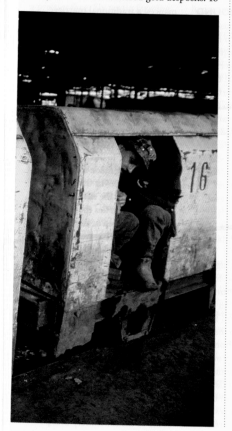

Left: Coal miners in Petroșani enter a mine by railcar.
Above: Changing shifts at Lupeni Mine in Petroșani

make way for the vast quarry, the mining company proposes to remove five mountains. The company plans a 1,440-acre (600 ha) cyanide tailings lake and wants 2,000 people to relocate. In return, Gabriel has funded archaeological digs, offered to build a new village elsewhere, and promised to rescue the area from poverty and landscape the site once the mine is tapped out.

Local opposition to Gabriel is strong. People are concerned about the threat cyanide waste poses to their health. They point out that the pit likely will be active for only 20 years, yet their unique archaeological heritage will be destroyed forever. They believe that most of the profits from the mine will go abroad. And finally, they do not trust that the company will recreate their beautiful mountains, forests, and pastures. ∎

Dobra River runs beside the road. In another couple of miles (3 km) you will encounter the DN67C, where you turn right. Known as the **Drumul Regelui,** this road was built for King Carol II when he wanted to reach a mountain resort. Follow the road north through Şugag and Mărtinie toward **Căpâlna.** The remains of one of the finest Dacian citadels in southern Transylvania lie 4 miles (6 km) southwest of this village. **Dealul Cetate** ❺ dates from the second half of the first century B.C. The oval fortress was attacked during the Daco-Roman wars but survived as a medieval refuge.

Eleven miles (18 km) farther down the road, you reach Săsciori. Stay with the Sebeş River as it flows down toward the town of **Sebeş** ❻. The main focal point here is the Romanesque-Gothic **church** *(Str. Piaţa Primăriei 6, tel 0258 731 693, $)* that stands in the center of town. It has an exceptionally tall choir and very handsome stone carvings.

Your drive through the Mărginimea Sibiului concludes shortly. From Sebeş, turn east and drive 6 miles (9 km) along the main road to Sibiu (DN1) and then turn right onto a smaller road signed for **Cetatea Câlnic** ❼ *(tel 0258 747 220, call for appt. or ask caretakers at Casa Parohială Sasească, 200 yards/200 m from the citadel, $).* The original fortress was built for Count Chyl de Kelling in the mid-12th century. Later in the Middle Ages it became a refuge for villagers, and a series of pantries were added inside the inner, fortified walls. The two rings of walls, magnificent donjon (a massive inner tower), and chapel have recently been restored. The citadel has been designated a World Heritage Site and now serves as a cultural center. ∎

A drive through the Cindrel Mountains affords dozens of romantic panoramas and vistas.

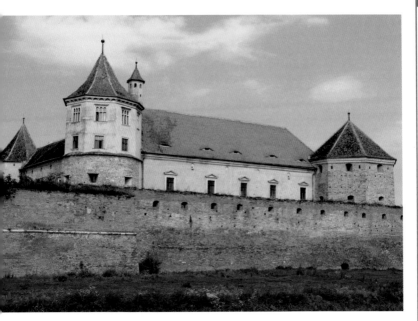

Ţara Oltului

Făgăraş Castle is the town's main focal point; today it houses cultural attractions, including a cellar restaurant.

THE LONG SLIVER OF LAND SQUEEZED BETWEEN THE WIDE Olt River and the southern Carpathians is known as Ţara Oltului (Olt Land). Named after the Olt, this medieval region was developed by the Saxons who arrived in the 13th century. For this reason, some people believe that the area was originally called the Altland, the Old Land. Ţara Oltului is farming country. In summer, tree-fringed fields full of freshly mown hay dot its rolling pasturelands.

Within its tight confines, Ţara Oltului has some interesting sights. The town of **Avrig** contains the **Palatul de Vară Brukenthal** (*Str. Lazăr 38, tel 0744 840 335*), the baroque summer palace that the wealthy governor Samuel von Brukenthal built for his family in 1771. You can visit the botanical garden that he laid out at the rear.

You can also visit **Clubul Copiilor,** where local craftswoman Rodica Ispas has established a **textile weaving project** (*contact Rodica Ispas, Str. Horia 8, tel 0269 523 465*) for the town's children.

The northern terminus of the exhilarating **Transfăgărăşan Highway** (*open summer;* see p. 67) is 10.5 miles (17 km) from Avrig. This seasonal road crosses the mountains into Muntenia.

A mile (2 km) beyond the highway terminus is the village of Cârţa and the ruins of a Cistercian abbey, **Abaţia Cârţa** (*tel 0269 521 125, call for appt., closed during Sun. service, $*). Consisting mainly of its stately choir, an impressive watchtower, and a length of arcaded wall, the abbey was built by monks from the French abbey of Pontigny in the early 13th century. Cârţa Abbey

Sighișoara's
medieval old
town stands
on a clifftop
high above the
valley floor.

Sighișoara

Sighișoara

▲ 102 D3

**Visitor
information**

✉ Centrul de
Informare Turistică
Str. Octavian Goga 8

☎ 0265 770 415

PERCHED ON A ROCKY OUTCROP WITH ITS PROTECTIVE
wall intact, romantic Sighișoara is one of the most attractive towns in
Transylvania. The adjective "fairy-tale" has never been more appropriately applied. Once inside its citadel, you will feel as though you
have been transported into the past.

Sighișoara's 13th-century fortress
stands in the middle of the modern, lower town and seems to
float overhead. Built after the ter-
rifying 1241–42 Tatar invasion, it
now contains hotels and inns,
restaurants, cafés, a school, several
churches, and a museum. The
citadel is in fact a fully functioning part of the town. At the height
of its strength, the fortress had 14
towers and bastions (nine remain)
and three rings of defensive walls.
Two gates guard entrance into the
citadel, one on the east and the

other on the western side. Cars
are not allowed inside.

Although the Saxons began to
settle in Sighișoara during the
12th century, most of the oldest
houses inside the citadel date
from the late 1600s, built after a
fire destroyed the town.

The magnificent 192-foot-
high (64 m) **Turnul cu Ceas**
(Clock Tower; *Piața Muzeului 1,
tel 0265 771 108, closed Mon., $*)
towers over the citadel's eastern
gate. Built in the 1300s but sub-
stantially altered since then, the

tower now houses a small history and science museum. Climb to the top for a great view of the surrounding countryside. On the hour, the mechanical carillon rumbles into action, and seven oak figures roll around the clock face. The figures represent the mythical gods who gave their names to the days of the week (Mercury, Jupiter, etc.); each one carries an alchemical symbol on its head. The carillon was probably installed with the clock mechanism in the mid-17th century.

A couple of notable buildings front Piața Muzeului, a square near the Clock Tower. **Strada Cositorarilor No. 5,** currently occupied by the restaurant Casa Vlad Dracul, is said to be the birthplace of Muntenian prince Vlad III Dracula (1431–1476). A former **Dominican monastery church** (tel 0265 771 195) founded in the 13th century sits on the square's north side. Although the church is now Evangelical, the beautiful 1680 baroque altarpiece from its previous incarnation is still there, together with a collection of 35 13th-century Islamic carpets. The rugs were donated by the town's much-traveled merchants. Concerts are often held inside.

From the Piața Cetății, Strada Școlilor heads south and dead-ends at a T-intersection; look for the nearby **Scara Școlarilor** (Students' Steps), a covered wooden staircase. It dates from the mid-17th century and was built for students who attended the German school higher up the hill.

Farther up the hill you come to the most handsome church in town, **Biserica din Deal** (Church on the Hill; tel 0265 771 195, $). Also known by its patron saint, Sf. Niculae (St. Nicholas), the church was probably built in

the early 1400s, but stands on the site of a much older chapel. The church seems to grow organically out of its foundations. Its simple exterior belies the magic inside. A 1704 fire damaged the gorgeous interior paintings, but they recently were restored by teams of conservators from Bucharest's fine art school. One highlight is an

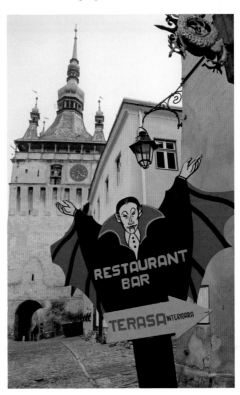

almost complete fresco of the "Last Judgment" on the east end of the north nave wall. Experts believe that a Tyrolean (Austrian) artist painted some of the paintings. With wonderful central European carvings from the late 1300s and an altarpiece by Johannes, the son of the celebrated German sculptor Veit Stoss, Biserica din Deal is a treasure not to be missed. ■

A Dracula-themed restaurant advertises itself near Sighişoara's medieval Clock Tower.

Târgu Mureş

IN CONTRAST TO THE DEEPLY RURAL CHARACTER OF THE surrounding countryside, Târgu Mureş is intensely urban. A thriving university city, it was a center of artistic dissent during the communist years and the cultural scene is as active as ever. You will hear as much Hungarian in the streets as Romanian.

Târgu Mureş
🗺 102 D3
**Visitor
information**
✉ Centrul de
 Informare Turistică,
 Str. Enescu 2
☎ 0365 404 934

The city's Hungarian name is Marosvásárhely (pronounced Marosh-va-SHAR-hay). First mentioned in 1300, Târgu Mureş grew from a market into a garrison town manned by the Secklers who protected Transylvania's borders for the Hungarian king. In the 18th century, it became a center of learning.

Most people start their tour of the city at **Piaţa Trandafirilor** (Roses Square), the rectangular square around which most of the city's traffic revolves. As well as shops, restaurants, and Internet cafés, the square contains many

cultural institutions. Standing tall at the square's eastern end is the **Orthodox Cathedral** (*Piaţa Trandafirilor 1*). It is the largest in Transylvania and was built in the 1920s shortly after Transylvania was handed over to Romania.

The opposite end of the square holds the **Palatul Culturii** (*Str. Enescu 2*). The Culture Palace is a masterpiece of late 19th-century Secessionist-style architecture, which combines geometrical and free-flowing lines. The building and many of its interior fittings were designed by Marcel Komor (1868–1944) and Dezsö Jakab

(1864–1932). Hungary's well-known ceramics firm, Zsolnay, made the vibrant blue, yellow, and red roof tiles. The first-floor **Sala Oglinzilor** (Mirrors Hall), so-called because it is lined with huge mirrors in riotously floral frames, is a wonder to behold. The only daylight comes from 12 colorful stained-glass windows that show scenes from a Hungarian legend.

The palace is home to Mureş County's **history and archaeology museums** (*Muzeul Judeţean de Arheologie şi Istorie, Str. Horea 24, tel 0265 263 960; Secţia de Artă, Str. Enescu, tel 265 267 179; both closed Mon., $*), whose highlights include a beautiful fibula from the 12th century B.C. and paintings by the great Romanian Impressionist, Nicolae Grigorescu. The building also contains a concert hall and library.

Nearby, the **Muzeul de Etnografie** (*Piaţa Trandafirilor 11, tel 0265 250 169, closed Mon., $*) is housed in an 18th-century baroque mansion. The collection was founded by Aurel Filimon (1891–1946), an archaeologist who laid the foundations of ethnographic and folklore research in Mureş. A few minutes' walk away is a lovely 19th-century building housing the **Secţia de Stiinţele Naturii** (*Str. Horea 24, tel 0251 236 987, closed Mon., $*). You can see exotic butterflies and the second largest stuffed Carpathian stag in the country at this natural history museum.

Târgu Mureş has three excellent theaters; try to catch a performance at the experimental **Teatrul pentru Copii şi Tineret Ariel** (Ariel Theater for Children and Young People; *Str. Poştei 2, tel 0365 407 950*). Although staged in either Hungarian or Romanian, its repertoire includes traditional puppet theater and mime.

To the north of Piaţa Trandafirilor, Piaţa Bernady György holds the medieval **citadel.** It was begun in 1492 for Count Ştefan Bathory (Báthori István in Hungarian). Extended

and redesigned in a late Renaissance style, it has a pentagonal plan and seven bastions. High brick walls protect a 15th-century Protestant church and medieval bakery. Recently restored, the citadel now hosts many cultural events.

The historic **Biblioteca Teleki-Bolyai** (*No. 17, tel 0265 261 857, closed Sun.*) sits on Strada Bolyai, a long street that heads south from Piaţa Trandafirilor. Founded by Count Sámuel Teleki, it was opened in 1802 and was one of the first public libraries in (what was then) Hungary. The holdings include rare books by Savonarola, Geleotto Marzio's *Liber de Homine* printed in Bologna circa 1475, and fascinating 18th-century publications describing the lives of contemporary Transylvanian noblewomen. ■

Romanian and Hungarian emblems stand peaceably side by side in Târgu Mureş, their political enmities forgotten in a concerted drive to improve life for all.

A Eurasian lynx *(Felis lynx)* perches on a fallen tree trunk.

Bears, wolves, & lynx

Romania is one of the last places in Europe where bears, wolves, and lynx still live in the wild. They inhabit the forest-cloaked Carpathian Mountains, most of which lie in Romania. Experts estimate that 60 percent of Europe's remaining brown bears, 40 percent of its wolves, and nearly all its lynx (excluding those which survive in Russia) can be found here. Recent statistics show that Romania has about 5,000 bears, 3,000 wolves, and 2,000 lynx.

These three species constitute the only surviving large carnivores on the continent. Thanks to trophy hunting, the protection of domestic livestock, and fear, the remaining population is extremely vulnerable. In some areas, huge efforts have been made to educate the public into understanding the animals and their needs. This is not only with conservation in mind, but with the aim of developing sustainable ecotourism as well.

There is very little likelihood of actually seeing a wolf in the wild. Bears and lynx may be less shy, but great care should be taken not to approach any of them. Generally these animals come lower down the slopes only in the winter, when food pickings are scarce.

In 1997, a group of ecologists founded a six-year project called the Carpathian Large Carnivore Project (CLCP), with the goal of gaining a greater understanding of the three endangered species. Many local and international organizations were involved in the Zărneşti-based project. Over the course of the project, 17 wolves and 12 bears were radio-collared and monitored, and a new national nature reserve, Parcul Naţional Piatra Craiului, was established. Although the project successfully gathered a lot of information, sadly by 2002 only one collared animal, a wolf, still lived.

Since 2003, the national park has taken over CLCP's scientific activities and Zărneşti has become a mecca for ecotourism. One of the founder members of CLCP, tour operator and guide Colin Shaw, cofounded the Asociaţia de Ecoturism din România. This ecotourism association now sets the standard for the industry.

Romania has signed the convention on the protection of rare species, but hypocritically allows bear hunting. The annual quota

Above: The endangered Carpathian brown bear (Ursus arctos). Below: One of the rarely seen wolves of the southern Carpathians.

is fixed by an institution that profits from the business. Sensational bear-watching has also become a problem: One of the most well-known places to see wild bears is the Braşov suburb of Rădădău, where overflowing trash cans attract the scavenging animals. Many tour operators now include the "sight" on their itineraries. Despite warnings and advice to keep the cans closed, one person has been killed by a bear. This act has fed an already high state of public alarm, raising concern that the bears are more likely than ever to fall victim to fear. ■

Braşov

BRAŞOV IS ONE OF TRANSYLVANIA'S GREATEST SAXON CITIES. The city was heavily industrialized under the communists, but the medieval center survived in remarkably good shape.

The busy **Piaţa Sfatului** (Council Square) makes a good focal point. In many ways, it serves as an open-air stage. The three-story building and watchtower in the center of the square houses the **Muzeul Judeţean de Istorie** *(Piaţa Sfatului 30, tel 0268 472 363, closed Mon., $)*. Beautifully presented, the displays include findings from the people's castle at Râsnov and the first known document written in Romanian, dating from 1521.

The area around Piaţa Sfatului has lots of terrace cafés and restaurants, many uniquely sited. For instance, the well-known **Cerbul Carpatin** (Carpathian Stag; *Piaţa Sfatului 14, tel 0268 417 612)* occupies part of an imposing 16th-century town house-cum-market hall.

Near the Town Hall is St. Mary's Evangelical Church, better known as **Biserica Neagră** (Black Church; *Curtea Honterus 2, tel 0268 511 824, closed Sun., $)*. The nickname stems from the fact that during the Habsburg siege of Braşov in 1689, a tremendous fire blackened the church walls—and left 3,000 people dead. In service since 1383, the Black Church became the flagship of Transylvanian Protestantism in the 15th century. Its most famous priest was Johannes Honterus (1498–1549), who spread Luther's message from here. His statue stands outside.

Braşov
103 E2
Visitor information
Centrul de Informare Turistică, Piaţa Sfatului 30
0268 419 078

Inside, take note of the decorated box pews; the paintings identify which guilds owned the pews. There's also a collection of 119 Anatolian rugs, the gift of Saxon merchants who bought them either on their travels or from Turkish soldiers on their way to fight the Habsburgs. During summer months, thrice weekly organ concerts are held here.

Be sure to experience the oddity that lies a five-minute walk to the northeast from the Black Church: **Strada Sforii** (Rope Street). Varying between 3.6 and 4.4 feet (111–135 cm) in width, it is said to be the narrowest street in Europe.

Between Piaţa Sfatului and Bulevardul Eroilor, the pedestrian **Strada Republicii** is lined with bakeries and food shops housed in attractive 18th- and 19th-century buildings. At the northern end, turn left for Braşov's superb **Muzeul de Etnografie** (B-dul Eroilor 21A, tel 0268 476 243, closed Mon., $). This ethnographic museum has been imaginatively organized as though it were a medieval market.

From 1395, Braşov's Saxon town was protected by walls. Small sections have survived, along with the remains of seven bastions, the most impressive of which is the tall, circular **Bastionul Ţesătorilor** (Str. Gheorghe Coşbuc 9, tel 0268 472 368, closed Mon., $), built by the weavers' guild in the 16th century; inside, its walls are lined with tiers of roofed wooden platforms where people took refuge during attacks. A small museum traces the history of Braşov; it contains a model of the medieval town and its fortifications.

The Saxon town walls also enclose a 16th-century **Cetatea.** This citadel crowns the summit of Dealul Cetăţii; walk or drive to the top via Strada Nicolae Iorga and Strada Eminescu for a marvelous view over the old center. The building houses the restaurant **Cetatea** (tel 0268 417 617), which serves local dishes.

To the southwest lies **Poarta Şchei.** Erected in 1827, this triumphal gate was one of two that segregated the German-speaking Saxon town from the outlying, ethnically Romanian village of Şchei. The other gate, **Poarta Ecaterinei,** dates from 1559 and stands nearby. Romanians wishing to enter Braşov could do so only on certain days of the week, and they were required to pay a toll.

Şchei's main orientation point is the late 15th-century Orthodox **Biserica Sf. Nicolae.** Built for Muntenian prince Neagoe Basarab, the church stands on one side of Piaţa Unirii. Its slender towers with their needle-sharp pinnacles pierce the sky like a castle in a fairy tale. Next door, the first Romanian school, dating from 1495, has been converted into a **museum** (Piaţa Unirii 2–3, tel 0268 511 411, $) dedicated to the history of Şchei, which dates back to pre-Roman times. The low, vaulted rooms contain a printing press that belonged to the school's founder. The village is rife with signs proudly proclaiming its people's Dacian heritage. Look for the door-knockers made to resemble the Dacian standard (a dragon's or wolf's head mounted on a serpent's body).

Opposite the Cetatea, the conical **Muntele Tâmpa** makes a striking backdrop to the old town. A **cable car** (Telecabina Tâmpa, Str. Brediceanu, closed Mon., $) goes to the top of the mountain— 1,080 feet (360 m) above the city—for a stunning bird's-eye view of the medieval roofscape. ■

Topping a tall crag, the historic frontier castle of Bran, known as Dracula's Castle, is up for sale for $78 million.

Around Braşov

FROM BRAŞOV THERE ARE ALMOST TOO MANY PLACES TO see. To the north you can find more superb citadel churches. Go southwest and the landscape offers magnificent hikes in largely unspoiled areas of the southern Carpathians. South lies the Prahova Valley, and to the east the mountains cross into a little-visited area of Moldavia called Vrancea (see pp. 210–11).

Hărman & Prejmer

103 E2

HĂRMAN & PREJMER

The neighboring Saxon villages of Hărman and Prejmer lie a few miles north of Braşov. In each one, solid terra-cotta-tiled farmhouses stand gable end to the streets like so many yoked oxen. (The arrangement dates from the reign of the Habsburg empress Maria Theresa and can be seen in 18th-century villages all over central and eastern Europe.) In the last two decades, many of the German-speaking inhabitants have emigrated, abandoning their homes to the Roma (see pp. 204–205).

In Hărman, the oval defense walls of the **Citadel** (*tel 0268 367 438, closed Mon., $*) enclose a now predominantly Gothic 12th-century church. The 36-foot-high (12 m) walls were built by the community in the 15th century to withstand violent attacks, be it from the Austrians, Muntenians, Moldavians, Secklers, Tatars, or Turks. These were rough times and people lived in constant fear. The four small turrets surrounding the base of the church spire indicated that the people of Hărman had the right to pass the death sentence. A 13th-century funerary chapel inside the church contains fragments of lively late Gothic frescoes.

The walls of Prejmer's **Citadel** (*tel 0268 362 052, closed Sun.–Mon., $; see pp. 148–149*) are yet more impressive. They were raised in three stages between the 15th and 18th centuries. The innermost walls were fitted with sleeping cells, refectories, and galleries to accommodate the entire community during a siege. Prejmer's simple Gothic shrine, modeled on Rhineland churches, must have been an oasis of calm in the midst of terror.

ALONG THE OLD MUNTENIAN TRADE ROAD

The road heading southwest from Braşov winds through the mountains into northern Muntenia. It follows one of the oldest known trade routes in Romania.

Râşnov lies about 10 miles (16 km) from Braşov. Besides its rambling streets of picturesque medieval houses, this town has an extraordinary hilltop **Citadel** *(tel 0268 230 078, $)*. Built by the Teutonic Knights in 1215, the fortress stands on a rock about 400 feet (150 m) above the town.

Râşnov was conquered only once, by Gabriel Báthory in 1612. Now in private hands, the buildings have been restored and give the impression that this was a hilltop village rather than a conventional, medieval castle. The Citadel has been converted into an upbeat tourist attraction, complete with its own museum. An observation point *($)* affords spectacular views of the surrounding mountains. Some of the scenes for the 2003 film *Cold Mountain* were shot near here.

To the southwest lies **Parcul Naţional Piatra Craiului.** This national park offers walking opportunities through beautiful scenery sprinkled with many rare, endemic plants. Its centerpiece is the conical mountain of **Piatra Craiului** (7,000 feet/2,238 m).

In another 10 miles (16 km),

the road reaches the village of **Bran.** The **Castel Bran** *(Str. Traian Moşoiu 489, tel 0268 238 333, closed Mon., $$),* known as Dracula's Castle, looks every inch the part. Protected by sheer walls and pointed defense towers, its few windows peer down at the village from several hundred feet. First documented in 1377, the castle housed a frontier garrison and customs post on the border between Muntenia and Transylvania. Its connections with Prince Vlad III of Muntenia (Dracula) are fairly tenuous: He captured Bran

Teutonic Knights

The Teutonic Knights were invited to southeast Transylvania by the Hungarian king Endre II in 1211. Given the task of protecting the region's borders from marauding Cumans (a nomadic Turkic people), the military monks established stone castles all over the Bârsa Land (surrounding Braşov). With the Saxons' help, Endre threw the Knights out in 1225 after learning that they were planning to seize the area for the pope. ∎

for a brief period while quarreling with Braşov's merchants in 1459, but there is little proof that he spent much time here.

At one time or another, virtually all of the opposing powers that struggled for control of the principality had to deal with Bran. The last, unsuccessful, assault was by the Turks in 1787. The castle belonged more or less continuously to the Saxons of Braşov from the late 15th century until 1920 when the city gave it to the Romanian royal family. After years spent as a summer palace, a field hospital, and a communist-

Râşnov
🗺 103 E1

Parcul Naţional Piatra Craiului
🗺 103 E1

Bran
🗺 103 E1
Visitor information
✉ Centrul de Informare Turistică, Str. Principală 509
☎ 0268 236 355

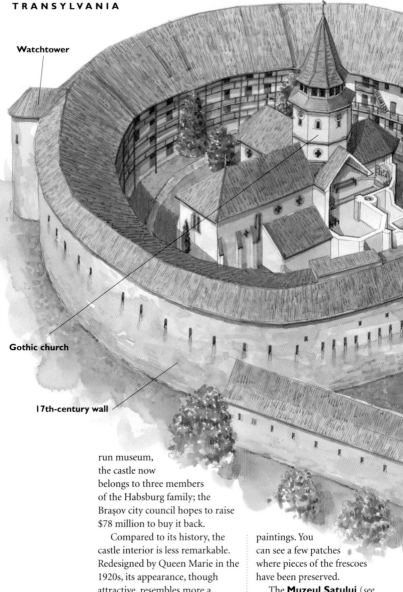

Watchtower

Gothic church

17th-century wall

run museum, the castle now belongs to three members of the Habsburg family; the Braşov city council hopes to raise $78 million to buy it back.

Compared to its history, the castle interior is less remarkable. Redesigned by Queen Marie in the 1920s, its appearance, though attractive, resembles more a modern Spanish hacienda than a battle-worn citadel. The fortifications are impressive, however; they include loop holes and an escape lift. In 1989, engineers discovered that the crag supporting the castle was crumbling under its weight. Excavations made during the process revealed medieval wall

paintings. You can see a few patches where pieces of the frescoes have been preserved.

The **Muzeul Satului** (*see details for Bran Castle, p. 147*) stands on the southern side of the castle hill. Housed in the former *vama* (customs building) on the Transylvanian-Muntenian border, this lovely village museum tells you more about the history and culture of the surrounding area.

From Bran the road becomes increasingly mountainous, with

272 habitable rooms on four levels. The top level is connected by a circular passageway.

PREJMER

Original 15th-century defensive wall

19th-century extension of wall and entrance passageway

Exterior portal

breathtaking views and enticing alpine villages. **Moieciu de Jos** and **Moieciu de Sus** are now well equipped with guesthouses. Farther on toward Câmpulung Muscel (see p. 74) take time to explore the superb rock formations and waterfalls of **Cheile Dâmbovicioarei** (Dâmbovicioara Gorges) and other villages both on and off the main road. **Podul Dâmboviţei** village has delightful Saxon architecture. ∎

Corund
103 E3

Praid
103 D3

Wooden gates at Mikó Citadel in Miercurea Ciuc: the castle is an ethnographic museum dedicated to the Seckler Land.

of a four-leaf clover. Inside is a reproduction of the pretty, 17th-century coffered ceiling.

A ruined 15th-century castle-fortress known as **Székely Támadt** (Fortress Attacked by Secklers) casts a powerful aura over the town. Standing in the northwest corner of Piața Libertății, the castle was used in the mid-16th century by Prince János Szigmund to control the Secklers who had risen against him. The remains of four bastions can still be seen.

CORUND

Some 18 miles (29 km) north of Odorheiu Secuiesc, the village of Corund lies in a beautiful setting renowned for its salt mines and potteries. This Székely community is one of two that have made a

successful business out of selling their own ceramics (the other is Dănești; see pp. 180–181). Corund's villagers have specialized in pottery since the 1700s. Today they are best known for their blue-and-white wares (the blue is a deep cobalt that the Saxons introduced in the 18th century). Ceramics and craft stalls line the main street, and you can often watch the craftspeople at work.

PRAID

Salt has been mined in Transylvania for at least 2,000 years. The village of Praid has one of the largest underground salt mountains in the region. At 4,800 feet (1,465 m) thick, it is a geological rarity, and the rock contains about three billion tons of salt. The entrance to the **mine**

(*Str. Gării 44, tel 0266 240 200,
closed Sun., $*) is near the main
street. Visitors are taken by bus
along a tunnel that is nearly a
mile (1.5 km) long and 240 feet
(75 m) below ground.

SOVATA

The 19th-century spa town of
Sovata developed around several
salt lakes. Although often crowded with vacationing Romanians
in the holiday seasons, the town
has retained some of its traditional character. **Lacul Ursu**
(called Bear Lake because it
looks like a bear's hide) has such
a high saline content that the
deep water retains the sun's
heat. Its depth is warmer than
the surface: At 5 feet (1.5 m)
deep, the temperature can reach
68°F (20°C).

REGHIN

A lively farming town that first
appears in documents in 1228,
Reghin spreads out along the
Mureş River on the northwestern
edge of the Seckler Land. Its
population is much more mixed
than in the Székely towns; the
majority of people living here are
ethnic Romanians. Its central
square, **Piaţa Petru Maior,** is
lined with splendid, two-story
19th- and early 20th-century
buildings. Sporting handsome
wrought-iron balconies and
painted in eye-catching colors,
these houses give a clue to just
how prosperous Reghin was in
the Austro-Hungarian period.
The **Muzeul Etnografic** (*Str.
Vânătorilor 51, tel 0265 512 571,
closed Mon., $*), the folklife
museum, is beguilingly rustic.

THE ROAD TO BICAZ

From Miercurea Ciuc or Sovata
there are several well-surfaced
roads that cross the Carpathians
into the neighboring province of
Moldavia. The most spectacular
route goes from Miercurea Ciuc
north to Gheorgheni and then
east on the DN12C over the
Bicaz Pass.

At the pass you'll come to
Lacu Roşu (Red Lake). It
acquired its name after a 19th-
century landslide turned the
water a shade of pink. Today the
surface of the lake is fractured by
the broken trunks of fir trees that
were smashed in the downpour.
For a small fee, you can rent a
rowboat and spend some idyll
time on the lake. A few miles east
of Lacu Roşu, the road plunges
down a series of vertiginous
switchback turns past **Cheile
Bicazului** (Bicaz Gorges). Stop
and admire the awe-inspiring
views of the cliffs, waterfalls, and
rock formations. ■

The ancient citadel church in Viscri has been serving the community since the 12th century.

More places to visit in Transylvania

CASTELUL BÁNFFY

The magnificent 16th-century Bánffy Palace (or Castle), known as the Transylvanian Versailles, stands in the village of Bonţida, 20 miles (32 km) north of Cluj. The original building underwent several alterations; the striking baroque facades were added in 1750 by the Austrian architect Fischer von Erlach.

The castle was badly damaged in World War II. In 1948, Count Miklós Bánffy was forced to abandon his ancestral home; he immortalized it in three novels about pre–World War I Transylvania (published in English under the title *The Writing on the Wall: The Transylvanian Trilogy*).

The communist period saw the mansion fall down, its furniture and paintings looted, and the grounds used by the local collective farm. In the 1980s, the habitable areas were turned into a pyschiatric hospital. Today, a massive restoration project is returning Bánffy Castle to its former glory, serving as training center of building conservation and crafts. Visitors can arrange a guided tour and relax in its attractive café.
🅰 102 C4 ✉ Bonţida ☎ 0264 439 858 (appt. req.) 🆂 $ 🚆 Trains and buses from Cluj

MĂNĂSTIREA NICULA

Attractively situated on a hillside about 6 miles (10 km) southeast of Gherla, the Nicula Monastery was founded by a hermit called Nicolae in around 1326. It is home to a 17th-century "miracle-working" icon of the Virgin Mary. The icon gave rise to one of Romania's best-known glass-icon schools (see pp. 190–191), and some of the finest examples are on display here in a small museum.

The communists closed the monastery in 1948 and eventually confiscated the miraculous icon in 1964. The painting was ultimately returned after a clumsy restoration. It hangs in the 19th-century church. The wooden church dates from 1770 and was transported here from Bistriţa. The monks of Nicula still paint icons on glass.
🅰 102 C4 ✉ Gherla ☎ 0264 241 835

VISCRI

Lying in rolling pastureland about 28 miles (45 km) east of Sighişoara, this Saxon village has become a by-word for self-regeneration. The town's dynamic mayor, Caroline Fernolend, used authentic building materials, such as wood lathes and lime plaster, to restore several traditional farmhouses and convert them into guesthouses. Fernolend is one of the few remaining Luxembourgers whose ancestors colonized this area in the 12th century. A magnificent citadel church overlooks Viscri. It dates from the 1100s, making it one of the oldest of its kind in Transylvania. Visitors often enjoy walking the paths between here and nearby Mâlâncrav.
🅰 103 D2 **Visitor information**
✉ Primăria, Buneşti ☎ 0268 248 711 🆂 $ ◾

The regions of the Banat and Crişana lie at Romania's western edges, where the Great Hungarian Plain meets the foothills of the Carpathians. Their large cities reveal an unmistakable Austro-Hungarian influence, while the rural areas exude Old World charm.

Banat & Crişana

Timişoara's Piaţa Libertăţii (Freedom Square)

Banat & Crişana

Stretching from Ukraine to the Danube River, the neighboring regions of the Banat (to the south) and Crişana (to the north) share a common history—from the late 11th or early 12th century to the mid-19th century, both regions were ruled successively by the Hungarians, the Turks, and the Habsburgs—but they have individual characters.

Memorial chapel at the Memorial of the Revolution Museum in Timişoara

Before 1918, the Banat (whose name comes from *ban,* a medieval word for "governor") formed part of a larger area of the Danube plains belonging to Austria-Hungary. After World War I it was divided into three portions (the other two now belong to Hungary and Serbia). Crişana is defined by three rivers which flow across it from east to west. In the fifth millennium B.C. the area was home to a highly artistic culture, known as Criş, whose strong sense of design is manifest in the region's folk art to this day.

Timişoara, the Banat's first city, is the brightest urban center in western Romania. Throughout the communist years, many of Timişoara's writers maintained a critical voice. One of them was Herta Müller, whose forebears emigrated to the Banat when it was under Habsburg rule. Her prize-winning novel, *The Land of Green Plums* (first published

as *Herztier* in 1994), describes with an extraordinary, almost surreal poetry the depths to which Romania's totalitarian regime could sink in brutalizing the people it controlled.

Between Timişoara and the Danube lie the foothills and mountains of the southern Carpathians. Their highest point is Mount Semenicul at 4,744 feet (1,446 m). In this area the countryside is sparsely populated and although there are skiing resorts in the Semenic range (east of the industrial town of Reşiţa), as yet the Banat has little to offer in the way of conventional tourism. Few would think it worth coming here, but the landscape, once inhabited by Romans and traversed by Europe's migrating nomads, has a melancholy grandeur. In high summer, its rolling vistas carry the eye across golden hayfields and patches of woodland into an untroubled distance under unbelievably deep blue skies.

North of the Banat, just over the Mureș River, lies the region of Crișana. The elegant city of Oradea sits among rolling countryside in central Crișana near the Hungarian border. The Romanian, Hungarian, Turkish, and Austrian influences can all be seen in its downtown area, an interesting change in scenery from the more rural villages scattered around the region.

Moving farther across the open pastureland of both Crișana and the Banat, adorned with fields of corn or potatoes, villages of wood-framed, adobe houses remind one that until the 1950s this was a predominantly agricultural country. Such visions make one believe that time can be arrested. The sight of an ox-drawn cart or a man scything a hay meadow in long, rhythmical movements provides a sense of continuity with medieval Europe. Before the communists took them over, many of the estates were run by Hungarian landowners. Here and there a forlorn-looking manor house or an onion-domed Catholic or white-walled Reformed church provides a reminder of this part of Romania's past.

Crișana and the Banat have managed to preserve some of the attractive "old ways" that appeal to romantics. In this area, the haystacks are so expressive that they almost speak for themselves. ∎

Piaţa Unirii

For a full sense of the triumphal Austro-Hungarian presence in Timişoara, head to Piaţa Unirii. This beautiful open space is so large it could accommodate a soccer field. The twin baroque towers of the 18th-century Roman Catholic cathedral keep goal at one end while Székely's 1907 Serbian

(1906–1997), who was best known for his expressive portraits. To the right of the museum the green-and-pink facade of the 1910 **Casa Brück** (*Str. Mercy 9*) catches the eye. This art nouveau/Secessionist confection is another László Székely design, as is the adjoining 1908 **Casa Emmer.** Be sure also to admire the fully rounded volumes

Two women conversing on Romanian National Day (December 1) in Piaţa Victoriei, Timişoara

Muzeul de Artă
- ✉ Piaţa Unirii 1
- ☎ 0256 491 592
- 🕐 Closed Mon.
- 💲 $

Orthodox metropolitanate stands guard at the other, clad in fetching pistachio-and-white stripes, next to the Serbian Episcopal church of St. Nicholas, built in the 1740s.

A phalanx of other magnificent buildings face each other on the long sides of Piaţa Unirii. Grandest by far is the 1733 **Palatul Baroc** (Baroque Palace), which first headquartered the Habsburgs' mining administration. Since 2006 the building has housed the **Muzeul de Artă.** Highlights of this art museum's wide-ranging collections include hundreds of 18th- and 19th-century icons from regional Romanian schools and a group of 90 pictures by the Romanian painter Corneliu Baba

of the 1906 **Banca de Scont,** designed by the Hungarian team of Dezsö Jakab and Marcell Komor. The bank sits at the southwest corner of Piaţa Unirii, where Alecsandri and Lazăr streets intersect.

In summer the proprietors of terrace cafés take advantage of the space in Piaţa Unirii to park a flotilla of umbrellas there. In the northwest corner stands the baroque **Monumentul Sf. Treime.** A vision of writhing humanity, the statue memorializes the thousands of people in the Banat who fell victim to the plague in the 18th century. It was made in Vienna and erected here in the late 1750s. A nearby fountain dispenses alkaline drinking water. One of the great achievements of the Austrian regime was to drain the marshes that surrounded Timişoara and to canalize the Bega River that now flows through the city between well-contained banks.

FABRIC DISTRICT

The industrialization of Timişoara began when the Habsburg governor of Transylvania, General Mercy, created the Fabric district in 1720. Fabric contains some of Europe's earliest and most ornate factory buildings. The development of Fabric provided the impetus for a new phase of building that linked it with the Cetate district.

As you walk west from Cetate toward Fabric along Bulevardul Revoluţiei 1989, take note of the decorative brackets of street lanterns on the buildings. In 1884, Timişoara was the first European city to have electric street lighting.

Walk over the newly restored, László Székely–designed **Podul Decebal** (Decebal Bridge), where the boulevard acquires a new name, 3 August 1919. The shady **Parcul Poporului** (People's Park) lies opposite; at the park's east end stand a church and the magnificent 1889 **Sinagoga din Fabric** (Fabric Synagogue; *Str. Caragiale*). The park marks the edge of the old industrial district.

East of Parcul Poporului, the paved square of **Piaţa Traian** is surrounded by historic buildings. The marvelously expressive Secessionist-style 1909 **City Alms House** (again by Székely) occupies the corner of Romanilor and Traian; it is decorated with stylized lions' heads that echo the building's severely geometrical lines. Nearby, at the corner of Strada Dacilor and Bulevardul 3 August 1919, is a handsome Secessionist apartment building called **Palatul Mercur**

(Mercury Palace); a **Serbian Orthodox church** (1740s) stands at the northern end of the square.

Other architectural gems to look for in this district include the 1718 **Fabrica de Bere** (Beer Factory; *B-dul Pestalozzi & Str. Dacilor*); the early 20th-century **Dura Battery Factory** *(Str. Pestalozzi 22)*, which looks postmodern before its time; and the majestic **Facultatea de Chimie, Biologie si Geografie** *(B-dul Pestalozzi 16)*, a university building housing the departments of chemistry, biology, and geography.

To see additional interesting architecture, return closer to the city center and **Piaţa Plevnei.** The west end of this square features the art nouveau 1905 **Casa cu Păuni** (House of Peacocks). Graceful figures of peacocks have been modeled in relief on its front wall and window frames. ■

The spark of the revolution

On December 15, 1989, a crowd gathered outside a vicarage on Strada Cipariu to protest the house arrest of Father László Tökes, a young and outspoken priest belonging to the Hungarian Reformed Church. Beaten up by members of the Securitatea (Romania's secret police), Tökes was due to be evicted that day. A delegation demanded Tökes's release but the authorities refused and called in the militia. That night, the Securitatea spirited Tökes to an outlying village for interrogation; in town, street battles broke out and raged for five days. The army eventually switched sides and by the end of December, the world had changed. A plaque on the church commemorates the event. László Tökes is now bishop of Oradea. ■

A drive to Valea Almăjului

A drive to Valea Almăjului amply rewards curious visitors. This rarely-visited corner of southwest Romania has little tourist infrastructure, but the area is one of the prettiest in rural Banat. The best time to come visit is in late spring, when flowers are in bloom, or in summer, when the hay is being harvested, the woods are in full leaf, and vast tracts of hill- and mountainside lay themselves open to long-distance hiking.

Oraviţa's 19th-century theater has four-carat gold-leaf detailing but is in desperate need of repair.

Begin your trip in the old mining town of **Oraviţa** ❶, at the neoclassic **Teatrul Vechi Mihai Eminescu** (*Str. Mihai Eminescu 8, tel 0255 572 215*). Created by Ion Niuni in 1817, this theater was the first Romanian theater in the country. Its compact rococo auditorium is a delicious throwback to a Viennese original. The foyer contains a modest museum that documents the town's history. A couple hundred yards to the right, wedged in among a series of single-story, 18th-century houses on Strada 1 Decembrie 1918, is the **Vulturul Negru** (Black Eagle; *Str. 1 Decembrie 1918 7, closed Mon.*). This was the first pharmacy shop to open in the Romanian mountains (1796). Now a

museum, it contains its original wooden fittings and medical instruments.

Drive northeast out of town along the DN57B toward **Marila,** passing a depressing sanatorium and rusting industrial machinery. The road then drops down toward a suburb of Anina called **Steierdorf** ❷. This coal-mining village was founded by Swabians (Germans) and Slovaks during the 18th century when the Habsburgs "planted" foreign colonists in the area to develop modern industries and discourage feudal landlords.

About 7 miles (12 km) farther on, the road climbs into verdant forests and a narrow, steep-sided defile known as the **Cheile Minişului** ❸. Roughly 3 miles (5 km) from

high. The Crişana Museum comprises sections dedicated to fine art, archaeology and history, natural sciences, and ethnography. The latter's highlights include displays of pottery from no less than 19 of Crişana's villages—astonishing for such a relatively small area—and a collection of patterned *lăzi de zestre* (wooden dowry chests).

The Episcopal Palace forms part of a larger architectural ensemble that Hillebrandt designed. It includes the **Catedrala Romano-Catolică** (*Şirul Canonicilor 19, tel 0259 418 235, closed Sun.–Mon., $*), drawing on Ricca's plans for the church of Il Gesù found in the Italian capital.

Pasajul Vulturul Negru (Black Eagle Passage; *Piaţa Unirii 2–4*) is an art nouveau shopping arcade that opens to the street on three sides. Created by the Hungarian architects Marcell Komor and Dezsö Jakab and dating from 1909, its extrovert, curving profiles, soaring ceilings, and stained-glass panels are crowned by an exotic clock tower. The complex incorporates a new four-star hotel, **Hotel Vulturul Negru** (*Str. Independenţei 1, tel 0259 450 000*), which fronts the river and counts the Primăria as a neighbor. For another dose of Central European atmosphere, drop into the Gothic-Secessionist-style 1902 **Hotel Astoria** (*Str. Teatrului 2, tel 0259 130 745*), where Hungary's radical poet, Endre Ady (1877–1919), used to come to meet his friends .

Another exuberant art nouveau fantasy is the **Palatul Moskovits,** which sits at the corner of Strada Independenţei and Strada V. Alecsandri. Its curvaceous facades are decorated with allegorical figures in relief and ceramic tiles. Designed by Kálmán Rimanoczy Jr., it was completed in 1905.

Oradea's most imposing sight is the spectacular **Cetatea Oradea** (*Piaţa Independenţei, tel 0259 435 140, fee for guided tours*). Immortalized in Rogerius of Apulia's *Carmen Miserabile* (or to translate its full title, *Lament for the Destruction of the Kingdom of Hungary by the Tatars*), written circa 1241, the citadel was actually founded in the previous century. It was destroyed and rebuilt several times, and occasionally exchanged hands. It even served as the permanent headquarters for the Ottoman sultan Suleiman the Magnificent between 1529 and 1538. The present five-point-star shape of the fortress was begun in 1569; its appearance is owed to the Italian military architect Domenico da Bologna, commissioned with the rebuilding by Transylvanian prince Ioan Sigismund. So impressive was the building on its completion that the Turkish traveler Evlia Celebi, who stayed in Oradea to watch an estimated 45,000 of his country's soldiers attack the fortress in 1660, wrote that the moat was 120 feet (40 m) wide and "as deep as a sea." When the Turks breached the citadel's defenses in August that year, Commander Ali Pasha triumphantly reported to the sultan that with its defeat, Transylvania had lost its heart.

Even in its present ruined state, Cetatea Oradea is still an imposing place. One of its many intriguing elements is a network of underground channels that were supplied by ducts of warm water that would not freeze even in winter. The citadel has been designated a World Heritage site and is currently undergoing restoration. In addition, the citadel hosts art exhibitions and crafts fairs and a portion of it is home to the fine arts department of Oradea University. ■

Sylvania's Plateau

Zalău
🗺 157 C4

Visitor information
✉ Primăria
Municipiului Zalău,
Piaţa Iuliu Maniu 3
☎ 0260 610 550

Muzeul Judeţean de Istorie şi Artă Zalău
✉ Str. Unirii 9, Zalău
☎ 0260 612 223
💲 $

Galeria de Artă Ion Sima
✉ Str. Gheorghe Doja 6, Zalău
☎ 0260 611 065
🕐 Closed Mon.
💲 $

Muzeul Maghiar Etnografic Sípos Lázló
✉ No. 85, Bogdand
☎ 0740 558 319 (ask for Mrs. Dede Eva)
🕐 Closed Mon.
💲 $

Bogdand
🗺 157 C4

Hodod
🗺 157 C4

SYLVANIA'S PLATEAU, SQUEEZED BETWEEN CULMEA COD-rului, the Meseş and Şes Mountains at the northern edge of the Apuseni range, is dominated by thickly wooded, rolling hills rather than full-scale mountains. This area rarely features in package tours and has retained a peaceful, low-key atmosphere, enhanced by an indefinable romantic air provided by neglected manor houses with peeling walls, weathered terra-cotta roofs, moss-covered carvings, and workaday agrarian villages.

Get your bearings in the county town of **Zalău** (pronounced Za-LOW). This cheerful town has a couple of excellent museums. **Muzeul Judeţean de Istorie şi Artă Zalău** is housed in a 19th-century building with an exceptionally pretty facade. The history section concentrates mainly on archaeological finds, including some rock paintings that are more than 100,000 years old. A five-minute walk from here takes you to the **Galeria de Artă Ion Sima,** which as its name indicates is dedicated mainly to the zestful canvases of the Romanian Impressionist painter Ion Sima (1898–1985).

Head west for the town of **Şimleu Silvaniei.** The handsome (but now ruined) 16th-century **Castelul Bathori** (Báthory Castle) stands in the center of town, above the marketplace. Between the 13th and 17th centuries, the Transylvanian Báthory clan produced many of the principality's leaders, including one king (István, ruler of Poland) and several princes, as well as cardinals, bishops, and judges. Descended from an ancient Hungarian tribe, inbreeding sent some of them mad, and the Báthorys eventually died out altogether. Today the castle is little more than a skeleton, but its graceful early 18th-century carriage entrance remains.

Farther up the valley (follow the stream and the railway line) turn into **Cehei** village to see the 18th-century **wooden church,** which is girdled with a rope motif called a *brâu,* a device that symbolizes the eternal nature of God's love. Some ethnographers believe that such motifs derive from the real ropes that used to hold timber churches together in previous centuries.

In nearby **Uileacu Şimleului** stands the **Biserica Reformată,** a Hungarian Reformed church with a polygonal tower. It was formerly part of a 13th-century Benedictine monastery founded by descendants of the Hungarian king Árpád I. It has a handsome coffered ceiling.

Small, charming farming villages dot the plateau. In **Bogdand** you might enjoy **Muzeul Maghiar Etnografic Sípos László.** This little museum is contained in a single-story, 19th-century farmhouse with a white facade and arcaded veranda. The interior's two small rooms have been decorated in a traditional Hungarian way, complete with cheerful ceramics, homespun cloth, and painted furniture.

A few miles east, the village of **Hodod** plays host to a semi-derelict manor house. It belonged to the Wesselényi family and was constructed between 1736 and 1776. At the top of the hill on the east side of the village is another **Hungarian Reformed church,** this time from the 15th century. The Wesselényi family emblem, consisting of a mermaid and a swan, adorns the coffered ceiling, and there is a stone pulpit by the 17th-century Transylvanian master, Dávid Şípos.

Farther east, a 14th-century castle once dominated the skyline of **Cehu Silvaniei** village. Abandoned after the 1703–1711 rebellion led by Hungarian prince Francis Rákóczi against the Habsburgs, the citadel has all but disappeared. All that remains is a 16th-century circular fountain in

between 1779 and 1810. Its park has been converted into one of Romania's best-known botanical gardens, **Grădina Botanică a Institutului de Cercetări Biologice.** The garden was founded in 1968 by an enthusiastic school teacher. Covering 58 acres (24 ha), its exotic varieties of shrubs and trees include syringa, berberis, and cypress. The greenhouses are geodesic domes.

Approximately 9.5 miles (15 km) away is the Roman camp of

Grădina Botanică a Institutului de Cercetări Biologice
🅐 157 C4
✉ Str. Parcului 14, Jibou
☎ 0260 641 617
💲 $

Cehu Silvaniei
🅐 157 C4

the town center *(near Str. Crişan 17)*. In 1944 the Nazis turned this village into a Jewish ghetto and most of the 551 registered Jews were sent to Auschwitz. The unmarked Jewish cemetery dates from the 19th century and contains about 20 headstones. You can find it in a field along an unmarked track beside Strada Cloşca 8.

In the heart of nearby **Jibou** stands **Palatul Wesselényi** (Wesselényi Palace), another baroque masterpiece that has lain neglected for decades. It was built

Porolissum, which guarded the northwest corner of Dacia in the second and third centuries A.D. A narrow road from nearby **Moigrad** village winds up to the remains of the military camp; it peters out into a grassy track near the top of the hill. Scattered over the lonely hilltop among the sheep, the site contains a gate tower, a stretch of paved Romana road, temple walls, and vestiges of a superb amphitheater. It also commands a fantastic view over the Transylvania Plateau. ■

A wooden house in Marişel village lies on the edge of the Apuseni Mountains.

Healing waters

Romania contains a third of Europe's mineral and thermal springs—some 3,000 found throughout the country: in the mountains, on the plains, and on the Black Sea coast. Many of them have been used for their therapeutic powers since the Roman occupation of Dacia in the second century A.D. Today, the waters of Romania's 70 natural spring spas offer relief from rheumatism, heart disease, digestive problems, nervous disorders, skin complaints, and many more ailments.

"Taking the waters" conjures images of 18th-century aristocrats idling away their leisure time in Baden Baden or Bath. There was a time when Băile Herculane (Hercules's Baths, named after the Roman god who was said to have stopped to bathe here) could compare favorably with both. Located in the narrow Cerna Valley of southwest Romania, where the wild, rugged walls of the Domogled Gorges tower overhead, the spa was founded by Roman legionaries who discovered that its hot, salty, and sulfurous springs helped to cure their aching limbs. Roman nobles also liked the waters of Hercules; they built elaborate votive altars that still survive. Other Romanian spas dating from Roman times include Geoagiu Băi near Deva and Băile Felix, which is close to Oradea.

The Habsburgs rediscovered Băile Herculane when the Austrian Empire established its borders along the Danube River in the early 18th century. Starting in 1736, they and their Austro-Hungarian successors built treatment centers with dressed stone walls; ornate, imperial hotels; and a casino with arcades of slender, wrought-iron columns. Băile Herculane was patronized by the central European elite. They included the Austro-Hungarian emperor Franz Joseph and his beautiful but ill-fated wife, Elisabeth, known as Sissi, who wrote affectionately about the spa in her journals.

The Habsburgs' spas set the mark for other Romanian resorts such as Buziaş near Timişoara (founded in 1819), which has an ornamental park and a covered, Byzantine-Turkish-style colonnade similar to the ones at Baden Baden and Karlovy Vary. During the 1960s, the communists extended the existing resorts by building high-rise hotels next to them. Now, although still in use, many of the stylish 18th- and 19th-century edifices look sadly dilapidated as they wait for long-delayed restoration.

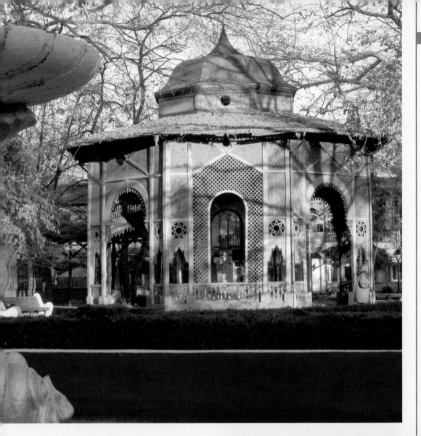

Run-down yet elegant Buziaş (above) still draws locals hoping to benefit from its sulfur-rich waters (far left). Hydrotherapy facilities at Băile Olaneşti spa (right).

A spa of a very different sort, Eforie Nord sits on the Black Sea coast. It was established as a health resort, with a sanatorium opening in 1894 and a bathing ward in 1904. Its attraction was not only the sea air and sun but also *nămol*, the rich, black, sapropelic mud from nearby Lake Techirghiol that is used in treatments. Eforie was one of several Romanian resorts that sprang up thanks to the encouragement of German-born King Carol I (1839–1914), who more than anyone helped make them popular. Today, Eforie is the second largest holiday resort in Romania (the largest is coastal Mamaia, located north of Eforie).

The waters are not just for soaking. Some of Romania's best-known bottled mineral waters come from the Carpathian

springs of Covasna and Borsec in eastern Transylvania. But the bottled varieties represent only a fraction of the many different compositions of naturally carbonated water. Emperor Napoleon III preferred the waters of Călimăneşti (in Wallachia) over those of France. And many Romanians take their water directly from springs that bubble up in places known only to them. ■

Satu Mare & around

The exuberant, art nouveau and Viennese Secession-inspired Hotel Dacia in Satu Mare

LYING A MERE 20-MINUTE DRIVE FROM ROMANIA'S NORTH-west border with Hungary, Satu Mare is a pleasant market town imbued with a distinctly Austro-Hungarian character. Mentioned first in 1181, it is the legendary site of Castrum Zotmar, a fortified stronghold first mentioned in tenth-century chronicles and from which the town derives its name.

Satu Mare
🗺 157 C5
Visitor information
✉ Centrul de Informare şi Promovare Turistică, Piaţa Independenţei 39, Oradea
☎ 0259 435 140

Satu Mare's old center lies close to Piaţa Libertăţii, a large, irregularly shaped square where the public gardens provide a welcome respite after a day of sightseeing. This town has always been a stopping-off point for travelers on their way to or from Hungary, since it is so close to the old international border crossing at Petea. At the southern end of the square, you can't miss the multicolored facade of the Secessionist-style **Hotel**

Dacia *(Piaţa Libertăţii 8, tel 0261 715 773)*, which was built in 1902 to a prize-winning design by Ödön Lechner. Today, the hotel forecourt is a well-known meeting point for the minibuses that make a twice-daily dash between Bistriţa (see pp. 107–109) in Transylvania and Budapest in Hungary.

Opposite the hotel stands the **Secţia de Artă** *(Piaţa Libertăţii 21, tel 0261 710 114, closed Mon., $)*. It contains Romanian fine and decorative art from the collections of the county museum. It is housed in a building with an impressive dark-pink-and-white, neo-Gothic facade from 1842. One of the wings dates from the 1700s.

The history and ethnography sections of the **Muzeul Judeţean Satu Mare** (*Str. Lucaciu 21, tel 0261 737 526, closed Mon., $*), are housed in the town's three-story former *primăria,* which is about three blocks east of Piaţa Libertăţii along Bulevardul Brătianu. The 1936 Town Hall building looks rather severe until you start to analyze how the Romanian architect, G. P. Liteanu, separated the facade into several different playful layers.

ŢARA OAŞULUI

Northeast of Satu Mare, sandwiched between the Igniş Mountains and the Ukrainian border, lies an ethnographic zone called Ţara Oaşului. The cultural and economic focus of this area is the town of **Negreşti-Oaş.** If you have only time for one visit in this region, choose the excellent local museum here. **Muzeul Ţara Oaşilor** has two sites, the *sediu* (headquarters) on Strada Victoriei (*No. 140, tel 0261 854 839, $*), which features ethnography and fine arts, and *muzeul in aer liber* (the open-air museum) in the center of Negreşti (*Str. Livezilor 3–5, tel 0261 854 860*). Apart from the appeal of its vernacular buildings, one of the museum's main attractions is the chance to see pottery being made and witness wooden mills, whirlpools, and a smithy in action.

Five miles (8 km) from Negreşti-Oaş, the view opens onto the breathtaking landscapes of **Luna Şes.** This area covers 600 acres (250 ha) at the northern edge of 3,940-foot (1,201 m) Mount

Pietroasa and 3,323-foot (1,013 m) Muntele Mic. Plans are being made to transform this area into a recreational destination, complete with skiing, motocross, fishing, and horse-riding facilities in Luna Şes as well as hotels, restaurants, and campsites.

Ţara Oaşului, be it ever so entrancing, is not Arcadia. After the fall of communism, many young people from this area were so desperate to escape what they saw as a hopeless future that they

Sâmbra Oilor

Each spring on a hillside overlooking Huta-Certeze, village people and farmers come together for Sâmbra Oilor (Sheep Owners Gathering). This centuries-old custom marks the day when the flocks leave their winter pastures for the mountains. Traditionally it is the time when the owners hire shepherds for the season, count their sheep, and ask the priest to bless them. Since the 1970s, the event has been transformed into a major folk festival, complete with singing and dancing exhibitions, which draws as many as 20,000 visitors. ∎

Negreşti-Oaş
▲ 157 D5

became illegal workers in Western Europe. Some have earned enough to return with great wealth. And so a new ethnographic phenomenon has emerged in the villages of this once modest, rural hideaway: Sumptuous three- and four-story villas have sprung up. Vying with each other in luxury, some are so grand that they are equipped with elevators and artesian wells. To get a better idea of the area's changing character, tour the villages of **Certeze, Huta-Certeze, Racşa, Tur, Bixad, Trip, Târşolţ** and **Cămărzana.** ∎

More places to visit in Banat & Crișana

BUCOVA

Lying near the narrow Iron Gate Pass, where the Dacians and Romans confronted each other in A.D. 101, this pretty village offers you a foothold into the wild and beautiful Munții Tarcului. The guesthouse **Casa de Vacanța Irina** *(tel 0721 347 864)* caters for mountain bikers and can organize hiking tours with an English-speaking guide. About 13 miles (20 km) to the northwest are the famous pink **marble quarries of Ruschița** *(contact Titan Mar–Marmosim SA, Str. Cuza Voda 24, Simeria, tel 0254 260 851)*. Romania's answer to Carrara, the quarries have been in operation since 1883.

🅜 157 C2

CHEILE BARCĂULUI

The remote and suprisingly beautiful Barcău Gorges lie west of Fildu de Jos, between the villages of Tusa and Șag. They form part of a nature reserve that contains wild boar and mountain stag. Tusa has a wooden Orthodox church from 1700, as well as vineyards, where you are welcome to taste the wines, and a trout hatchery.

🅜 157 C4

CRAMELE RECAȘ

Located near Timișoara, Recaș has been home to a vineyard since the 15th century. Visitors can book a wine-tasting with a meal, visit the winery, and in season, help gather the harvest. Once in the village of Recaș, look for the signs to Cramele Recaș.

🅜 157 B2 ✉ S. C. Cramele Recaș S.A.
☎ 0256 330 296 🚗 By car: 15 miles (24 km) from Timișoara via DN6/E70

FILDU DE JOS

The *comuna* (district) of Fildu de Jos—four villages in the southern half of Sălaj County, near the Apuseni Mountains and the border with Transylvania—is one of the most attractive places in Crișana. As you go south, the landscape becomes more varied, interesting, and green: Hills grow from a ripple into a wave of mountains, meadows sprout haystacks, and streams tumble over rounded stones. Unspoiled by progress, the villages in question are Fildu de Jos itself (in existence since 1249, when it belonged to the manor of Fyld), **Fildu de Mijloc, Fildu de Sus,** and **Tetișu.**

The residents have gone down in history for their part in the struggle to unite Transylvania, Crișana, and the Banat with the rest of Romania. Today, the residents are mainly a mixture of Romanians, Hungarians, and Roma. Once you turn west off DN1G, the narrow road urges you to go at a much gentler pace. Beside the road, the Almaș stream runs under bridges made from single logs. What sets these simple constructions apart is the thought that has gone into them: Often there is also a handrail made from a slender branch.

People here live by what they can earn from raising livestock, growing potatoes, and manufacturing wood. As in most parts of rural Romania, the villages are losing their younger generations to the cities; they have little interest in maintaining old, slow, and painstaking farming methods.

Fildu de Jos has a superb timber church that was erected in 1727. The woodwork shows a wonderful mixture of inventiveness, elegance, and solidity and is all of a piece with the rough-hewn farmstead gates that survive throughout the village. Inside the church, there are wall paintings from 1856.

Other wooden churches can be found in the nearby villages of **Sânmihaiu Almașului, Baica,** and **Racăș.** There are many more of these highly individual and visually engaging buildings all over Crișana and not only in the more famous woodworking region of Maramureș.

🅜 157 C4

MONEASA

The spa resort of Moneasa stands at an elevation of 840 feet (256 m) in the densely wooded Codru Moma Mountains to the west of Vascău. Many of the resort hotels look as though they have been left behind in a different era, but the area provides great opportunities for trekking on the western edge of the Apuseni Mountains.

🅜 157 B3 ✉ On the DN76 ∎

M aramureş is a living embodiment of medieval Europe. It is a place where ancient traditions still play an accepted part of everyday life— and where people know how to enjoy them to the full.

Maramureş

A brightly colored tomb painting at the Happy Cemetary, Săpânţa

Restored **Piaţa Libertăţii** lies at the heart of **Baia Mare**, the seat of Maramureş county.

Maramureş

RICH IN OAK AND FIR FORESTS, MARAMUREŞ IS OFTEN CALLED THE LAND of wood. Its people, the Moroşeni, are widely respected for their carpentry skills, developed over the past 900 years. Their masterpieces are the tall-spired, shingle-roofed, double-skirted timber churches that have become a significant feature of the landscape.

Lying on the northwestern edge of Romania, Maramureş is an isolated enclave in the Carpathian Mountains. A region of largely unspoiled beauty, it covers an area of 3,900 square miles (6,304 sq km), about the size of the state of Delaware. Ever since the 14th century, the Maramureş has been considered part of Transylvania, but its remote location and independent traditions have always given the region its own distinctive character. After the partitioning of land after World War I, only one-third of the "original" Maramureş

region (that south of the Tisa River) reverted to Romania.

The landscape of Maramureş reflects the fact that it has been well cared for by hand rather than machinery for centuries. Nowhere is this more true than in the four valleys that constitute "Historic Maramureş." Named Cosău, Iza, Mara, and Vişeu, they are the region's "inner circle," each one preserving its rural heritage of folk customs, architecture, music, and dress in a slightly more concentrated form than elsewhere in Maramureş.

Other deeply rural areas adjoin Historic Maramureş to the west and south. They include the countryside around Sighetu Marmaţiei (the region's second largest town), which lies close to the Tisa River, and the *ţările* of Lăpuş and Chioar. (Literally, *ţările* means "the lands," but "independent medieval domains" makes the meaning clearer.) Ţara Oaşului (see p. 173) is also closely related to Maramureş, but it lies outside the *judeţ* (county) boundaries in Crişana.

Following the road east along Valea Vişeului (Vişeu Valley) along the northern edge of this region brings you to the Rodna Mountains, where Maramureş meets Moldavia (see pp. 193-214), which is said to have been founded by a Maramureş nobleman. The administrative center of the region is Baia Mare, an industrial city that teems with life.

There are nearly a hundred wooden churches in Maramureş; eight of them are on UNESCO's World Heritage List. But the region's wood culture extends far beyond the churches: The timber houses are also magnificent, with steep roofs and arcaded verandas. The tall, farmyard gates, covered in decorative carvings and equipped with their own roofs, often signal that the family within are *nemeşi*, local Romanian peasant nobles, and that these apparently easygoing communities have a sense of self-respect that goes beyond mere material possessions.

The Maramureş year still revolves around the agricultural seasons, which are often marked by celebrations that date back to pre-Christian times. Throughout the summer, every farming family worth its salt puts its collective mind to scything, drying, gathering, and stacking *fânul* (hay). And from April to October, hired shepherds stay in the mountain pastures to tend communal flocks of sheep, taking turns so that the sheep are watched around the clock to protect them from wolves and sheep thieves.

Apart from mining operations (itself an ancient Maramureş tradition) in Baia Sprie, Borşa, and Cavnic, heavy industry has by-passed Historic Maramureş. But the loveliness of this area is much more than the sum of its picture-postcard views. Despite the pressures of modernity, Maramureş lies right at the heart of ancient Europe. ∎

Baia Mare

Baia Mare

🅰 177 B1

Visitor information

www.VisitMaramures.ro

✉ Centrul de Informare Turistică, Hotel Mara

☎ 0262 226 656

BAIA MARE, THE COUNTY TOWN OF MARAMUREŞ, SITS against an attractive green backdrop of the Guţâi Mountains. Unfortuneatly, Baia Mare is one of Romania's most polluted industrial cities. Its name appropriately means "big pit," and it is best known as a mining center. The extraction of gold, silver, and other nonferrous metals in this area dates back more than 2,000 years. The city itself has a few gems worth exploring.

Central Baia Mare looks totally modern, but it has a medieval heart. In 1329, the town was mentioned in a contemporary Hungarian chronicle as Rivulus Dominarum (Women's River). The name is said to celebrate the fact that the townswomen had charmed the invading Hungarian army into leaving the citadel walls intact.

Most of the visible signs of Baia Mare's more distant past lie in or around a single square, **Piaţa Libertăţii.** Translated as "Freedom Square," this space and its surrounding buildings have been recently restored, becoming an oasis of elegance. The oldest house, **Casa Elisabeta,** dates from the 1440s and stands on the square's east side; it is named after the wife of the Transylvanian leader Iancu de Hunedoara. It is all that remains of the castle that he built for her. Iancu and his son, the Hungarian king Matei Corvin (R. 1458–1490), received the town and its mines as a reward from the local lords for keeping the Turks at bay. Only the first floor and basement are original and today the building is used as a space for temporary exhibitions.

Iancu de Hunedoara also built the 120-foot-tall (40 m) watchtower on Strada 1 Mai, **Turnul lui Ştefan,** and the nearby **Catedrala Sf. Ştefan** (St. Stephen's Cathedral). Between Strada 1 Mai and Strada Crişan you can see the remains of a 15th-century building that housed a Latin school called **Schola Rivulina.** The school was one of the first in Romania; it taught students from the mid-16th century until 1755.

The **Muzeul Judeţean de Artă** (County Art Museum; *Str. 1 Mai 8, tel 0262 213 964, closed Mon., $*) is devoted almost entirely to paintings by members of the Baia Mare School, which is also known as the Nagybánya School or colony (Nagybánya is the Hungarian name for Baia Mare). Founded in 1896 as a private art college by Simon Hollósy (1875–1918), the school was at the forefront of European painting and attracted some of the finest Hungarian artists of the day, including Károlyi Ferenczy (1862–1917) and Jenő Maticska (1885–1906). The building dates from 1784.

Just a few minutes away, the **Piaţa Izvoarelor** (Square of the Springs) is home to the town's weekly open-air market. The rotund, 15th-century **Bastionul Măcelarilor** (Butchers Bastion) looms over the square. The rebel leader Pintea Viteazul was executed here in 1703 for his part in the Rákóczi uprising against the Habsburg overlords.

If you walk north from Piaţa Libertăţii along Strada Podul Viilor and then turn right into Strada Dacia, you will reach the narrow lane called **Strada Monetăriei** (Coiners Street). Nearby is a pretty courtyard containing the **Muzeul Judeţean de Arheologie şi Istorie** (*Str. Monetărie 3, tel 0262 211 927, closed Mon., $*), the regional archaeology and history museum. The collections are housed in the royal mint, which was founded in 1411 although the existing building was constructed in the 1730s. Traces of human settlement have been discovered dating back to the paleolithic era

Expoziţia Pavilionară, the museum's indoor section across the road, explains the Chioar district's involvement with apiculture (beekeeping) since the Middle Ages.

The main axes in Baia Mare's commercial center are the east-west-running Bulevardul Bucureşti and the north-south artery of Bulevardul Unirii. Some of the smartest cafés and bars can be found on Bulevardul Bucureşti.

around Baia Mare. The most striking local finds on exhibit include several Bronze Age hoards that contained gold rings and some copper hatchets.

A ten-minute walk west from Piaţa Libertăţii, crossing the Şaşar River, brings you to the **Muzeul de Etnografie şi Artă Populară** (*Str. Dealul Florilor 1, tel 0262 276 895, closed Mon., $*). This open-air museum is divided into two sections. The **Muzeul Satului** (Village Museum) covers 14.5 acres (6 ha) of a hillside and features a wooden church, homesteads, and barns from around the region. One of the striking exhibits in

Close to Bulevardul Unirii stands one of Baia Mare's less well-known but rewarding visitor attractions, the **Muzeul de Mineralogie** (*B-dul Traian 8, tel 0262 227 517, closed Mon., $*). Even if you cannot read the Romanian explanations, this museum is a real find. The Mineralogy Museum's charm lies in its welcoming and informative atmosphere, encouraging visitors to browse at their leisure. On the ground floor, wooden display cabinets show samples of every kind of local rock and crystal, while a gallery upstairs exhibits some wonderful crystal flowers. ∎

Pitching hay for their livestock's winter feed, near Baia Mare

Historic Maramureş

**Valea
Marei**
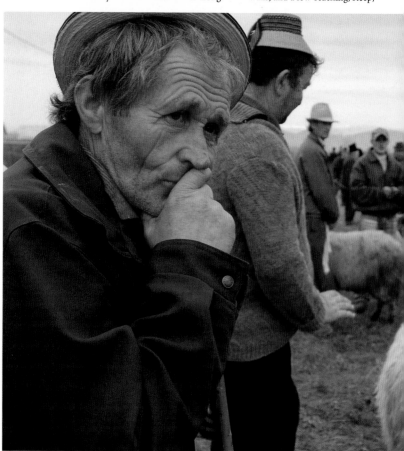 177 B2

"MARAMUREŞ ŢARA VECHE CU OAMENI FĂRĂ PERECHE—
Maramureş is an ancient land whose people are beyond compare." So
goes an immodest Maramureş *doină* (lament). The people of the four
valleys—Mara, Cosău, Iza, and Vişeu—that make up this area have
preserved a spirited sense of their own identity.

MARA VALLEY

**Decisions,
decisions: Ocna
Şugatag's weekly
livestock market
is a great social
as well as
agricultural
attraction.**

From Baia Mare, the Guţâi Pass
provides passage into the Valea
Marei. As the road descends to the
picturesque village of **Mara,** the
view through the trees gives
mesmeric glimpses of a herd of
wild mountain peaks that race
away into Ukraine. Farther along

the road, **Deseşti** has a beautiful
wooden church dedicated to **Sf.
Paraschiva.** Built in 1770 and
listed as a World Heritage site by
UNESCO, it is both sturdy and
beautiful with a tall spire that
tapers to a needle point; a lookout
platform; chunky, block-work
walls; and a low-reaching, steep,

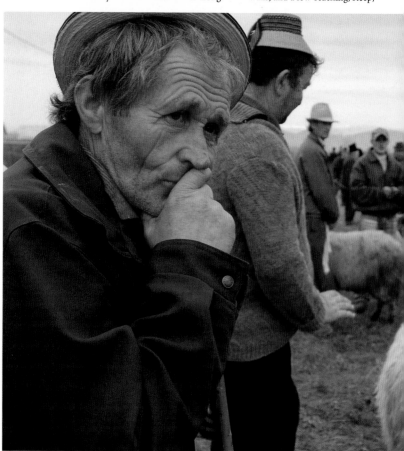

shingled, double-skirted roof. The lookout platform acted as a watchtower, a necessary early-warning system against repeated Tatar invasions. Steep roofs are essential to stop heavy falls of snow from crushing the timbers. Deseşti's church has some of the finest examples of folk art in Maramureş. Direct and full of purpose, the paintings were created by two local masters, Radu Munteanu and Gheorghe Visovat. The scenes include "Arbore lui Ieseu" ("The Tree of Jesse"), above the altar, and "Judecata de Apoi" ("The Last Judgment") in the exonarthex or first chamber.

Three miles (5 km) away, on a broad plateau surrounded by hills, the delightful village of **Hoteni** features a wealth of traditional wooden farmsteads with magnificently decorated gates. It has become famous for **Tânjaua**, a festival rooted in a ritual that dates back to Roman times if not earlier. Meant to identify the village's best plowman, its focal point is a long ceremonial "plow" made of fir branches and decorated with streamers that is carried through the main street of the town. Meanwhile, the village lads chase, catch, and then dunk the chosen plowman in the river. Recently, the festival has evolved into an open-air folk music festival.

COSĂU VALLEY

The Valea Cosăului lies beyond Hoteni to the east of the DN18. On the eastern edge of **Călineşti,** a little church from 1630 stands alone on a hill. Constructed from thick oak beams tied together with wooden pegs, it contains the remains of some 18th-century frescoes. In the village center, check out the *vâltoare* (a water-powered, fan-shaped wooden whirlpool for washing and fulling textiles) and *cazan* (still) for *ţuică* (plum brandy). Both are for the villagers' communal use. Ask for directions when you get to Călineşti.

A few miles farther south, the main road brings you to **Sârbi** and its rows of handsome carved gates. The rope patterns of rosettes and stick figures can be traced to the neolithic people who inhabited the Maramureş region 7,000 years ago. The two small but sturdy wooden churches are evidence that the village was once divided into two parishes. Both shrines, one from 1665 and the other from 1667, sit on hills above the main through road.

Deseşti
△ 177 B2
Visitor information
✉ Primăria, Str. Principală 190
☎ 0262 372 601

Valea Cosăului
△ 177 B2

Budeşti is almost like a continuation of Sârbi. Named after a 14th-century landowner called Bud, it contains about 5,000 people and is one of the largest villages in Historic Maramureş. In 2003, the village was featured in a British documentary called *The Last Peasants,* which highlighted the life of the Moroşeni.

Of Budeşti's two wooden churches, the superb 1628 **Biserica Josani** was built for local nemeşi (Romanian peasant nobles). The four turrets around its tower's base show that the village once had the right to hold its own judicial trials. The frescoes (1762) inside are by Alexandru Ponehalschi, and the church has a collection of icons, some of which date back to the mid-15th century. A *toacă* (wooden sounding board) hangs outside the entrance; it is beaten with a hammer to call parishioners to services. The nearby large row of stone slabs form the *masa moşilor* (the elders' table), where the faithful place decorated baskets of food representing funeral alms and Easter offerings. At Easter, every family has its own traditional place at the table.

IZA VALLEY

Valea Izei

🅰 177 B2–C1

One of the highlights of the Valea Izei is the road that heads east from the hamlet of **Vadu Izei**, located 4 miles (6.5 km) south of Sighetu Marmaţiei (see pp. 186–187). Several weavers and woodworkers can be found in this attractive village, as well as in the neighboring settlement of **Valea Stejarului** to the east.

Farther east again, the most striking thing about **Bârsana** (named after *bârsani*, local shepherds who breed long-haired sheep) is its newly built Orthodox monastery. The complex consists entirely of wooden buildings built in a traditional style; most of them postdate the 1989 revolution. Half a mile (1 km) back along the road on a hill surrounded by orchards stands a graceful, early **18th-century wooden church** (the unique two-tiered, arcaded porch was added in 1900). It was moved here, closer to the village, after the monastery to which it belonged closed in 1791. Its interior frescoes were painted by Toader Hodor and date from 1806. Showing baroque and rococo influences, these folk paintings are exceptionally good and are the main reason why the church is listed as a World Heritage monument.

Continue southeast to **Poienile Izei** to see another superb wooden church on the World Heritage List. Constructed of fir logs between 1604 and 1632, it stands on a gently sloping hillside. The entrance doors are beautifully painted and show the figures of Sts. Paul and Peter. The highlight of this church is the frescoes created in 1794 by Gheorghe din Dragomireşti. The most famous and arresting scenes are from "The Last Judgment" in the first room: On the north wall, the damned are borne inexorably toward final retribution by Gehenna, the river of hellfire, which in turn is swallowed whole by a monstrous Leviathan with remarkably human eyes.

Southeast of Poienile Izei and linked to it most directly by a dirt road, **Botiza** lies on a tributary of the Iza River and has become a thriving tourist center thanks to the initiative of its women. A score of guesthouses have opened, and local artisans sell traditional Maramureş carpets, which often feature stylized dancers, fir trees, and churches.

Across the mountains to the

east, via Şieu and Bogdan Vodă, lies **Ieud**. Of its two parish churches, the older and more fascinating is the late 17th-century **Biserica din Deal** (Church on the Hill), which was built on the site of a much earlier shrine. It, too, is a World Heritage monument. While its exterior is lovely, its interior is a wonder to behold. Murals cover every inch of available space. They were completed in 1782 by Alexandru Ponehalschi and are considered his best work. Ponehalschi was trained in the Byzantine tradition but his mature style shows that he drew on the baroque style.

Hidden away in a field on the village outskirts is a **Jewish cemetery.** It is one of the few, poignant witnesses to a once thriving community of Jews who lived peacefully in Maramureş. Most of the Jews from this region perished in fascist death camps.

VIŞEU VALLEY

The long, narrow Valea Vişeu skirts the Maramureş Mountains, which separate Romania from Ukraine. To the north lie a few isolated villages of Huţuls, a people who speak a form of Slavonic and who share numerous customs, traditions, and even features of their folk costumes with Romanians from Maramureş and Bucovina. The Huţuls have also given their name to a breed of sturdy mountain ponies.

Vişeu de Sus has the only working **narrow-gauge logging railway** (*contact OK Travel, B-dul Ştirbei 38, Bucharest, tel 021 311 2390, www.oktravel.ro*) left in Maramureş. The privately run line offers an unforgettable trip into the mountains as far as the Vaser river near the Ukrainian border. If you wish, hike back from the Vaser to more fully experience the woodlands of the valley.

East of the mining town of Borşa, the ski resort of **Staţiunea Borşa** stands among the high-sided hay barns that pepper the meadows on the edge of **Parcul Naţional Rodna** (Rodna National Park). This alpine nature

reserve offers plenty of scenic hiking opportunities.

Beyond Staţiunea Borşa the road climbs over the **Prislop Pass** into neighboring Moldavia. On the way up is an unremarkable memorial to a remarkable story. In 1717, after the Crimean Tatars had wreaked havoc on the people of Maramureş yet again, a group of Moroşeni led by a priest from Borşa ambushed the marauders in the valley with such ferocity that they never returned. Appropriately enough, the priest's name was Popa Lupu, Reverend Wolf. ∎

Valea Vişeu
 177 C1–D1

With a spire of 180 ft (56 m), the church at Bârsana's monastery complex is said to be the tallest wooden structure in Europe.

Many Maramureş women still weave their own textiles at home from hand-spun wool.

A drive through Historic Maramureş

This excursion ventures into a breathtaking area of Maramureş. It winds through a part of Ţara Chioarului over the Neteda Pass to Budeati.

Start from the center of **Baia Sprie** and take the road that branches to the right up a hill to **Şişeşti**. In Şişeşti, stop at the Orthodox church and visit the **Muzeul Memorial Vasile Lucaciu ❶** *(No. 250, tel 0262 298 070, closed Mon., $)*, the Vasile Lucaciu Memorial Museum. Known as the Lion of Şişeşti, Lucaciu (1852–1922) was a Greco-Catholic priest who fought for the rights of ethnic Romanians in Transylvania. The museum complex comprises the parish house, school, library, and 1890 church. Beyond the church, look carefully and you will find the tiny, sun-bleached body of an earlier wooden church that is covered with beautiful patterns.

Continue southeast to **Şurdeşti**, where you turn right onto the road that heads to Copâlnic Mănăstur; follow the signs for the *Biserica*. At the end of a drive lined with walnut trees stands **Sf. Arhangheli ❷** *(ask for key at parish house beside gates)*, a Greco-Catholic church. An inscription tells us it was built in 1766. Its steeple alone measures over 162 feet (52 m) high and until recently it was the tallest wooden church in Europe (it has been superceded by Peri Monastery in Săpânţa). The interior is decorated with late 18th- or early 19th-century murals by an unknown hand. In Şurdeşti, the peal of the church's bells signal the start and finish of each haymaking day—another astonishing sign of just how much has survived of Maramureş's ancient rural heritage. In addition, craftspeople in the village make wooden hay rakes and forks, beaded necklaces, and hairy woolen jackets called *gube*, the ancestry of which can be traced back to the skin cloaks worn by the nomadic shepherds of Central Asia.

Retrace your route to the main road, and turn right, heading toward Cavnic. As you leave Şurdeşti, keep an eye out for a cliff on the left-hand side of the road with the Romanian flag painted on it. Underneath the cliff, hidden from the road, is group of boulders, resembling haystacks, called **Clăile de Piatră** ❸. Legend has it that one Sunday St. Peter was walking through Şurdeşti and saw a man making haystacks. Peter was so angry that he cursed the farmer and transformed the haystacks into rocks. Local folklore still decrees that hay cannot be made on certain saints' days.

Cavnic is a workaday mining town, but once you have driven up beyond it, the world opens out. The road starts winding between fir forests and up and over the **Neteda Pass** ❹. Just beyond the pass, find a place to stop to take in the view. You can see across

the open velvet meadows dotted with haystacks down along the poplar-lined road toward Budeşti and way beyond to where the Carpathian peaks enter Ukraine. As far as the eye can see was once part of Maramureş, too, but the land north of the Tisa River (today's border with Ukraine) was partitioned at the end of World War I. The Soviet Union laid claim to this corner of the Carpathians at the end of World War II because it provided direct access to the union's satellites in Eastern Europe.

Drive down the winding hill road past the myrtle groves and haystack-peppered pastures until you reach **Budeşti** (see pp. 181–82). ∎

✚ See area map p. 177
➤ Baia Sprie
↔ 30 miles (48 km)
🕐 I hour (plus stops)
➤ Budeşti

NOT TO BE MISSED
- Şurdeşti
- Neteda Pass

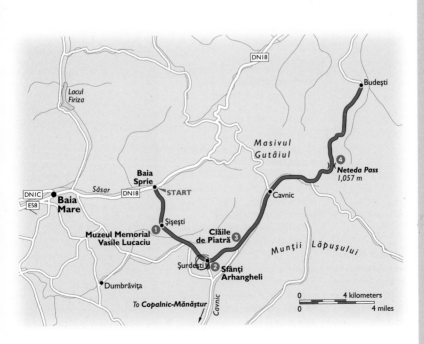

Sighetu Marmaţiei

Sighetu Marmaţiei
177 B2
Visitor information
✉ Centrul de Informare Turistică, Str. Piaţa Libertăţii 21
☎ 0262 312 5528

A FAST-GROWING TOWN, SIGHETU MARMAŢIEI (OR SIGHET, as it is known) is Maramureş's historic capital. Increasingly popular with tourists, this industrial and university center lies close to the Tisa River, Romania's border with Ukraine. The old center revolves around Piaţa Libertăţii and Strada Mihaly de Apşa, parallel one-way streets, in an area lined with handsome Austro-Hungarian buildings.

Datini

Each December, the two-day Festivalul Datinilor de Iarnă (Festival of Winter Customs), or Datini for short, gives everyone the chance to don their best (or most outrageous) traditional clothes: Boys wear scary wolf's head masks or garish military uniforms and girls wear thick white jackets or embroidered sheepskin waistcoats, striped double aprons, and high black boots. The 2006 festival coincided with the reopening of a bridge over the Tisa that had been closed more than 60 years earlier. It joins Sighet to the Ukrainian town of Solotvino. ∎

early 1950s, scores of intellectuals, journalists, government ministers, priests, and others were sent here without trial. Most of them died by torture and starvation, including Iuliu Maniu (1873–1953), the leader of the Romanian Peasants' Party, one of Romania's greatest democrats. Today, it is now an extensive museum and study center devoted to

On Piaţa Libertăţii you will find the **Muzeul Maramureşului** (Maramureş Museum; *Piaţa Libertăţii 15, tel 0262 311 521, closed Mon., $*). This charming ethnography museum is housed in a baroque-style building from 1730. It is packed with gorgeous handmade textiles, woodwork, and other items connected with the region's rich rural heritage, including some fearsome New Year's masks.

The **Memorialul Victimelor Comunismului şi al Rezistenţei** (*Str. Corneliu Coposu 4, tel 0262 319 424, closed Mon. in winter*) stands at the other end of nearby Strada Coposu. The building housed one of the most oppressive prisons in communist Romania—during the

Săpânţa village: The crosses in the Happy Cemetery carry witty verses that make light of death.

the memory of the prisoners and to the history of the resistance movement in communist Romania.

The childhood home of author and Holocaust survivor Elie Wiesel stands at the corner of Dragoș Voda and Tudor Vladmirescu streets. Furnished as a typical pre–World War II Jewish home, it is now a **museum** *(Str. T. Vladimirescu 1, closed Mon.)* that celebrates the Jewish way of life in Maramureș.

Do not miss the **Muzeul Maramureșului, Secția în Aer Liber** *(access via DN18, closed Mon., $)*, Sighet's open-air village museum. Located in the town's outskirts, the museum is laid out as if it were a traditional Maramureș village. Each house transplanted here shows a particular style or period; the oldest buildings date back to the 16th century. Some are equipped with intriguing tools. ∎

Above: The scenic valley just south of Sighetu Marmației

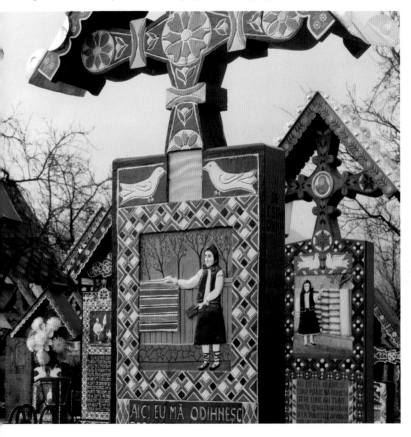

Valea Lăpuşului

Valea Lăpuşului
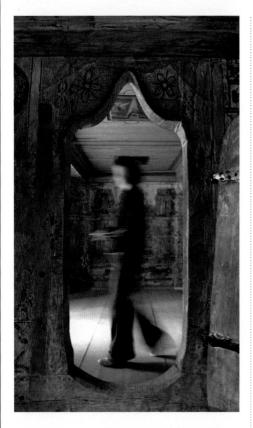
177 B1

SEPARATED FROM HISTORIC MARAMUREŞ BY HIGH mountains, the Lapus Valley has an attraction and identity all of its own. It is similarly cloaked in an all-pervasive greenness from rolling meadowlands, but the pastures are wider and the slopes gentler than in Historic Maramureş, a result of its closeness to the Transylvanian Plateau that lies to the south. This area is also known as Ţara Lăpuşului, denoting a medieval landholding that was inhabited and organized by ethnic Romanians before the Hungarians arrived. An easy road from Baia Mare reaches into the valley.

Drive northeast to **Rogoz,** where an 18th-century wooden church hugs the ground. The overhanging roof protects some stylized horse-head carvings placed at the ends of extended wall joints. Their presence is a mysterious carryover from the widespread pagan belief that horses keep evil spirits away. Inside, the church is gnarled and sturdy like the oak it was made from. The entrance into the main body of the building is extremely low and shaped like an open mouth; only very short people can pass through without stooping. The priests of these little parish churches demanded that worshipers bow their heads when they came in, willingly or not.

This valley is superlative walking and climbing country: Abandon your car and follow any of the mountain trails to fully enjoy the land *(trail maps available from travel agents in Baia Mare).* Some paths reach deep into the forests beside the Lăpuş River, giving access to rock caves, slender cascades that tumble hundreds of feet down vertical cliff faces, and wild plants such as fritillary and juniper, which grow in great profusion in the river meadows together with a mass of other beautiful flowering plants, herbs, and grasses. ■

A tourist walks by a doorway in Rogoz's 18th-century wooden church in Valea Lăpuşului.

The main town of this area, **Târgu Lăpuş,** has about 13,000 people. As its name suggests, the town has a market *(târg),* where in season you may buy all kinds of fresh, locally produced fruit, vegetables, meats, and cheeses.

Ţara Chioarului

Dirt road
to Paradise?
Romania's unique
blend of richness
and poverty in
a rural setting

WESTERN NEIGHBOR TO THE LAPUS VALLEY, LOVELY ŢARA Chioarului offers plenty of walking opportunities. Its picturesque countryside is a wonder of verdant pastures, isolated plowed fields, and congregations of farmhouses painted a deep blue with their high-ridged, thatched roofs and collapsed wooden fences. The people plowing their fields with oxen or raking the soil with wooden harrows recall medieval images showing Adam tilling the earth. Comparisons between biblical scenery and this historic land of "free Romanians" present themselves almost unbidden.

Although the main road from Baia Mare to Cluj cuts through Ţara Chioarului, this area is less well-developed for tourism than even Historic Maramureş, but plans are afoot to publish books about its ethnography, folklore, and crafts and to help visitors find its many craftspeople.

Şomcuta Mare is the largest town in the area and a good focal point. To the north of the town lie more hidden architectural treasures in the form of old wooden churches that look as though they have been built of massive oak logs; their individual, asymmetrical shapes and built-to-last solidity will catch your eye. The villages of **Coaş, Coruia, Remetea Chioarului,** and **Vălenii Şomcutei** all have some exquisite examples.

The village of **Mesteacăn—** its name means "birch tree" but the birch forests have been replaced by orchards—has a novel way of keeping its rural customs alive: an annual competition to find the best female scyther, *plăcinta* (pancake) maker, and poet. The competition, the brainchild of a retired army colonel, was first held in 1997 on Sânzienele (Fairies' or Midsummer's Day). The festival is an attempt to rekindle pride in local skills and self-respect as well as a draw for tourists. Everybody wears their traditional clothes of embroidered white cotton and colorful aprons and waistcoats. The day is fleshed out with performances of *învârtite,* fast round dances; the ones danced here are called Şapte Paşi and Patru Paşi. ■

Ţara Chioarului
🛆 177 A1-B1

Glass icons

One of the most fetching aspects of Romanian folk art is the practice of painting religious icons on glass. Painted in an immediate, colorful style that grabs your attention, they have become recognized as a quintessentially Romanian phenomenon. But where did these icons come from, and why paint on glass in a country where there is no shortage of wood?

The story begins in antiquity when the Byzantines used to paint images on glass. So did the Bohemians and Moravians. No one knows exactly when or how the Romanians learned this skill. It is always said to have started in Nicula, a small village in the mountains to the northeast of Cluj.

For several centuries, Nicula had remained a staunchly Orthodox community in the midst of Hungarian Catholics. Parishioners were proud of their little church, which dated back to 1552, and of the Virgin Mary icon that hung on its walls. The icon was painted by a local man called Luca of Iclod. When the Habsburgs defeated the Turks and conquered Transylvania, they also tried to stamp out the Christian Orthodox faith. But some of the Austrians were curious to see for themselves how the "schismatics" conducted their religion. In 1694, a group of officers from the Imperial Army came to Nicula and visited the church. Luca's icon particularly drew their attention, and when they came closer they saw what looked like real tears falling from the Virgin's eyes. They were not the only witnesses; the phenomenon was recorded as fact when the soldiers and others swore in court that the icon had wept continuously for 26 days.

People started to come from far and wide, convinced that the miracle was a sign that the image had healing powers. Soon there was a demand for copies. Preparing wood to be the canvas of an icon takes time, and when demand exceeded supply, the Niculeni began painting the Virgin's likeness on glass made by the Armenians of nearby Gherla. The glass was not only easier and quicker to handle, but cheaper as well.

Romanian glass icons became very popular in the 18th and 19th centuries, in part because they were less expensive than the wooden ones. Painting an icon on wood took a great deal of skill, caused a considerable waste of material, and involved the use of expensive materials such as gold leaf; all of these things contributed to the high cost of wooden icons. Painting glass icons required skills as well—the image needs to be reversed and the paint applied in the correct sequence of layers—but the cost was minimal.

The bright, cheerful images on glass rapidly gained adherents among artists, spawning many different schools, which have been recognized, cataloged, and displayed in important museum collections such as the Muzeul Ţăranului Român in Bucharest (see pp. 62–63) and the glass-icon museum in Sibiel, Transylvania (see pp. 132–33). You can still see glass icons in country churches and in rural homes, where they often hang in special corners that have been set aside as domestic shrines. The icons are sometimes draped with embroidered ştergare (towels).

In Maramureş, many traditional churches are decorated with glass icons; they include those at Budeşti's Biserica Josani (see p. 182), Ieud din Şes (in Ieud), and Nicula's own wooden church. Interestingly, many of the icons on glass offer visual proof that in Romania's rural areas, Christianity and pagan beliefs are inextricably linked. Many of the popular images show saints such as Elijah, George, Haralambie, and Nicholas, who are believed to control fertility and weather conditions, as though they were pagan gods.

Today the market for glass icons is as healthy as ever. Several artists specialize in creating them for sale, and not all the images are religious: Some contemporary painters interpret famous events in Romanian history. ■

Right: A late 19th-century Transylvanian glass icon of St. George killing the dragon (from the Museum of the Romanian Peasant in Bucharest)

218 324, $). Prince Vasile Lupu paid Italian masons to extend and embellish the existing 1546 church, hence its interesting facade, which is a hybrid of baroque and Byzantine styles. Although he was a Turkish vassal, Lupu regarded himself as an heir to the Byzantine throne. He forged strong links with Orthodox monasteries outside Moldavia, encouraged the printing of Christian texts, and founded an academy. At Golia, his Cyrillic initials (BB for Vasile Voivode or the Basil the Prince) and the Moldavian aurochs-head symbol can be seen in discreet locations around the interior.

From Golia Monastery, a five-minute walk further east along Cuza Vodă and across Strada Sărariei brings you to Strada Sinagogelor

The beautifully decorated 19th-century Barboi Monastery church is located on Str. Costache Negri, on the east side of Iasi.

and **Sinagoga Mare,** one of the oldest Jewish synagogues in Romania. It was founded in 1671, rebuilt in the 18th century, and restored in the 1970s.

Walk south from Strada Cuza Vodă to the neoclassic extravaganza of the **Teatrul Naţional Vasile Alecsandri** (*Str. V. Alecsandri 5, tel 0232 255 999*), which is also home to the national opera company. It was built in the 1890s by the Austrian team of Fellner and Helmer. The opulence continues inside. Opposite the theater at Cuza Vodă 29 is the home of the Iaşi Filharmonia, dating from 1815.

OTHER SIGHTS IN IAŞI

Walk north along Strada Brătianu and turn left into Bulevardul Independenţei to reach the lovely

mid-18th-century building that was the first home of the university (founded 1860). It now houses the **Muzeul de Istorie Naturală,** one of Romania's finest natural history collections. Walk to the end of the street, turn left and first right, and head up the hill into Bulevardul Copou. Keep going north until you reach Grădina Copou. The nearby **Muzeul Mihai Eminescu** is dedicated to the life and work of Romania's national poet, a radical thinker who studied in Iaşi.

In the hilly Ţicău district of Iaşi you will find **Bojdeuca Ion Creangă,** a tiny wooden cottage that one of Romania's best-known and most radical 19th-century writers, Ion Creangă, used between 1872 and 1889. Delightfully informal, the museum contains

memorabilia and photographs relating to his life.

AROUND IAŞI
Mănăstirea Cetăţuia
Overlooking the city from a hill near the vineyards, the Cetăţuia Monastery gives yet more insight into Iaşi's complex history. Founded by Prince Gheorghe Duca, this handsome (and still functioning) Orthodox monastery was completed in 1672. Duca was envious of Trei Ierarhi (see p. 197) and commissioned superb stone carvings both inside and outside the church—notice the *brâu* (cord) motif that runs around the church exterior, imitating the wooden ropework in some of Romania's older wooden churches. The frescoes were painted by two Aromanian artists, Gheorghe and Mihai Dima. ("Aromanian" is the generic word for several different ent groups of ethnic Romanians who formed enclaves in various southeastern European countries.)

Bârnova
One of the most attractive roads out of Iaşi leads to Bârnova through woods of laurels and rhododendrons. This rural village has a beautiful early 17th-century fortified monastery. The Greek-plan church with its massive walls was built for Prince Miron Barnovschi in the 1620s, when the Moldavians were still struggling against the Turks. The monastery is run by ascetic-looking Orthodox monks with long beards. The brothers play an important role in village life, such as running a primary school. In many rural communities in eastern Moldavia, the outlying monasteries are often the primary providers of assistance.

Mănăstirea Dobrovăţ
The Dobrovăţ Monastery near Bârnova stands in an even more

Muzeul de Istorie Naturală
- ✉ B-dul Independenţei
- ☎ 0232 201 339
- 🕐 Closed Mon.
- 💲 $

Muzeul Mihai Eminescu
- ✉ Universitatea Veche 16
- ☎ 0747 499 405
- 🕐 Closed Mon.
- 💲 $

Bojdeuca Ion Creangă
- ✉ Str. Simion Bărnuţiu 4
- ☎ 0747 499 488
- 🕐 Closed Mon.
- 💲 $

Mănăstirea Dobrovăţ
- 🅰 195 D3
- ✉ Dobrovăţ-Ruşi
- ☎ 0232 321 321

Mănăstirea Catăţuia
- 🅰 195 D3

Bârnova
- 🅰 195 D3

Cotnari

195 C4

romantic spot on the edge of an extensive woodland. The six monks that live here look after one of the region's finest churches, built for Ştefan cel Mare in 1503 on the site of a much older monastery. This church was the last of about 40 shrines that Ştefan erected in Moldavia, Transylvania,

Outside one of Moldavia's many painted monasteries

and what is now Ukraine, as he fought for the independence of his realm. Ştefan's greatest enemies were the Ottoman Turks, and his successful campaigns, which often involved guerrilla warfare, are enshrined in Romanian history. The larger of the church's two chambers are covered in fading frescoes. They were the inspiration of Ştefan's illegitimate son, Petru Rareş, who took the Moldavian throne twice in the mid-16th century and wanted to strengthen his popularity and claim to the throne. The paintings date from 1529. As well as the more general Christian stories, which include a rare appearance of "Scara

Virtuţilor" ("Ladder of Virtue," see also Suceviţa, pp. 206–207), there is a votive painting showing a model of how the church looked when it was first built. It emphasizes the roof's graceful sweep, which is a distinctive Moldavian feature. The smaller chamber is a *paraclis* or winter chapel, contemporary with the main one. The gate tower at Dobrovăţ dates from 1743.

Cucuteni archaeological site
To the northwest of Iaşi on the road between Târgu Frumos and Hârlău, lies the archaeological site of Cucuteni. Located on Dealul Gosan at the northern end of Cucuteni village, it contains some tumuli and vestiges of an Iron Age Dacian citadel and tools. It was here that archaeologists realized that a highly sophisticated culture, now known as the Cucuteni or Tripolie, had flourished in what are now Moldavia, Moldova, and Ukraine between 4200 and 3200 B.C. Great builders and craftsmen, the Cucuteni were destroyed by nomadic Indo-Europeans before the great Egyptian and Sumerian cultures had even begun. You can see some breathtaking examples of their pottery in Piatra Neamţ.

Cotnari
The vineyards of Cotnari northwest of Iaşi produce a delicious dessert wine, Grasă de Cotnari. Prince Ştefan cel Mare himself imported the vines from the Hungarian region of Tokay in the 15th century. The famous wine has an extraordinary green color that becomes more intense with age. The 17th-century diplomat Dimitrie Cantemir (see p. 197) was delighted to find that he could drink several glasses without getting a hangover. The **company headquarters** (*S. C. Cotnari S.A., Cotnari village, No. 10, tel 0232 730 296*) contains a museum and tasting center. ■

Suceava

ONE OF THE MEDIEVAL CAPITALS OF MOLDAVIA, SUCEAVA IS the capital of southern Bucovina. Its handful of historic buildings and museums, most of them found near the town center, Piaţa 23 Decembrie, merit a couple hours of attention. People often stop in Suceava on their way to the Carpathians and the famous painted churches of Bucovina.

Suceava
🗺 195 B4
Visitor information
✉ Centrul de Informare Turistică, Str. Vasile Bumbac 14
☎ 0230 551 241

The **Mănăstirea Sf. Ioan cel Nou** (Monastery of St. John the New) in Strada Mitropoliei is dedicated to one of Moldavia's patron saints, chosen because he was martyred by Turks after refusing to convert to Islam. The monastery was founded in 1514 by Bogdan III. The exterior walls of its great church, Sf. Gheorghe, completed in 1522, are covered with faded murals that hint at the glories of the painted churches farther west.

Five minutes' walk away along Strada Ciprian Porumbescu is the charming late 16th–early 17th-century *han* (inn) that houses the rewarding **Muzeul Etnografic**. The first floor is arranged to look like the inn, and highlights include a splendid chimney piece decorated with traditional, locally made green-and-yellow Kuty tiles, which are loosely modeled on Byzantine motifs. The second floor displays domestic tools, clothes (be sure to see the *sumane*, magnificent felted and frogged cloaks), crafts, and other items from several different regions of Bucovina.

The ethnographic museum's open-air sister stands in a forest clearing on the eastern edge of town. **Muzeul Satului Bucovinean** contains 80 vernacular buildings from around the Ţara de Sus (Highland Bucovina region), including the late 19th-century Casa Roşu, a stunning little 18th-century church from Vama decorated with horse-head motifs, and a water mill from Humor.

The **Cetatea de Scaun** (Crown Citadel; $), the impressive ruins of Suceava's medieval fortress, looms above town. Drive 2 miles (3 km) to the citadel via a winding road or take the shorter footpath from the town center. Founded circa 1388 by Prince Petru I Muşat (R. 1375–1391), the castle was virtually rebuilt by Ştefan cel Mare, who added a moat and the 6-foot-thick (2 m) perimeter walls and circular bastions. The citadel resisted repeated attacks by the Turks until 1673, when janissaries succeeded in blowing it up.

Head west from the citadel to visit the oldest church in Suceava, **Biserica Mirăuţi** (*Str. Mirăuţilor 17*). Founded by Petru I Muşat, it was the first Orthodox cathedral in Moldavia; all Moldavia's princes were crowned here until 1522. The church was completely rebuilt in the 17th century. ∎

Kuty pottery tiles decorate a fireplace inside Suceava's handsome ethnographic museum.

Muzeul Etnografic
✉ Str. Ciprian Porumbescu 5
☎ 0230 216 439 ext. 115
🕐 Closed Mon.
💲 $

Muzeul Satului Bucovinean
✉ Platoul Cetăţii
🕐 Closed Mon.
💲 $

Bucovina's medieval churches

Mănăstirea Dragomirna
🅰 195 B2
✉ Comuna Mitocul Dragomirnei
☎ 0230 533 839
💲 $

Mănăstirea Humor
🅰 195 B4
✉ Str. Mănăstirea, Humor
💲 $

Mănăstirea Voroneț
🅰 195 B4
✉ Voroneț
☎ 0230 235 323
💲 $

IMMORTALIZED AS *DULCE BUCOVINA* (MEANING "SWEET land of beech woods") by Romania's national poet, Mihai Eminescu, Bucovina is renowned for its physical beauty and for its medieval churches that are enveloped in gorgeous frescoes.

During the Turkish invasions of Bulgaria and Serbia, thousands of Orthodox clerics sought refuge in the Carpathian Mountains, where they were welcomed by Moldavia's princes. Between the 15th and 17th centuries, the number of religious institutions rose so fast that Moldavia—and Bucovina in particular—became known as a second Mount Athos. The fortified monasteries sheltered villagers and soldiers during attacks. The exterior scenes of biblical stories both entertained and educated the masses who would not enter the church or who could not understand the liturgy. If you don't have time to visit Voroneț, take half an hour to see Dragomirna Monastery, another fine building (although not painted externally) very close to Suceava.

MĂNĂSTIREA DRAGOMIRNA

The Dragomirna Monastery lies only 6 miles (10 km) north of Suceava (see p. 201). Metropolitan Archbishop Crimca built it between 1602 and 1609. Its style marked the start of a new phase of religious building in Moldavia in which stone facades replaced exterior frescoes. The Ottoman Turks were gradually taking control of the region, so the monasteries were putting more resources into protection rather than decoration. Protected behind immensely tall, fortified walls, the church's stone facade contains all the elements of the distinctive "Moldavian style": a magnificently sweeping roof, a Byzantine ground plan, Gothic detailing around doors and windows, relief work fronds and flowers, and a brâu or twisted belt motif. The church's most remarkable feature is its proportions: Dragomirna is incredibly tall for its width, 138 by 31 feet (42 m by 9.5 m). Look at the building from the eastern end to get the effect.

Dragomirna is one of a handful of monasteries in this area that remained open during the communist period. Today the nuns run a hostel that accommodates pilgrims, as well as visitors who are seeking a retreat or a cure.

MĂNĂSTIREA HUMOR

Mănăstirea Humor lies 3 miles (5 km) to the west of Câmpulung Moldovenesc. Built in 1530 for Prince Petru Rareş and his chancellor, Teodor Bubuiog, the precinct resembles a mini-citadel; it even has

On the trefoil-shaped east side of the church, row upon row of holy figures dance attendance on the personages of God the Father and Christ, who occupy the easternmost panels. Various incidental panels on the church contain images of

The early 17th-century Dragomirna Monastery lies north of Suceava.

a freestanding watchtower (1641).

The monastery's church was painted in 1535. An artist called Toma created the exterior paintings; the chief color here is red. One of the highlights is the lush "Arborele lui Jesse" ("Tree of Jesse") in the center of the south wall. Individual scenes are shown like vignettes within a stylized acanthus plant. The painting literally traces Jesus's family tree to its roots. As described in Isaiah, Jesse lies at the bottom with a branch protruding from his stomach.

seraphim as well as floral decoration.

The church's interior paintings are also superb; look for the flights into and out of Egypt in the middle tomb chamber, where Teodor Bubuiog and his wife lie at rest.

Humor survived the communist period as a parish church; it regained its monastic status in 1991. If you're staying over, the village of Humor has plenty of guesthouses.

MĂNĂSTIREA VORONEŢ

Located at the southern end of Voroneţ village, the fortified Voroneţ

Roma

To most of us, the Roma (also called Romanies or Gypsies, or *Ţigani* or *Rroma* in Romanian) are an enigma. Feared but also secretly admired, and even envied, unofficially they constitute about 10 percent of Romania's population and are among the country's most disadvantaged people.

They live in towns and cities, but also in rural villages, where they often live in houses set apart from the rest. The most recognizable Roma are those who still wear their traditional clothes, which vary from group to group. Among the most distinctive items are the broad-rimmed, black felt hats worn by men in some parts of Transylvania and the long,

floating, brightly colored skirts of the women.

Sadly, the Roma were often much better off before 1989 than they are now, even though the communists did not recognize their minority status. Today, many Romanians see the freewheeling Ţigani, as they are more often known, as a threat to their property and livelihoods. A few Ţigani have amassed huge fortunes on the black market, and resentment against them has been compounded by the vast pagoda-style houses they have built to show off their wealth (you can see some of them in Ciurea, near Iaşi, in Paşcani, between Suceava and Iaşi, and in Buzescu, near Alexandria). In addition, years after the fact, non-Roma still use the case of the Gypsies

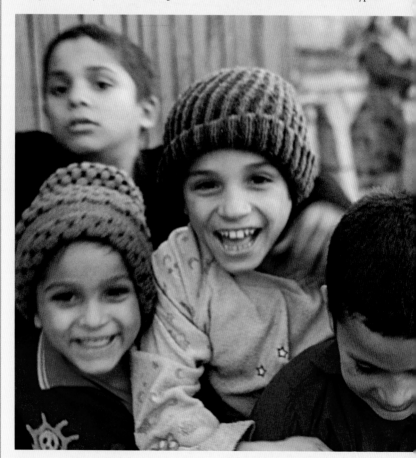

who supposedly ate the swans in Vienna's
Schönbrunn Park as a reason to hate the
Ţigani; they believe that the rest of the world
deplores Romanians as a whole because of the
event. As a result, the relationship between
Gypsies and the non-Roma has since become
troubled, and occasionally violent.

The Roma's negative reputation in
Romania developed over hundreds of years.
During most of that period, they were born
into slavery. In the 14th and 15th centuries,
highly respected princes such as Mircea cel
Bătrân and Ştefan cel Mare purchased whole
families of Gypsies from the slave markets of
Crimea. They were often sent as "gifts" to
monasteries, where they were expected to do
the most menial, backbreaking jobs and had
no rights of any kind. But not all Roma shared

the same fate: Groups emerged who were able
to move around, earning a living from a
variety of marketable skills.

Romania's Gypsies were released from
slavery in 1862 by Mihail Kogălniceanu, one of
Romania's great liberal statesmen. During
World War II, hundreds of thousands of Roma
were deported to death camps. The Romanian
communists treated them better, and until the
1970s, some Roma continued to survive on the
road, obeying their *bulibasha* (king) rather than
the state authorities. Even today, some remain
seminomadic, traveling by horse and cart.

Many well-educated Roma have begun to
make their voices heard, and attempts are
being made to help the less fortunate integrate
more fully into mainstream society. But non-
Gypsies find it hard to understand the
richness and complexity of the Roma culture;
many are not even aware that there is one. The
Roma originated on the Indian subcontinent;
their language is close to Sanskrit and modern
Punjabi and should not be confused with
Romanian (or Romansch, spoken in parts of
Switzerland). In Romania, they are usually
bilingual and often mix their own language
with Romanian.

The Gypsies traditionally belonged to a
range of professional groups that each had
strict codes of conduct. The most famous
are the *lăutari* (musicians) and *căldărari*
(tinkers and coppersmiths), but there are also
cărămidari (brickmakers), *ursari* (bear tamers),
and others. Some Roma continue to follow
their traditional occupations, and music is still
a vital part of their lives. One of the most
influential communities of lăutari is in Clejani,
a village to the south of Bucharest, where an
informal academy has operated for several
hundred years. One of its most famous singers
is Dimitru Baicu, better known as Cacurică,
who is a member of the internationally known
band Taraf de Haïdouks.

Literature abounds with romantic tales
about Gypsies, but Walter Starkie's delightful
*Raggle Taggle: Adventures with a Fiddle in
Hungary and Roumania* (1933) has become a
classic. For documentary films on the Roma,
search out Dumitru Budrala's *The Curse of the
Hedgehog* (2004), *The Land Is Waiting* by
Laurenţiu Calciu (2004), and Tony Gatlif's
Latcho Drom (Safe Journey, 1993). ■

**Mănăstirea
Moldoviţa**

⚑ 195 A4

✉ Vatra Moldoviţei

☎ 0230 336 348

💲 $

**Mănăstirea
Suceviţa**

⚑ 195 A4

✉ Suceviţa (25
miles/40 km NW of
Gura Humorului)

☎ 0230 417 110

💲 $

**The church at
Suceviţa was the
last of the painted
churches built in
the region.**

Monastery was founded by Ştefan
cel Mare. This working monastery
stands as one of the most striking
examples of the Moldavian style.
Built by military masons during the
summer of 1488, its shingled roofs
are shaped like a tent to help shoot
snow and water well away from the
exterior walls, which bear stunning
frescoes. The paintings—the domi-
nant color used here is a vibrant
azure called Voroneţ blue—date
from the 1540s, and the man
behind them, Metropolitan
Archbishop Grigore Roşca, faces
you in an arresting full-length portrait to the left of the main
entrance. All around him, row upon
row of feisty narratives illustrate the
lives and trials of Sf. Gheorghe, Sf.
Nicolae, and Sf. Ioan cel Nou.

Two exquisite exterior frescoes
stand out: the superb "Judecata de
Apoi" ("The Last Judgment"), which
fills the entire west end, and the
"Arborele lui Ieseu" ("Tree of Jesse"),
which occupies the middle of the
south wall. Interestingly, portraits of
ancient Greek philosophers, including
Plato and Aristotle, are included on
the extreme right-hand side of the
tree on the grounds of their moral
authority. If you have binoculars, you
will be able to make out the unusual
picture of Satan tempting Adam to
sell his soul in a sequence of frescoes
called "Păcatul lui Adam" ("Adam's
Contract") at the top of the east end
of the north wall.

MĂNĂSTIREA MOLDOVIŢA

The Moldoviţa Monastery, which
stands in the village of Vatra
Moldoviţei, was built for Prince
Petru Rareş in 1532. The materials
used here were less costly than at
Voroneţ; however, the effect is still
wonderful, and Moldoviţa has some
lovely, special features.

Perhaps the most intriguing fresco
is the "Asediul Constantinopolului"
("Siege of Constantinople"), on the
lowest register of the south wall, next
to the porch. This painting ostensibly
tells the story of the Virgin Mary
saving the Byzantine city by beating
off its Persian and Avar enemies in
626; the Orthodox patriarch is shown
invoking the Virgin's help as he
parades a famous icon along the
city's ramparts. However, the entire
episode (taken from the Akathist
sequence, or Marian Hymn) is
portrayed in a contemporary 16th-
century environment: The clothes,
the Turkish turbans worn by the
advancing cavalry, cannon, and ships
would compel a viewer of that period
to read the scene as an injunction to
heaven to save Moldavia from their
invaders, the Turks. As a sign of the
crisis facing Rareş (whose portrait
graces the city walls; his wife, Elena,

is there, too), this commissioned mural is one of the most important in all of the painted churches. The military saints who occupy the pillar to the left were another thinly veiled call to arms. (The representation of the Virgin here may come as a surprise: She is shown symbolically as bands of semicircular white paint and the fiery storm, which rains on the attackers in red and white speckles.)

MĂNĂSTIREA SUCEVIŢA

The rectangular fortifications of this late 16th-century monastery are extremely impressive, but when you walk through the archway, the first thing you will notice is a wall painting. This is the famous "Scara Virtuţilor" ("Ladder of Virtue"). Rare both for its size and its location (most of the other versions of this scene occur either as illuminations in gospels, as small icons, or on interior walls), it is a wonderfully engaging piece of work. A ladder with 32 rungs stretches from the Earth to heaven. Monks try to scale the ladder. Christ leans far out of heaven's window, arms open as he wills the monks to succeed. A band of angels with multicolored wings supports his efforts. Below, the weaker monks writhe in agony as they, having succumbed to devilish temptation, are pulled and prodded as they fall into the jaws of Cerberus.

Suceviţa was the last built of the 22 painted churches in Moldavia; they stopped being painted almost as quickly as the phenomenon had started. The reason is easy to discern: Politically, Moldavia was on the brink of a period of Turkish rule; its leaders needed to curtail their actions. At Suceviţa you will find none of the overt political propaganda of the kind seen at Voroneţ and Moldoviţa. Instead the paintings are more ascetic, inward looking, and ethereal.

Suceviţa's main color is a deep sea green, from the malachite used in the paint, but its walls glow with many colors, including gold. It was founded by a powerful family of bishops and princes who had close ties with Poland. A sign of that influence can be seen on the south wall, to the left of the wonderful "Tree of Jesse" (do not miss the philosopher kings here), in a scene showing the Virgin holding a veil over the heads of bowing priests. The narrative is called "Pocrov" (from a Slavonic word for "veil") and is framed by an open-fronted onion-domed church of a type that was far more Polish than Romanian. The village of Suceviţa is full of friendly guesthouses for weary travelers.

ARBORE

The church at Arbore does not belong to a monastery. It was built by the *hatman* (general) Luca Arbore in 1503. The frescoes date from 1541. Only the exterior's west-end murals have survived the passage of time, but the interior frescoes have been beautifully restored and are lovely. The church stands in an attractive village setting, facing a wide valley, where people still work in the fields. Stop and say "*Buna ziua*—Hello"—you never know where it might take you. ■

Detail of the Paradise Garden, a fresco on the west wall at Voroneţ Monastery

Suceviţa
✉ Centrul de Informare Turistică, Str. Principală (next to the Han Suceviţa)
☎ 0230 417 083

Arbore church
🄰 195 B4
✉ Arbore
☎ 0744 892 538
💲 $

Stephen the Great's tower and the fine art and ethnography museums (left) in Piatra Neamţ

A drive around Neamţ

The spectacular Carpathian foothills in the *judeţ* (county) of Neamţ form the backdrop of a wonderfully rural part of northern Moldavia. This route meanders through pastoral landscapes and past some interesting monasteries.

Take the DN15 north from Bicaz past the dam at the southern end of **Lacul Izvorul Muntelui ❶,** a reservoir with wooded banks that will be on your left for about 25 miles (40 km). Turn right onto the DN15B in Poiana Largului and head north over **Pasul Petru Vodă,** a 2,700-foot (820 m) pass that brings you through the villages of **Pluton, Dolheşti, Pipirig, Pâţăligeni,** and **Stânca** to **Leghin.** Most of the settlements have stunning single-story clapboard houses with long, wooden verandas. The finest are decorated with beautiful woodwork that looks like lace, revealing how close this region is to Ukraine.

In Leghin, turn right down a mountain road to see three picturesque monasteries. **Secu ❷** *(tel 0233 251 862, $),* 3 miles (5 km) south, was completed in 1605 on behalf of Nestor Ureche (father of Grigore Ureche, a famous Romanian chronicler). It has been extensively altered but is a very pretty ensemble. In another 3 miles (5 km), you'll reach **Sihăstria ❸** *(tel 0233 251 896).* Walk up the hill to where an early 19th-century church and a much larger modern one stand in prime positions overlooking the peaceful, forested valley. The monastery's name

means "refuge," an appropriate name for such a secluded place. The last 2 miles (3 km) of this detour follows a rough forest road into the clearing of **Sihla ❹.** This charming 16th-century *skete* (small monastery) comprises a wooden hermitage from 1763 and, a 10-minute walk away, **Peştera Sfintei Teodora de la Sihla,** the cave in which a local 17th-century holy woman called Teodora made her home for 20 years. She was canonized in 1992. Signs mark the way to the hermitage from Sihăstria.

Return to Leghin and continue east along the DN15B, then turn left for **Mănăstirea Neamţ ❺** *(tel 0233 251 851).* Prince Alexandru cel Bun built the monastery on the site of a preexisting church in the early 1500s; Ştefan cel Mare's masons further elongated the traditional plan. Tall cupolas shed pinpoints of light on the frescoes, which cover practically every wall. If you visit during a service, you may hear the monks intoning a liturgy that dates back to the earliest years of the Byzantine Empire. Neamţ is the largest Orthodox teaching monastery in Romania.

On your way back to the main road, you will pass the signposted entrance to the 468-

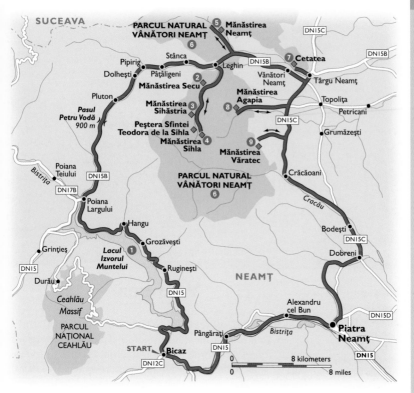

acre (180 ha) **Parcul Natural Vânători Neamț** ⑥, one of three reservations for the *zimbru* (European bison) in Romania. The park hopes to release its 16 animals to the wild. The park's visitor center *(Str. Zimbrilor 2, tel 0233 251 060, $)* is in Vânători Neamț.

Continue east along the DN15B and turn left into the town of **Târgu Neamț.** Take a side road to the left signposted for **Cetatea** ⑦. This castle was built for Prince Petru I Mușat in the late 14th century. Its nearly sheer walls are a remarkable engineering feat. The castle proved to be impregnable; in 1476, even Mehmet II, the conqueror of Constantinople, could not break into Neamț citadel.

Return to Târgu Neamț and head south 2.5 miles (4 km) along the DN15C, then turn right and drive about 5 miles (8 km) to the mid-16th-century **Mănăstirea Agapia** ⑧ *(tel 0233 244 736, $).* The church contains paintings completed in 1862 by the Romanian artist Nicolae Grigorescu. In addition to their routine domestic and agricultural work, the 500 or so nuns weave carpets and paint icons.

🚹 See area map p. 195

▶ Bicaz

⟷ 150 miles (240 km)

🕓 5 hours

▶ Bicaz

NOT TO BE MISSED

- Mănăstirea Sihla
- Parcul Natural Vânători Neamț
- Cetatea Neamț
- Mănăstirea Agapia

There is a religious museum and a gift shop.

Go back to the main road, turn right and in 2.5 miles (4 km) turn right again for **Mănăstirea Văratec** ⑨ *(tel 0233 244 741, $),* Romania's largest convent, whose main church dates from 1802. The monastery enjoys a breathtaking position in a wide and wooded landscape. Then head south to **Piatra Neamț,** an attractive town full of history (see p. 214). From there, drive west to return to Bicaz. ■

The frothy,
baroque-style
facade of the
history museum
in Focşani is
almost the only
survivor of the
town's pretty
19th-century
architecture.

Vrancea

FAMOUS FOR ITS VINEYARDS AND SPECTACULAR MOUNTAIN
scenery, Vrancea lies in the southwest corner of Moldavia. The region's
eastern fringes merge with the Bărăgan Plain, a seemingly endless
expanse, while to the west the Munţii Vrancei (Vrancea Mountains)
rise to 5,100 feet (1,600 m), their pointed peaks marking the sites of
long-dead volcanoes. Vrancea was the epicenter of Romania's massive
1977 earthquake, and you may see signs of the frequent landslides that
have earned this area a treacherous reputation.

Vrancea
🗺 195 C1-C2

Focşani
🗺 195 A4

Vrancea is rich in folklore: The ewe
in the famous legend of Miorița
(see p. 110) reputedly was born
here. Like so many areas of rural
Romania, Vrancea's pastoral culture opens a totally different window on Romania's history. Until
well within living memory, shepherds used to bring their flocks
over the mountains into Vrancea
on their long, solitary trails
between Mărginimea Sibiului in
Transylvania (see pp. 132–34) and
the Crimea.

The main town of Vrancea is
Focşani, which was harshly sys-
tematized during the 1960s. With
hardly any signposts, the town is a
nightmare for foreign drivers, but
a mile (2 km) or so northeast of

the town (across the DN2) is the
modest but delightful **Secţia de
Arthitectură şi Tehnică
Populară "Crângul Petreşti"**
*(Crângul Petreşti, com. Vânători,
tel 0237 212 130, closed Mon., $).*
This open-air village museum
gives you a lesson on the differences between peasant buildings in
the mountains and the plains. In
addition, marvel at the arcane
delights of a machine designed to
dry and smoke plums.

The *podgoriile* (vineyards)
cluster around a group of villages to
the west of Focşani. At harvesttime
you may have the chance to buy
huge bunches of fat, sweet, freshly
picked grapes by the roadside.

After Romania joined the Allies

in World War I, the Germans gradually pushed the eastern front back to the Vrancea Mountains, where, in August and September 1917, the Romanians managed to prevent the Germans from advancing any farther. Many lives were lost on both sides, but the Romanians counted it a great victory. At **Mărăşeşti,** 12 miles (19 km) north of Focşani (on the main north-south DN2), an impressive but forbidding **mausoleum** *(tel 0237 260 574, closed Mon., $)* marks the event and gives insight into Romania's beleaguered position. It contains some personal items belonging to Ecaterina Teodoroiu, who was killed after disguising herself as a man so she could join the fight.

The DN2D heads northwest out of Focşani and brings you through pretty beech woods into the Vrancea Mountains. About 30 miles (50 km) from Focşani, past Valea Sării and Bârseşti, turn right into the village of **Negrileşti.** Many of the farmhouses here are made of wood or of wattle and daub. This kind of traditional community may still retain a bakery and a smithy. Explore and see what you can find.

Another 15 miles (24 km) west along the DN2D from Negrileşti, and just before the village of Lepşa, turn south onto a country road to admire the multiple waterfalls of **Cascada Putna.** The cascades tumble dramatically down a 228-foot (69 m) chute through sculptural rock formations left by ancient lava flows in Cheile Tişiţei, the Tişiţa Gorges. The surrounding area is beloved by hikers.

The spa town of **Soveja** is famous for its sulfurous and sodium-rich waters. It also has a

Ţara Vrancei

The regional name of Vrancea is sometimes said to come from Baba Vrâncioaia, the mother of seven boys who joined Prince Ştefan cel Mare's army to fight the Turks. They were so brave that the prince gave them each a mountain in the southeast Carpathians, and told them to call their lands Ţara Vrancei (Land of Vrancea). A village called Vrâncioaia in the mountains lends credibility to the tale. ∎

somber World War I memorial and chapel. More romantically, Soveja is the place where in 1853 the writer Alecu Russo is said to have heard the archetype of the epic ballad, "Miorița" ("The Ewe Lamb"). It was published the same year by his friend, the playwright, folklorist, and politician Vasile Alecsandri, in an outburst of national consciousness, which was soon to be rewarded by the union of Moldavia with Muntenia in 1859. East of Soveja, the road gives you more glorious views of the Carpathian Mountains. ∎

Mărăşeşti
◭ 195 C2

Negrileşti
◭ 195 C2

Cascada Putna
◭ 195 B2

Soveja
◭ 195 C2

The First World War Memorial at Mărăşeşti commemorates Romania's brave stand against advancing German forces in 1917.

Southeast Moldavia

Galați
195 D1

Brăila
195 D1

EMPTY SPACE OR HIDDEN TREASURE, THE PLAINS OF southeastern Moldavia can be one or the other, depending on your viewpoint. The plains are defined by the Siret and Danube rivers. The Siret makes a dramatic entrance from the north, and the Danube plows its majestic course from the south. Before it splits into three main delta channels, the Danube passes two cities worthy of a visit.

GALAȚI

Inhabited since 500 B.C., Galați (pronounced Ga-LATZ) is Romania's largest and most dynamic river port. The city's commercial origins date back at least as far as the 16th century, when the Turks exploited its deep moorings. The city has been devastated many times, most recently in 1944, when the Germans halved its largely Jewish population. Today Galați is best known for its shipyard and for a massive iron and steel combine built during the communist period and privatized in 2001; however, the city has an attractive old center and benefits from its riverside views, fronted by miles of esplanade.

Prince Vasile Lupu commissioned the massive, fortified **church of Sf. Precista** *(Str. Traian 1)* in 1647. The church served as a place of refuge during attacks; it has a curious lookout platform on one side of the bell tower and an internal bridge over the nave and altar. Closed during the 1950s, it is now a working Orthodox church.

The handsome, two-story **Muzeul de Arta Vizuală** *(Str. Domnească 141, tel 0236 413 452, closed Mon., $)* has an impressive collection of 20th-century paintings, sculptures, and prints, including a cubist portrait of poet Ilarie Voronca by Victor Brauner (1903–1966).

Gara Fluvială *(Str. Portului 34),* which houses the Port Authority, is a fine three-story brick-and-stone building built in

the neo-Romanian style by Petre Antonescu (1915). With an imposing single watchtower at its eastern end, it dominates the riverside.

BRĂILA

The city of Brăila sits just over the border with Muntenia. Occupied many times throughout its history, it is now a bustling backwater where life rattles along at a cheerful pace. Brăila has many well-cared-for 19th-century buildings. The **Muzeul Județean Brăila** *(Piața*

Traian 3, tel 0339 401 002, closed Mon.–Tues., \$) occupies the former Hotel Francez, a graceful two-story building from 1855. The archaeology section of this county museum is particularly strong; it focuses on local neolithic and Bronze Age sites, highlighting among other things a jeweler's workshop from Grădiştea.

Secţia de Etnografie şi Artă Populară *(tel 0339 401 004, closed Mon., \$)*, the folk arts museum, is an unexpected delight. Located in a pretty, glass-fronted pavilion in Grădina Publică, the public gardens, its colorful collections are a joy to behold. *(Both museums undergoing restoration; closed through 2007.)*

For more river views, cross the river on the car ferry and drive to Tulcea (see p. 225) and the Danube Delta (see pp. 227–29) via the DN22. ∎

Maica Veronica

Vladimireşti Monastery, a convent on the DN25 between Galaţi and Tecuci, was founded in 1938 by Vasilica Barbu Gurău. Known as Maica Veronica, the abbess led an amazing life, which included helping many people flee the Stalinist purges of the 1950s— a story told in Silviu Crăciunas's *The Lost Footsteps* (1961). Arrested as an "enemy of the state" in 1955, she was condemned to 15 years in the abominable Jilava Prison near Ploieşti. The communists took the monastery in 1956 and arrested the nuns for wearing "illegal uniforms." Released in 1964, Veronica kept in secret contact with many of the sisters. She led 160 of them back to Vladimireşti in 1990. She died, much lamented, in 2005. ∎

A Moldavian woman gathers maize leaves to feed her livestock.

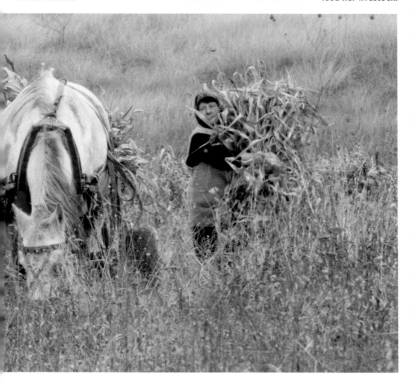

More places to visit in Moldavia

CÂMPULUNG MOLDOVENESC

Lying on the main route between Maramureş and Moldavia, Câmpulung Moldovenesc is an old market town. Its name means "Moldavian long field," which is a fairly accurate description of its elongated shape and of its surroundings, which comprise the magnificently expansive mountainsides of Obcina Feredeu to the north and Munţii Rarău-Giumalău to the south. Its alpine position invites hikers to take to the hills. North of Câmpulung you'll find scattered villages of Huţuls, a Slavic-speaking people descended probably from the Celts. Some of the Huţuls' beautiful traditional craftsmanship can be found among the collection of Câmpulung's **Muzeul Arta Lemnului** *(Calea Transilvaniei 10, tel 0230 311 378, closed Mon., $)*, the woodcraft museum, which is a wonderful place to leisurely browse.

🗺 195 A4 **Visitor information** ✉ Biroul de Promovare–Consultanţa şi Publicitate în Turism, Str. Sirenei 21 ☎ 0726 577 560

DOROHOI

This small town of 30,000 lies about 100 miles (160 km) northwest of Iaşi. The 1495 **church of Sf. Nicolae** was commissioned by Ştefan cel Mare, and the **Muzeul Ştiinţele Naturii** *(Str. Cuza 43, tel 0231 611 773, closed Mon., $)*, housed in the former 19th-century prefecture building, holds an impressive insect collection; however, the unique **Muzeul George Enescu** *(Str. Enescu 81, tel 0231 615 450, closed Mon., $)* is Dorohoi's real attraction. This museum is dedicated to the life of composer George Enescu. Enescu was born in the village of Liveni (now the village of George Enescu), 10 miles (16 km) to the east; his parents' 19th-century Moldavian house has been turned into a memorial, **Casa memorială G. Enescu** *(tel 0231 515 446, closed Mon.–Tues., $)*.

Although most of Dorohoi's population lives in modern apartments, a small, leafy district of older, single-story houses dates from before the World War II. While it looks peaceful today, it has a violent past—this is where most of the town's prewar Jewish community lived. Most were killed in a savage pogrom organized by the Romanian Army in 1940; many of the survivors and the other Jews of Dorohoi were deported to Transnistria.

🗺 195 B5

PIATRA NEAMŢ

This pleasant town of just over 100,000 people lies in the lee of a group of hills where the Dacians once had a major settlement, Petrodava. Its name means "German rock"— German settlers arrived in the Middle Ages—but many people just call it Piatra. The center is relatively small and the town is easy to negotiate. Its focal point is a municipal garden that runs alongside Strada Alexandru cel Bun; everyone seems to congregate here. Piatra Neamţ has an effervescent atmosphere, despite the broken steps and paving stones that tell their own familiar story of neglect.

Looking down on the park from Piaţa Libertăţii, the Moldavian-style **Biserica Sf. Ioan** (St. John's Church, 1491), **Turnul lui Ştefan** (Stephen's Tower), and a medieval archway that stands on its own are all that remain of Ştefan cel Mare's 15th-century court. Opposite the court, the **Muzeul de Artă** *(Piaţa Libertăţii 1, tel 0233 216 808, closed Mon., $)* stands in a handsome 1930s villa. The art museum offers a relaxing view of 19th- and 20th-century Romanian paintings. The building next door, though confusingly it shares the same address as the art museum, houses the **Muzeul de Etnografie** *(tel 0233 216 808, closed Mon., $)*. This small ethnographic museum presents a very lively picture of local traditions. Be sure not to miss the **Muzeul de Istorie şi Arheologie** *(Str. Mihai Eminescu 10, tel 0233 217 496, closed Mon., $)*. This history and archaeology museum displays some of the finest collections of prehistoric pottery in Romania outside of Bucharest: Highlights include the burial urns, miniature figures, and altars of the Cucuteni culture (see p. 200).

🗺 195 B3 **Visitor information** ✉ Centrul de Informare Turistică, B-dul Republicii 15 ☎ 0233 211 524 ∎

A place of dry steppe, forest, and marshland, Dobrogea has a Mediterranean feel. Vineyards flourish in the interior, while the coast attracts thousands of visitors, some to luxuriate in Black Sea resorts and others to the Danube Delta, one of the world's great wildernesses.

Dobrogea

Ruins of the Greek city of Histria

Dobrogea's capital, Constanţa, is a thriving port on the Black Sea.

Constanţa

THE HISTORIC SEAPORT OF CONSTANŢA, ONCE PROMOTED as a spa by King Carol I, offers a quirky mix of industry and culture. Oil terminals and shipyards dwarf the town's modest pleasure beach and promenade, but Constanţa lies in the center of Romania's seaside resorts and has become a regular port of call for cruise ships.

Constanţa
- 🅰 217 C2
- **Visitor information**
- www.infolitoral.ro
- ✉ Info Litoral
- Str. Traian 36
- ☎ 0241 555 000

Muzeul de Istorie Naţională şi Arheologie & Edificiul Roman cu Mozaic
- ✉ Piaţa Ovidiu 12
- ☎ 0241 614 562
- 🕐 Closed Mon.–Tues.
- 💲 $

Constanţa traces its history back to a sixth-century fishing village. Greeks from Miletos transformed the Black Sea settlement into a thriving port called Tomis. Later conquered by the Romans and Byzantines, it was named after the Roman emperor Constantine.

Piaţa Ovidiu is a convenient focal point. A statue of the Roman poet Ovid muses on a tall column in the middle of the traffic. Roman emperor Augustus relegated Ovid to Tomis in A.D. 8 for unknown reasons. Ovid poured out his sorrows in two volumes of poetry. *Tristia (Lamentations)* dwells at some length on the bitterness of the Black Sea winters and the vast amounts of wine that the locals swallowed "in whole buckets" at a time. Ovid was never recalled and died in Tomis.

Behind Ovid's statue is the entrance to the **Muzeul de Istorie Naţională şi Arheologie,** where you could browse for hours among the Greek and Roman statuary. Excavations began seriously in Constanţa in the 1960s. During the systematization that destroyed scores of 19th-century buildings, archaeologists discovered a very well-preserved network of streets, houses, and even early Christian churches belonging to ancient Tomis. The partially reconstructed and faded remains of a fourth-century Roman mosaic pavement can be seen behind the museum in its **Edificiul Roman cu Mozaic.** It was part of the Roman forum that replaced the ancient Greek agora of Tomis.

Walk south from Piaţa Ovidiu to the beautifully decorated

Mahmudiye Mosque (*Str. Crângului 1, tel 0241 611 390, closed Mon., $*). A copy of the mosque in Konya, Anatolia, it is the largest mosque in Romania. King Carol gave it to the Muslim community of Dobrogea in 1910. The huge carpet inside, woven in the famous Hereke workshops of Istanbul, was a gift from Abdul Hamid II, the last Ottoman emperor, to the Turkish community on the island of Ada Kaleh in the Danube. The 150-foot (50 m) minaret provides stunning

(Museum of the Romanian Navy). Housed in the former Naval Academy, its highlights include models of ancient Greek triremes and photographs of the Russian mutineers who moored in here during Russia's 1905 revolution.

No visit to Constanța would be complete without a stroll along the **esplanade.** The promenade dates from the reign of King Carol I, who took a liking to Constanța. He made it fashionable as a spa town. The wedding-cake building on the

Muzeul de Artă Populara
✉ B-dul Tomis 32
☎ 0241 616 133
🕐 Closed Mon.
💲 $

Muzeul Marinei Române
✉ Str. Traian 53
☎ 0241 803 301
💲 $

views of the city. The mosque serves a large Mulism community.

North of Piața Ovidiu, the **Muzeul de Artă Populara** occupies a red-and-white-striped 1893 building that stands out from the crowd at the northern end of Bulevardul Tomis. The folk art museum's collection of brightly colored textiles, stylish traditional dress, and curious household tools is an oasis of fusty innocence in the timeworn city.

From the folk art museum, walk eight minutes to the handsome **Muzeul Marinei Române**

front is the **Cazino Paris** (1909), built in the French Secessionist style for Carol's wife, Queen Elisabeth. Today the casino functions as a restaurant and bar.

To familiarize yourself with the denizens of the Danube Delta and the Black Sea, visit the **Aquarium de Constanța** near the entrance to the esplanade. At the esplanade's opposite end, the **Farul Genovez** stands watch. It is a lighthouse built by a British firm in 1860 to commemorate the Genoese merchants whose ships frequented the Black Sea in the 13th century. ■

The casino and esplanade in Constanța were created by King Carol I, who turned the town into a popular holiday resort.

Aquarium de Constanța
✉ B-dul 16 Februarie 1
☎ 0241 611 277
🕐 Closed Mon.
💲 $

A winemaking culture

Winemaking is a natural part of everyday life in Romania. The tradition goes back a long way. A legend holds that Dionysos, the god of wine, was a Thracian born on Romanian soil. Hollowed-out drinking cups from Cucuteni suggest that wine was made in Moldavia as long ago as the fifth millennium B.C. Coins and jewels showing grapes have been found in Dacian graves from the fourth century B.C.

The Dacian king Burebista (ca 82–44 B.C.) ordered all the vineyards destroyed to prevent migrating tribes from exploiting them. One theory says that the Romans revived the Dacians' vines; another asserts that the Romans introduced the plants to Romania. Wherever the truth lies, as far north as Maramureş you will see the tell-tale lines of ancient vine terraces scoring the hillsides.

In Romania, vines are prized for both their usefulness and their decorative qualities. The graceful plants are draped like a canopy in the humblest of courtyards, providing not only wine, but beauty and shade in the summer.

Many vineyards have been in production since the 17th century, or even earlier. They include Dealu Mare between Buzău and Târgovişte in Muntenia, Nicoreşti and Odobeşti in Vrancea, and Niculiţel (famous for its red and white wines and the sweet Muscat Ottonel) in Dobrogea. The varieties of wine range from dry and sparkling whites to dark, almost purple, reds that exude the heady smell of licorice.

Cotnari (northeast of Iaşi; see p. 200) is famous for its dessert wines, especially the greenish Grasă de Cotnari, which is sometimes aged for 20 years. The vineyard at Cotnari was founded by the Moldavian prince Ştefan cel Mare, who imported Hungarian Tokay vines in the 15th century. During the 16th and 17th centuries, wine accounted for a sixth of Moldavia's exports, and Cotnari was the most popular. The secret of Cotnari's success is said to be the area's calcareous soil and the "noble

Left: Much of Romania's winemaking industry still relies on manual labor.
Above: Collecting grapes to make young wine for a wedding
Right: A wine cellar in Braşov. Each barrel is about six feet long.

rot" (*Botrytis cinerea,* a beneficial mold). The wine impressed some of Europe's most famous princes and luminaries, including Peter the Great and King Jan Sobietszki of Poland.

Romanian wine was traditionally stored and shipped in barrels made from Moldavian oak, which had strong preservative qualities and was resistant to deathwatch beetles. Romanian vintners still prefer to mature their wine in old oak barrels or stainless steel barrels lined with oak. There is a saying that the drinker absorbs the qualities of the tree through the wine.

Favored by its extremely hot summers and the region's chalky and sandy soils, Dobrogea's vineyards have always had a head start on the rest of the country. The wines of Murfatlar were mentioned by the Roman poet Ovid, who noticed that the Dobrogeans sometimes concentrated their wine by freezing it. Today, Murfatlar produces more white than red varieties of wine, but most people know the region for a full-bodied Merlot. Recaş, to the east of Timişoara, was founded as a Romano-British company in 1998 and is carving a niche for itself in the international market.

The Transylvanian vineyards of Târnave lie along the Târnavă River to the west of Mediaş. The label specializes in white wine made from grapes such as Riesling and Traminer.

Some of Romania's folklife museums display massive wooden grape presses dating from the 18th and 19th centuries, showing how serious the art of winemaking was in the past. People still use wooden presses to squeeze *must* (freshly pressed grape juice). And at Romanian weddings, a gourd-shaped pottery jug with two long necks is part of the traditional paraphernalia at the reception. Called a *plosca,* it is designed so that the bride and groom can drink at the same time. ■

Basarabi & Adamclisi

Basarabi

217 B2

Adamclisi

217 B1

THE SMALL TOWN OF BASARABI, JUST 12 MILES (19 KM) WEST of Constanța, is named after the Basarab dynasty that ruled Muntenia from the 14th century. The town is best known for its monastic complex and its proximity to the famed Murfatlar vineyards. The nearby village of Adamclisi exudes charm and boasts a Roman monument.

South of Basarabi, the nearby **Complexul Monastic de la Basarabi** comprises six rudimentary Orthodox churches and chapels, together with monks' cells and tombs—all cut into an outcrop

A detail from Tropaeum Traiani, a Roman monumental trophy, at Adamclisi

Note: Visitors to Basarabi need to obtain a special permit in advance from the Ministry of Culture.

of soft, calcareous rock. Nobody knows the age of the churches, but an inscription gives clues that the site was occupied until 992 at the latest. Beware the deep holes; they were intended to trap intruders.

The church walls are covered in signs. With a flashlight, you'll be able to make out Christian crosses, zoomorphic and anthropomorphic symbols, stick figures, and inscriptions in Cyrillic, Glagolitic (the oldest known Slavic alphabet), ancient

Greek, and maybe Dacian runes. A graffito showing a pair of serpents twisted around each other suggests that the Vikings may have been here. The plan to reopen the complex as a fully accredited monastery has not yet been realized; you may face difficulties in visiting the site.

Podgoria Murfatlar *(Str. Murfatlar 1, tel 0241 706 850),* a Murfatlar vineyard, abuts the northern edge of Basarabi. Specializing in red and white wines, including the alluring-sounding Lacrima lui Ovidiu (Ovid's Tears), the vineyard has a wine museum and can arrange tastings with traditional Romanian meals.

ADAMCLISI

Isolated in the river plains to the southwest of Constanța, beautiful Adamclisi is full of atmosphere. Its main focal point is the **Tropaeum Traiani,** a giant circular stone "trophy" erected in A.D. 106–09 to celebrate Trajan's conquest of Dacia. The monument stands at the end of a tree-lined avenue and is a 1977 copy of the original; however, the base is authentic. The walls are decorated with copies of the Roman relief carvings. Some show Dacian shepherds and village folk between the military images of centurions.

Archaeologists have discovered the remains of a Byzantine town and some Byzantine churches here, too. Some of the finds, including pottery from the neolithic Hamangia culture, are on display in a **museum** *(DN24 to Tichilești, then DJ223, tel 0241 614 562, $).* ∎

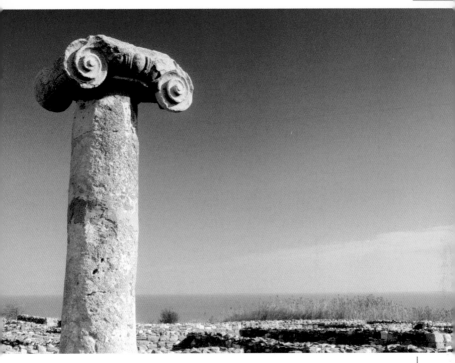

Histria

The ruins of the ancient Greek port city of Histria are strewn over 173 acres near the Black Sea coast.

KNOWN AS THE "ROMANIAN POMPEII," HISTRIA IS THE MOST important archaeological site on Romania's east coast. It comprises Greek, Roman, and Byzantine remains that date from the seventh century B.C. to the seventh century A.D. Now landlocked on the bank of Lacul Sinoe, it was the first major seaport on the western shores of the Black Sea. It lies about 48 miles (77 km) north of Constanța, accessible by a coastal road, or by the DN22 via Tariverde and Nuntaşi.

Histria is the oldest Greek site and the oldest urban structure on Romanian soil. Unfortunately, time has not been kind to Histria. The 173-acre (72 ha) site is overgrown, and a road cuts it in half. Ambitious restoration plans were drawn up in 2005, but little has been done. Although some of the walls reach 24 feet (7.5 m) high, you will still need some imagination to appreciate Histria as it once was.

The most important elements are the six city walls dating from the fifth century B.C. to the Byzantine period, a Roman forum, temples to Aphrodite and Zeus, two Roman baths, the eight basilicas (including Christian and pagan shrines), workshops, and trading areas. Histria was eventually abandoned for Tomis (Constanța) because the port silted up.

The site is now a part of the Danube Delta Biosphere Reserve and is under its management. An on-site museum helps make sense of all the history. ■

Histria
- 217 C2
- Danube Delta Biosphere Reserve (DN2A & DN22, then DJ226)
- 0241 614 562
- $

Babadag & Enisala

Babadag
🅰 217 C3

Enisala
🅰 217 C3

THE TOWN OF BABADAG REFLECTS A STRONG TURKISH AND Tatar influence. Dobrogea is home to most of Romania's Muslims, and thousands of them worship at Babadag's centrally located mosque. The nearby village of Enisala exhibits traces of other influences, in particular the Genoese merchants of the 13th century.

Babadag may owe its name to Sari Saltuq Baba, a Seljuk Turk and mystic who received the surrounding land from Byzantine emperor Michael VIII Paleologus in the mid-13th century. He helped spread Islam in the Balkans and is said to

Babadag has maintained a strong Muslim presence over the centuries. The central Gazi Ali Paşa mosque has been calling the faithful to prayer since the 17th century.

be buried here. Another source attributes the town's name to the Turkish words *baba*, meaning "Turkish," and *dag,* meaning "mountain." The 14th-century Arabian traveler Ibn Battuta wrote that Babadag was the last town to be ruled by Tatars before Wallachian prince Mircea cel Bătrân conquered Dobrogea. The discovery of a Byzantine-Tatar treasure on a nearby hill helps confirm this view. In the late 1600s, the pasha of Silistria moved his headquarters here, making it the regional headquarters of the Turkish army. After the Russo-Turkish War of 1771, Babadag fell into decline.

The cluster of Islamic buildings in Babadag's center belong to the **Moscheea lui Gazi Ali Paşa,** easily recognized by its 69-foot (21 m) minaret. Named for Ali Gazi, a governor of Turkish Dobrogea, the Ali Gazi Pasha Mosque dates from 1610. Recently lavishly restored with money from Istanbul, the mosque is under the administration of the mufti of Romania. The nearby **Muzeul de Artă Orientală** (*Str. Mihai Viteazu 1, closed Mon. & Nov.–Feb., tel 0240 516 204, $*) gives more insights into the history of Tatars and Turks in Dobrogea.

ENISALA

The village of Enisala lies east of Babadag. Visit the attractive little folklife museum, **Gospodăria Tărănească** (*DN22C, closed Mon., $*), housed in a traditional single-story dwelling from the early 20th century. It contains beautiful textiles.

The restored ruin of **Cetatea Enisala** perches on a tall crag overlooking the village. The castle dates from the late 13th century; it's one of many fortresses built by Genoa's merchant venturers, who dominated the eastern Mediterranean and the Black Sea at the time. Mircea cel Bătrân briefly installed a garrison here in the late 14th century, after ousting the Tatars. The views of the surrounding marshes and the distant sea are worth the climb (or drive) up. Evidence of Roman and early medieval (eighth century) settlements have also been found here. ∎

Tulcea

Many excursions to the waters of the Danube Delta begin at the port in Tulcea.

THIS LITTLE RIVER PORT LIES AT THE WESTERN EDGE OF the Danube Delta and is the main jumping-off point for journeys into the delta. The river makes a dramatic loop at this point, creating a natural shelter. The busy harbor teems with ferry boats (and in summertime, floating hotels), while rowing boats skitter to and fro between Tulcea and the village of Tudor Vladimirescu on the opposite shore. Tulcea's small, attractive old quarter is worth a visit.

A handsome 19th-century building on the right-hand side of Faleza (the promenade) holds the small but lively **Muzeul Judeţean de Artă.** Chiefly interesting for early 20th-century views of Dobrogea by such artists as Nicolae Dărăscu, Ştefan Dimitrescu, and Cecilia Cuţescu, the county's art museum also has a surprisingly good collection of surrealist paintings by the Romanian Jewish artist Victor Brauner (1903–1966), who visited here in 1920.

The **Secţia de Etnografie,** the folklife section of the county museum, is housed nearby in a former 19th-century bank. It contains some fascinating examples of Dobrogea's multiethnic culture, in which Greek, Aromanian, Turkish, Russian, and Bulgarian influences have all played a part. Don't miss the lovely textiles.

The 1904 **Monumentul Independenţei,** a monument commemorating Romania's liberation from Ottoman Turkey in 1878, crowns Citadel Hill at the park's center. Climb to the top for good views over the town.

Tulcea's other chief sight is the Parcul Monumentul Independenţei, an archaeological site. The archaeology museum, **Muzeul de Istorie şi Arheologie,** occupies the site of Cetatea Aegyssus, a Dacian and later Roman fortress. The museum tells in an entertaining manner the history of Dobrogea's most important archaeological sites— among them the Dacian citadels of Dinogetia (near Garvăn) and Troesmis (near Igliţa), the Greek settlement of Argamum (Jurilovca), and Roman Noviodunum (Isaccea) and Halmyris (Murighiol). Other highlights here include relief carvings of Thracian horsemen. ■

Tulcea
- 217 C4

Muzeul Judeţean de Artă
- Str. Grigore Antipa 2
- ☎ 0240 513 249
- Closed Mon.
- $ $

Secţia de Etnografie
- Str. 9 Mai 4
- ☎ 0240 516 204
- $ $

Muzeul de Istorie şi Arheologie
- Str. Gloriei, Parcul Monumentul Independenţei
- ☎ 0240 513 626
- Closed Mon.
- $ $

Reedbeds in autumn, west of Tulcea

West of Tulcea

THE ROLLING COUNTRYSIDE WEST OF TULCEA IS PEPPERED with attractive Orthodox monasteries. A quick tour will take in three of the loveliest set in this vineyard-strewn landscape.

Mănăstirea Celic Dere
🏛 217 B3-B4

Mănăstirea Cocoş
🏛 217 B4

Mănăstirea Saon
🏛 217 B4

From Tulcea, drive about 20 miles (32 km) west of Tulcea, through the town of **Somova,** whose lake attracts large numbers of migrating aquatic birds, and then turn south onto a country road. Follow this road 2 miles (3 km) past Teliţa to the peaceful **Mănăstirea Celic Dere** *(Poşta village, tel 0721 278 417, $).* Named after the nearby stream (which is Turkish for "steel brook"), the foundation was established in 1841 by two Russian Lipoveni monks. Today it is managed by 80 nuns. The modest museum *(closed Mon.)* contains a collection of rare religious books, antique carpets, and Romania's oldest icon, brought here from Mount Athos in Greece. You can also visit the carpet-weaving workshop. The splendid wooden *moară cu vânt* (windmill), transplanted from the Black Sea coast, is one of the few remaining examples of the thousands of wind- and wave-mills that were a common sight in the region well into the 19th century.

Return to the main road and head farther west between the vineyards to the village of **Niculiţel,** where you'll find the remains of a **paleo-Christian chapel and crypt** *(Str. Muzeului, tel 0745 769 874, closed Mon., $)* built in A.D. 370 during the reign of Emperor Valerius. The site was discovered in 1971, after a violent rainstorm washed away the earth to reveal one of the earliest churches in Romania. Beautifully restored and presented, the chapel contains a crypt that houses the bones of four Christian martyrs (Zotikos, Attalos, Kamasis, and Phillipos). Their four coffins can now be seen at the nearby 19th-century **Mănăstirea Cocoş** *(on main Tulcea-Galaţi road, 4 miles/6.5 km NW of Niculiţel, tel 0240 542 131).*

Near Niculiţel, visit the serene **Mănăstirea Saon,** founded by monks from the Celic Dere Monastery in 1846; the older church dates from 1881. Saon became a convent in 1916, but the communists closed it in 1960; it reopened in 1990. The nuns work the land, fish, and keep bees. The gardens are full of apple and cherry trees. ∎

Danube Delta

COVERING NEARLY 2,000 SQUARE MILES (5,800 SQ KM) OF sandy islands, floating reedbeds, dikes, forest, and marsh, the Danube Delta is the youngest part of Romania. It formed only 13,000 years ago, when the Gulf of Tulcea silted up. Large vessels can navigate only three of the thousands of waterways and lakes that crisscross the land. The dynamic delta's sandbanks and reedbeds constantly shift as the river deposits millions of tons of mud and silt here, at the end of its 1,788-mile (2,860 km) journey to the Black Sea.

The Danube Delta is the third most important wetland in the world and attracts millions of migrating birds. More than 300 species either live in or visit the delta. Breeding birds include the white pelican (the largest breeding population outside Africa), Dalmatian gray pelican, great diver, pygmy cormorant, glossy ibis, swans, and squacco heron. The delta also has 45 species of freshwater fish.

Despite its obvious importance as a wetland, the area's ecosystem remains vulnerable. Ukraine recently has proposed to develop the new Bistroe Channel to the Black Sea. Romania and the European Union have protested against the channel; as a result, Ukraine has agreed to let professionals decide its fate.

VISITING THE DELTA

The delta is spectacular between April and early September (note: the mosquitoes peak at this time, too). Many tour operators offer bird-watching packages. The best agents understand the importance of sensitivity and sustainability, and many of them also speak English. To find some of the most experienced operators of this type, contact **Asociaţia de Ecoturism din România** (see p. 263).

Few roads traverse the delta. A popular town reached via car is Murighiol beside **Lacul Murighiol** (Murighiol Lake), one of the best

lakes for bird-watching and a breeding ground for pelicans.

The most relaxing way to see the delta is by boat. Regular and fast ferries from Tulcea service the three main channels that link the city to the Black Sea. The most popular route travels the central arm, **Braţul Sulina**, which connects Tulcea with the old Danube River Authority port of Sulina (see p. 229) on the coast. You may disembark at one of several fishing villages, the most tourist-friendly of which is Crişan (see p. 231).

Braţul Chilia, the northern channel, separates Romania from Ukraine. The ferry service from Tulcea terminates at the Russian Lipoveni (see sidebar p. 229) village of Periprava (site of a Dacian settlement and, less palatably, a notorious communist prison) on Grindul Letea (Letea Sand Dune or Island; see below).

The southern channel, **Braţul Sf. Gheorghe,** leaves Braţul Sulina a few miles east of Tulcea. Ferries from Tulcea ply the channel three times a week, terminating at the fishing village of Sf. Gheorghe (see p. 229), at the channel's mouth.

GRINDUL LETEA

This island made entirely of sand supports an amazing variety of plant and animal life, including mature deciduous forests in which two species of sand-loving oak tree thrive. Some of the trees are 400

Danube Delta Biosphere Reserve
217 D3-C4
Visitor information
Administraţia Rezervaţiei Biosferei Delta Dunării (ARBDD), Str. Portului 34A, 820 243 Tulcea
0240 518 945
The ARBDD controls access to certain parts of the delta, fishing, and other activities that are possibly harmful to the ecosystem.

STAYING IN THE DELTA
The modern **Hotel Cormoran** (in Uzlina, near Murighiol) offers a range of accommodations at reasonable prices and can help with hiring boats and guides. There are also small, floating hotels that ply the smaller channels as well as the main branches. See Travelwise pp. 260–261 for a fuller listing.

A bird-watching hideout in a tree hangs over a waterway in the Danube Delta.

Grindul Letea
🏕 217 D4

years old. ARBDD (see Visitor Information, p. 227) has organized three tourist trails on Grindul Letea. Each connects the island's five villages and winds through different wildlife habitats; the hikes vary from two to four hours in length. Pamphlets mapping the routes are available from the ARBDD headquarters in Tulcea.

Semiferal horses graze the island, which is also home to the *enot* (raccoon dog), black-bellied fox, otter, and the venomous *Vipera renardi* snake. White-tailed and bald eagles, honey buzzards, and kestrels often wheel overhead, while the villages attract colorful red-and-turquoise bee-eaters and rollers. Collared pratincoles and black-winged stilts frequent the reedbeds and salt marshes.

Archaeologists have found Roman and medieval Genoese

remains on Grindul Letea; evidence shows that the island has been continuously occupied since then, but the existing villages are little more than hamlets. The streets are often no more than wide, grassy tracks lined with the palisade fences of single-story wooden clapboard houses. Most people get about on foot, bicycle, and horseback, or with a horse and cart.

Like Periprava, **Sfiştofca** and **Cardon** (the smallest village on the island—a 1992 census listed 19 people) are mainly inhabited by Russian-speaking Lipoveni. **Letea** (pop. 456 in 1992) is more Ukrainian in character. There is a *skete* (small monastery) in the village. The village of **C. A. Rosetti** acts as the island's communal center; it has a majority of Romanians. Look for the island's onion-domed churches. Most of the

Lipoveni

The Lipoveni—followers of a priest called Filip, hence their original name, Filipoveni—fled to the Danube Delta from Russia after the reforms of 1653 split the Russian Orthodox Church into two factions. Believers in the Old Rite were subjected to such extreme restrictions that they emigrated. They chose Serbia, Poland, Moldavia, and, surprisingly, the Ottoman Empire (which included Dobrogea). ∎

Sulina
🅐 217 D4

Sf. Gheorghe
🅐 217 D3

islanders participate in traditional occupations: a small amount of farming and animal breeding, along with fishing, hunting, beekeeping, and willow cutting. They are prohibited from carrying out these activities in the areas designated as part of the wildlife and wilderness reserve, **Pădurea Letea.**

SULINA

The coastal town of Sulina has a great past: From 1856 until 1938, it was home to the European Commission of the Lower Danube, established after the Crimean War to safeguard the interests of all the countries through which the Danube flowed. Consequently, the fishing village grew rapidly into a lively, cosmopolitan town of 40,000. The threat of war with Germany prompted the commission to leave Sulina in 1938, precipitating an equally rapid decline.

The **Farul Comisiei Europene a Dunării de Jos** (*Str. II 15, 0240 542 131, closed Mon., $*), an 1870 lighthouse built by the European Danube Commission, is now a museum. Its two small rooms detail the town's history. The lighthouse offers a grand view of the delta.

The nearby cemetery, **Cimitirul Maritim,** reveals the multinational character of Sulina. You'll find French, English, German, Italian, Russian, and Romanian names here. It is divided into four main sections according to religion; an Anglican section holds a few poignant, drunken-looking headstones recording the names of people who drowned in ships off the coast.

SF. GHEORGHE

The fishing village of Sf. Gheorghe at the mouth of Brațul Sf. Gheorghe is the perfect place to enjoy the sea air and sunshine, sample the delicious fish, and explore the sand dunes. The restricted **Rezervația Sf. Gheorghe-Palade-Perișor-Sacalin** lies opposite the channel mouth. You may explore the forest's rich animal and plant life with a registered guide. You might hear great bitterns booming nearby and see redshanks, warblers, and buntings. ∎

Cruising the delta

A trip through some of the magical side channels and lakes in the heart of the Danube Delta is an opportunity to see another facet of the delta. The wealth of animal and plant life will amaze and astound.

The following route is approved by the Delta's administrative body, Administraţia Rezervaţiei Biosferei Delta Dunării (ARBDD; see p. 227), which restricts access to some areas. You will need to hire a boat and an ARBDD-licensed, English-speaking guide as well. Both can be found through some of the delta hotels *(for a list, contact ARBDD)*, or a reputable travel agency such as those registered with Asociaţia de Ecoturism din România (see p. 263). For the types of boats available, see p. 263.

Begin your trip at Tulcea and head east along Braţul Sf. Gheorghe. After passing the riverside villages of **Nufăru** and **Ilganii de Jos**, turn left into **Canalul Litcov** (the man-made Litcov Canal).

The canal plows through a network of narrower channels and lakes. Ask your guide to tell you which ones you may explore. Willows overhang some of the channels, and the banks brim with water alder and poplars, brook mint and water hemlock, while deep pink and yellow water lilies often cover the water's surface. The larger lakes are all named and include **Lacul Gorgova, Lacul Potcoava,** and **Lacul Isac.** Egrets, ducks, and swans often nest in the reeds.

Head south along **Canalul Caraorman** for **Caraorman** ① village, which lies 35 miles (55 km) from Tulcea. Standing on a sandbank that stretches for some 12 miles (19 km), the village (whose name means "black forest" in Turkish) has about 490 people, who are mainly of Russian, Lipoveni (see sidebar p. 229), and Ukrainian origins. Facing the canal banks are fetching, reed-roofed houses, traditionally decorated with white walls and blue paintwork. High-prowed wooden fishing boats called *lotci* moor here like so many Venetian gondolas. Thanks to a phenomenal rise in fish prices since 1989, the villagers of Caraorman now concentrate on fishing rather than cattle breeding. On the east side of the village is the long, low, reed-thatched **cherhana.** The locals store the fish, including bream, carp, perch and zander, that they catch in the nearby lakes in this building's ice-cooled refrigeration rooms before the catch is sold to Murighiol or Tulcea.

Nearby, the beautiful **Rezervaţia Pădurea Caraorman** contains massive,

The wetlands of the Danube Delta formed only 13,000 years ago.

400-year-old oak trees that grow in the sand, creepers that reach 45 feet (15 m) in length, and a wealth of animal and birdlife—numbering among them owls, eagles, wildcats, boars, and wolves. You will need a permit to visit this protected forest reserve.

Backtrack north along the Canalul Caraorman and turn right into the **Canalul Crişan.** The Caraorman-Crişan Canal was broadened in the 1980s as part of Ceauşescu's plans to industrialize the delta. West of Caraorman you'll see dunes that contain some of Europe's finest sands.

About 7.5 miles (12 km) from Caraorman, you'll encounter the village of **Crişan ②.** The traditional-looking **Hotel Lebăda** *(tel 0240 543 778),* whose restaurant serves local fish specialties, stands on the northern bank. Farther west, a plaque marks the 1859 opening of the Braţul Sulina as a major navigation channel, after the British engineer Charles Hartley had it dredged and widened. There is another picturesque cherhana on Crişan's southern bank. (If you want to stay overnight, several modest guesthouses line the north bank of the Braţul Sulina.)

About half a mile (1 km) upstream of Crişan, on the northern shore near the junction with **Dunărea Veche** (the Old Danube), you will find the ARBDD's **Centrul de Documentare şi Educaţie Ecologică** (Ecological Information & Education Center;

tel 0240 519 214, closed Mon.), which contains wildlife displays, videos, and a library. It's an excellent resource on the delta.

Head west along Braţul Sulina. About 16 miles (25 km) east of Tulcea, the town of **Maliuc** has several hotels and guesthouses, where you can enjoy the local hospitality and sample regional fish dishes. Hotels include the **Complex Turistic Salcia** *(tel 0240 546 539)* and **Hotel Maliuc** *(tel 0748 200 372).* You can also hire a rowing boat to take you to **Lacul Furtuna ③** to the north, which offers wonderful bird-watching. Continue west to the village of **Partizani ④,** where you can hire fishermen to row you to the three lakes—Tataru, Lung, and Mester—also to the north.

End your tour by returning to Tulcea, drinking in the sights and sounds of the delta along the way. ∎

⊹ See area map p. 217
► Tulcea
↔ 80 miles (128 km)
◉ 5 hours (more with detours and stops)
► Tulcea

NOT TO BE MISSED
• Caraorman
• Crişan
• Lacul Furtuna

Arabian horses from the nearby stud farm at Mangalia in a schooling session on the beach

Mangalia

RENOWNED FOR THE QUALITY OF ITS SUNLIGHT AND ITS Mediterranean climate, the attractive beach town of Mangalia is also famous for its Greek, Roman, and Byzantine heritage. Known in antiquity as Callatis, the town was founded by Greeks from Megara on the orders of an oracle in the fourth century B.C. It lies south of the modern coastal resorts and 30 miles (45 km) south of Constanţa.

Mangalia

🏔 217 C1

Visitor information

✉ Primăria Municipiului Mangalia, Şoseaua Constanţei 13

☎ 0241 751 060

Chief among Mangalia's highlights is the **Romano-Byzantine street** that has been excavated and is now part of the dining room in the **Hotel President** (*Str. Teilor 6, tel 0241 755 861*). Midway between Şoseaua Constanţei and the sea, the hotel stands on 1,000 square yards (836 sq m) of stone pavement and water conduits from the southern part of the Callatis citadel, which dates from the sixth and seventh centuries A.D. The street measures 18 feet (6 m) wide, and the site has been left open for visitors to enjoy. Outside the hotel you can see part of the Roman city wall that was constructed on the remains of the earlier Greek wall; some of the blocks are beautifully shaped, showing signs of true Hellenistic skill and artistry.

A two-minute walk inland from the hotel takes you to the outlines of a fourth-century Syrian basilica, which was probably a bishopric. Return to Mangalia's main through-road, Şoseaua Constanţei,

of this charming Islamic mosque from 1525 contains Muslim gravestones and fragments from ancient Callatis. The mosque still functions, but non-Muslim visitors are welcome provided they observe the mosque's courtesies.

MANGALIA'S OUTSKIRTS

Two miles (3 km) north of Mangalia, in a pretty seaside location near Stațiunea Venus, the stud farm and riding center of **Herghelia Mangalia** (*SN Cai de Rasa Herghelia Mangalia, Șoseaua Constanței km 3, tel 0241 751 325, $*) has been breeding horses since 1926. The farm's more than 300 horses are mainly Ibn Galal (Egyptian) Arabs, but there are some Shagyar Arabs (an Arab-Moldavian cross). Visitors are welcome and you may be able to arrange a horseback ride (*$*). The riding horses are said to be very gentle. The surrounding countryside also provides pleasant walking opportunities.

A few miles west of Mangalia, in the area called La Movile, lies one of the world's most famous subterranean caves: **Peștera Movile.** Measuring only 720 feet (220 m) long with a very low roof, it was discovered by chance in 1986 and contains a unique ecosystem, which is driven entirely by the oxidation of hydrogen sulfide or chemosynthesis. In laymen's terms, this means that the organisms living there manage to exist entirely without light. Today the cave is protected by Primăria Mangalia and Grupul pentru Explorație și Speologie Subterane. You'll have to settle for admiring the area above the cave. Access is strictly restricted to researchers and students. (*For more information, contact Primăria Municipală Mangalia or Cristian Lascu, Str. Frumoasă 31, Bucharest, tel 021 312 4051*) ■

to reach the superb, not-to-be-missed **Muzeul de Arheologie Callatis** (*Șoseaua Constanței 23, tel 0241 753 580, $*). The archaeological museum features a treasure trove of Greek, Thracian, and neolithic objects, from little gold figures to clay water pipes. Far from being staid and academic, the displays stimulate visions of daily life here as it once was, as a strenuous battle for expression, identity, and survival.

Other fascinating archaeological remains lie scattered around town (*ask at tourist information center for more details*), and divers have discovered vestiges of Callatis's port under the sea as well.

From the archaeological museum, a five-minute walk south will take you to the **Moscheea Esma Han Sultan** (*Str. Oituz 1, tel 0241 754 250, $*). The cemetery

Members of Slava Rusă's large Russian Orthodox community worship at Uspenia Monastery.

More places to visit in Dobrogea

HALMYRIS

Spread across mounds of long grass near the village of Murighiol, this archaeological site may look deserted, but it is in fact the archaeological excavation site of an important Roman fort. Work continues to excavate the barracks and the sixth-century bishopric, whose remains include the painted tombs of two martyrs. Emperor Trajan fought two wars to take this vital strategic location from the Dacians, giving the Romans control over the fertile Danube Delta and a gateway to Asia. For the next 600 years, Halmyris served as a legionary base, naval port, and supply depot for Roman colonization and cultural exchange. In all, Halmyris was occupied for 1,100 years, from the Iron Age to the Byzantine period. You can help excavate the site (contact Earthwatch, 3 Clock Tower Place, Ste. 100, Box 75, Maynard, MA 01754, USA, tel 978 461 0081 or 800 776 0188). 217 C3 For more information, contact **Institutul de Cercetari Eco-Muzeale** ✉ Str. 14 Noiembrie 3, Tulcea ☎ 0240 513 231

SLAVA RUSĂ

The village of Slava Rusă, southwest of Babadag, is one of those quiet, unexpected, and magical places in Dobrogea. Although half of its 1,400 inhabitants came originally from Italy and Spain, it was founded by Lipoveni and is the main center of Old Rite Russian Orthodoxy

in Dobrogea. The Russian Orthodox monasteries of Uspenia and Vovidenia are nearby and the village has two Russian churches. Have a look at some of the beautiful wooden houses; many are ornamented with superb carvings. You may see the Lipoveni wearing their traditional clothes—the men in tunics tied with belts and the women in long skirts.

Slava Rusă stands on the site of the Roman and later Romano-Byzantine city of (L)Ibida (second to seventh centuries A.D.). Walk around the perimeter of the village to see the ongoing excavations. Exciting discoveries made at the archaeological site include a glassmaking kiln, beautifully formed ceramics and bronze figurines, carved capitals, silver buckles, coins, a triple-nave basilica, and several large necropolises (the Cavoul Tudorka, or Tudorka Tomb, contained 39 bodies and is decorated with frescoes). The walled city covers 67 acres (27 ha), making it one of the most important Roman cities ever found in Dobrogea.

Two miles (3 km) from the village, archaeologists also discovered an early Christian monastery dating from sometime between the second half of the fourth century and the first half of the seventh century. It is one of the earliest monastic foundations in the Roman province of Scythia Minor and in Romania as a whole. 217 B3 **Visitor information** ✉ Muzeul de Istorie și Arheologie, Tulcea ☎ 0240 513 626 ■

Travelwise

A Bucharest tram stop

TRAVELWISE INFORMATION.

PLANNING YOUR TRIP

WHEN TO GO

Romania has a standard European continental climate, with long, hot summers and cold, sometimes very cold, winters. The best time to visit depends on where in Romania you plan to go and what you want to do.

Bucharest is best seen in the spring or fall; winters are often too wet and cold to enjoy and the summers can be brutally hot, with temperatures typically reaching well into the 90s Fahrenheit (mid- to upper-30s Celsius).

The mountains and highlands of Transylvania are ideal for touring and hiking in the warm-weather months from May until the end of September. The season here starts to wind down in October, and by November some of the smaller hotels and attractions outside the main cities close their doors for the winter.

The Danube Delta and the Black Sea coastal resorts come into their own in July and August, when it seems the entire country is on vacation. The delta is especially pleasant in late spring, before the crowds come, and fall, after they go home. The water in the Black Sea is warm enough to swim in from June until about mid-September. During the winter, Black Sea resorts like Mamaia practically shut down, and you'll have to search long and hard for an open hotel. Constanța, however, is large enough to be a year-round destination.

The winter ski season, centered in the resorts around Brașov, runs from mid-December to mid-March. The most popular skiing month is February, when resorts can be crowded to bursting. Brașov itself is a lively, year-round destination—just when the skiers pack their bags and head home, the hikers and summer vacationers descend on the town.

There is no particular Romanian festival season. The main Transylvanian folk festivals, including the popular medieval festival in Sighișoara, are timed for mid-summer to take advantage of the influx of visitors. Cultural and music festivals in the large cities are usually held in the spring and fall. Aside from the festivities connected to Christmas and New Year's, winter is a relatively quiet season.

WHAT TO BRING

There are no special packing needs for Romania, and what you bring very much depends on what you plan to do.

If hiking is on the itinerary, be sure to bring sturdy walking shoes with ankle support, as well as something waterproof to protect you from late afternoon showers, and a sweater or fleece for the cool mountain evenings (even at the height of summer). Mosquitoes are a problem, especially in wooded areas and the Danube Delta, so pack or plan to buy good mosquito repellent. If a trip to the Danube Delta is on the agenda, pack a small pair of binoculars for wildlife sightings. Although Romania has a comprehensive and well-stocked network of pharmacies, it's always a good idea to bring along an ample supply of any prescription medications you need.

While casual dress will see you through nearly any occasion, if you intend to spend time in Bucharest, consider bringing at least one nicer outfit (a sport coat for men, dress skirt for women) for concerts and evenings out at restaurants. Don't forget comfortable shoes, and plan on doing a lot of walking once you're here. You also might want to pack an eye mask. Many hotels and pensions,

oddly, don't have thick drapes, so more often than not you'll find yourself waking up with the sun.

In general, don't panic about forgetting anything. Anything you leave at home can always be purchased once you've arrived.

INSURANCE

No vaccinations are necessary to enter Romania, and there are no particular health hazards to be aware of. That said, be sure to check with your health insurer to confirm that you have proper coverage on any trip abroad. Most U.S. plans are not recognized in Romania, and if you fall ill, you'll likely have to pay for your services in cash and seek reimbursement from your insurer later. Be sure to retain any receipts for making later claims. The cost of medical services is relatively low by U.S. standards.

ENTRY FORMALITIES

VISA

Visitors with a valid passport from the United States and Canada can enter Romania visa-free for stays up to 90 days. Citizens of the European Union, including the United Kingdom, do not need a visa. The Romanian police can stop you and ask for identity at any time; while this is not likely to happen, it's a good idea to carry a photocopy of your passport with you.

CUSTOMS

There are no special customs requirements for visiting Romania. You are permitted to bring in currency equivalent to about $12,000. You are not obliged to declare small amounts of gifts (of up to about $130 in value), alcoholic beverages, or tobacco for personal use. Your bags are unlikely to be searched, but laws forbidding the importation of illegal drugs are strictly enforced.

HOW TO GET TO ROMANIA

BY AIRPLANE

Romania's flagship carrier, Tarom (www.tarom.ro), maintains regular air service from major North American hubs (New York's JFK, Washington's Dulles, Toronto, and Montreal) to Bucharest's Otopeni Airport. These flights usually involve a stop in western Europe (Paris or Vienna) before continuing on to Bucharest. Many other international airlines, including major U.S. carriers, offer one-stop service between the United States and Bucharest, sometimes under code-share agreements with Tarom.

Once you're in Europe, there are frequent (often several times a day) air connections between nearly all of the major European hubs and Bucharest. Eastern European capitals like Budapest, Prague, Warsaw, and Sofia are well served by their respective national carriers.

If you're departing from a European city, it's worth looking into the possibility of flying with a budget carrier. These are increasingly common throughout Europe, and though they've been slow to add Romanian cities, that's expected to change now that Romania is a full-fledged member of the European Union. The Romanian-based budget carrier Blue Air (www.blueair-web.com) now flies from Madrid, Paris, Rome, and several other European cities to Bucharest's Băneasa Airport. Similarly, Bratislava-based SkyEurope (www.skyeurope.com) offers regular service to Băneasa from its wide network of European cities with a stopover in the Slovak capital. If you don't mind arriving in Timişoara, another budget carrier to consider would be Carpatair (www.carpatair.com), which flies to the western Romanian city from Paris as well as several German and Italian cities. Carpatair also offers connecting flights to smaller

Romanian cities, including Cluj-Napoca, Iaşi, and Sibiu. Budget airlines, in general, are cheaper than the larger national carriers, but can be difficult to coordinate with overseas flights. They frequently fly from smaller, out-of-the-way airports, meaning that you usually have to arrange an airport transfer as part of the overall flight plan.

Most international carriers arrive at Bucharest's Otopeni (tel 021 230 0022), officially known as Henri Coanda International Airport. Otopeni lies about 12 miles (20 km) from the city center and is easily reached by bus or taxi. Leave at least an hour to get to and from the airport during weekdays, owing to rush-hour traffic, and about 30–45 minutes during evenings and weekends. Use caution when choosing a taxi, since rip-offs abound. Refuse any offers of a ride you might get in the arrivals hall and instead walk outside to see the row of yellow cabs lined up at taxi stands. A taxi ride from the airport to the center should cost about 50–60 RON (about $20–$25). Bus no. 783 makes the trip from the airport to several main central destinations every 30 minutes from about 6 a.m. until midnight. The journey costs 2 RON ($0.80), and you can buy tickets from the small window near where the bus stops. The airport itself is relatively small and efficient. You'll find car rental agencies, currency exchange bureaus, and an ATM just outside the main arrivals hall.

Budget carriers, including Romania's Blue Air arrive at Băneasa (tel 021 232 0020), about 6 miles (10 km) from the center of the city. Băneasa has relatively few facilities for arriving visitors. A taxi from the airport to the center of the city will cost about 30–40 RON ($12–$15). Bus no. 131 can take you downtown, while bus no. 205 will transfer you to Bucharest's main train station, Gara de Nord (North Station).

In addition to Bucharest's airport, several other cities, including Timişoara, Arad, Cluj-Napoca, Iaşi, Târgu Mureş, Baia Mare, Bacău, Suceava, and Constanţa, have small international airports with air service to some European destinations. During the summer, charters fly from elsewhere in Europe to Constanţa and the resorts on the Black Sea.

BY TRAIN

Romania's rail network is well integrated into the European grid, and rail connections to the country from the main European capitals are frequent. At least one train per day links Bucharest with Budapest, Vienna, Prague, and other regional capitals. Be forewarned that traveling by rail can be painfully slow—especially once you enter Romania. The one daily train from Prague, for example, takes a full day (23 hours, 42 minutes) to cover the less than 900 miles (1,500 km) distance. Sleepers are available on long international hauls.

Most trains to Bucharest arrive at the city's Gara de Nord, located about 3 miles (2 km) northwest of the city center and reachable by taxi or subway line. The Gara de Nord might appear pretty seedy at first, but it's come a long way in recent years in cleaning itself up and offering a range of services for rail travelers. There's a decent coffee shop, a McDonald's, and several small grocery stores to buy provisions for the journey. Ticket offices are located in the corridor just outside the main departure hall. Train platforms and departure times are usually clearly marked.

BY BUS

Eurolines (www.eurolines.com), Europe's primary international bus carrier, maintains regular bus service from the main European cities to Bucharest and other large cities in Romania. Ticket prices and journey times are generally comparable to the trains, with buses being perhaps slightly quicker. Book tickets well in advance, since buses are popular with students and tend to fill up fast, especially during the summer holidays. Buses to Bucharest usually arrive at the bus station adjacent to the Gara de Nord (see p. 237). To reach the center of the city, take the subway or a taxi.

BY CAR

Romania is easily reachable by car, with the main frontier crossings from western Europe along the Hungarian border—though it's also possible to cross into Romania from Serbia, Bulgaria, Ukraine, or Moldova. If traveling from Hungary, follow the signs to the Romanian cities of Oradea (if you're heading to the north) or Arad (to the south), both of which lie on main trans-European highways. Expect long lines at frontier crossings, particularly on Fridays when people are traveling for the weekend. To minimize waiting times, time your arrival for late evening or early morning. Note that smaller crossings may not be open 24 hours a day.

GETTING AROUND

BY CAR

Driving in Romania is legal with a valid driver's license from your country of origin (U.S. state and Canadian provincial licenses are permitted) and proof of insurance. To travel on highways, you must also purchase a sticker (rovinieta), available at border crossings and some large gas stations for around $5 for a week's worth of travel, and $8 for 30 days. If you rent a car, it will come with insurance and registration documents, and possibly also a highway sticker. Rules of the road follow the European norms, and U.S. drivers should first familiarize themselves with European traffic signs.

Car travel in Romania is, in general, a mixed bag. On the positive side, driving will give you much more flexibility for visiting smaller cities and villages, particularly in Transylvania and Maramureș, that are not easily reachable via trains and buses. It can also be quicker on some stretches, though Intercity (IC) trains remain the fastest way to travel between major cities. On the negative side, roads are narrow and often in poor condition, drivers are aggressive, and traffic can be heavy. Don't even attempt to drive in Bucharest aside from getting in and out of the city. The traffic is maddening. Add to that the relatively high cost of gasoline (about $5 a gallon). Consider car travel only if you're planning extensive travel to out-of-the-way areas or if you're on an extended stay and can easily handle the delays and inconveniences as they come. In any event, always have a good map or road atlas on hand (available at large gas stations) since roads are often poorly marked.

The legal speed limit on highways is 120 kph (about 70 mph). This drops down to 90 kph (50 mph) on two-lane open roads outside of built-up areas and 50 kph (30 mph) in cities. Speed limits are strictly enforced and fines can be steep. Note that the blood-alcohol limit is zero for drivers, and drivers are prohibited from using their cell phones behind the wheel (though this last law tends to get ignored in practice).

Renting a car is easy to arrange from your home country over the phone or the Internet. Most of the major rental agencies, including Hertz, Avis, Thrifty, and others, have local offices at the Bucharest airport or in town with airport pickup and drop-off. In most cases, drivers must be at least 21 years old, have a major credit card, and have had their driver's license for at least one year. Rentals will usually come with

some form of insurance, but it's best to ask what is covered and what supplemental coverage, if any, you'll need. Cars are likely to be late-model Romanian or other European makes, though you're unlikely to find one with automatic transmission (and if you do, it will be much more expensive than a stick shift).

Unleaded gas is easy to find, and most filling stations will take international credit cards.

BY CITY BUS

Most cities and large towns have extensive municipal bus systems that provide the backbone of the public transportation system. Tickets generally run between 1 and 2 RON per trip (depending on the city) and can almost always be bought at magazine and tobacco kiosks or at ticket windows adjacent to bus stops. Validate your ticket in stamping machines once on the bus and hold onto it until the end of the journey. Depending on the city, you may have to buy an additional ticket to cover any large luggage you might be carrying. If in doubt, buy and validate two tickets. Bus travel is relatively easy; the only trick will be sorting out the stops and routes from confusing timetables.

BY LOCAL BUS

Intercity bus travel is cheap and convenient and is usually a better option than the train for traveling relatively short distances (up to 100 miles/160 km) within a particular region.

There's no national bus company per se. Most companies are privately owned and operate regional fleets. If you plan on traveling by bus, don't worry about putting together a detailed nationwide itinerary; that would be nearly impossible (one website that might help is www.autogari.ro). Instead, plan pretty much on traveling on the fly, arriving in one destination and then working out from there how to get to your next one.

Romanian bus stations (*autogara*) are usually located close to train stations for convenient hopping from one to the other. Be forewarned, though, that bus stations can be highly confusing places, with competing companies often offering service to the same places. Timetables won't always be posted, and it won't always be apparent at first glance how and where to buy tickets. Sometimes you'll have to buy tickets at the counter and other times from the driver. There doesn't seem to be any set rule, but a little perseverance pays off, and if in doubt simply ask someone to point you in the right direction.

Buses—especially the ubiquitous minibuses—are usually packed, and it's a good idea to try to buy tickets at least a day in advance. Sometimes this won't be possible; you'll simply be told to show up at a certain time and buy a ticket from the driver. If you can get an advance ticket, you'll usually be assigned a reserved seat.

BY PLANE

Air travel within Romania is possible and relatively affordable, though still much more expensive than trains or buses. It's a serious option if you don't have much time and you want to see one or more far-flung destinations. Tarom (www.tarom.ro), the national air carrier, maintains flights from Bucharest to several large cities around the country, including Timişoara, Iaşi, and Cluj-Napoca. Budget carriers Blue Air (www.blueair-web.com) and Carpatair (www.carpatair.com) also offer limited domestic service, with Blue Air flights originating from Bucharest's Băneasa field and Carpatair from Timişoara. You can buy flight tickets from travel agencies scattered around major cities. Note that service between some cities may not be offered every day.

BY TAXI

Taxis are generally reliable and cheap, and for negotiating large cities they will probably be your transportation of choice. Drivers are required by law to post their rates on the outside of the cab. In an honest cab, the posted fare should run somewhere between 1.00 and 1.50 RON per kilometer. If it's any higher, don't get in. Taxi rip-offs are not as common as they once were, but always be sure to choose a cab run by a bona fide company. This is especially important when taking taxis from train stations or from Bucharest's Otopeni Airport, where taxi fraud is still occasionally a problem. In general, refuse any offers of rides you may get while still inside a train station or airport, and instead proceed outside to legitimate cabs lined up at taxi stands.

BY TRAIN

Train travel remains the best way of covering long distances in Romania relatively quickly and cheaply. The country's national train network, CFR, is extensive, and trains link just about every city and town in the country. That said, train travel in Romania is a significant step down from what you may be accustomed to in western Europe. Travel on all but the top-of-the-line Intercity (IC) trains can be painfully slow, and the trains themselves can be dirty and in poor repair. Added to that is the fact that timetables can change from day to day without warning. The CFR website (www.cfr.ro) maintains a fairly accurate online timetable with English translation, but even that has been known to carry outdated information.

Romanian trains are divided into four categories reflecting their respective comfort and speed. The best are the IC trains. These are modern and well maintained, and compare favorably with western European trains. You'll find IC trains linking most of the major cities; the downside is that they don't run frequently and you'll have to plan carefully in advance to use them. IC trains are more expensive than other trains—though still reasonable—and require a seat reservation. Going down the line to the other train categories, "Rapid" (marked with an R on timetables) and "Accelerat" (A) trains are slower than IC trains, but they are usually acceptably clean and run more frequently. "Personal" trains (P)—essentially locals—are poorly maintained and tend to stop in every village along the way. Take those only if necessary.

Buy train tickets either at ticket windows at train stations or at special CFR travel offices in town. Nearly every city and large town will have a CFR office (look for the sign "CFR—Agentia de Voiaj" or ask at your hotel for the address). Note that tickets for same-day travel are usually available only at station ticket windows. If possible, try to buy your tickets a day or two in advance, since trains on popular routes (for example, Bucharest–Constanţa in summer) can sell out. In addition to the ticket, you'll be required to buy a seat reservation (1.80 RON). Though you'll usually have the option of buying first- or second-class seats, in practice there's little difference between the two.

Romania is a member of the Eurail pass (www.eurail.com) network. A Eurail Romania pass costs $262 and allows for 10 days of first-class rail travel within a two-month period. Whether or not this makes sense depends on how much you will travel, but in general fares are low and even if you're on the go the entire time, it's unlikely to be better than a break-even proposition. And if you're traveling on a rail pass, you still have to buy a seat reservation in advance.

Romanian train stations (*gara*) tend to be dirty and unpleasant, and while there's little real danger, they are no place to linger. As is the case throughout Europe, arrivals (*sosiri*) are listed on white timetables, while departures (*plecari*) are on yellow.

As of 2006, all cars on all trains are nonsmoking, and rules are strictly enforced.

PRACTICAL ADVICE

COMMUNICATIONS

Post Offices

You'll find post offices (marked *Poşta Română*) near the center of every city, town, and village in Romania. Post offices are usually open during standard business hours, though the central post office in Bucharest (Str. Matei Millo 10) is open from Monday to Saturday from 7:30 a.m. to 8 p.m. (closed Sun.). Other large post offices may keep Saturday hours as well. Post offices are popular places, and lines can be long. If you're just stopping in to buy stamps or mail a postcard, try first at your hotel reception (sometimes they keep stamps on hand for guests). You'll need 3.40 RON in postage to send a postcard to the United States or Canada. Post offices often offer fax services and have phone booths from which you can place international calls.

Telephones

Romania's country code is 40. To call a Romanian number from the United States, dial 011-40, followed by the area code of the city you are calling (dropping the zero) and the number. For example, to reach a number in Bucharest, with an area code of 021, you would dial 011-40-21 and then the local number. To dial between cities in Romania, dial the area code of the city (retaining the zero) and then the number. For example, to call to Braşov, which has an area code of 0268, from Bucharest you would dial 0268 and then the local Braşov number.

Area codes for some large cities are as follows:
Braşov 0268
Bucharest 021
Cluj-Napoca 0264
Constanţa 0241
Iaşi 0232
Sibiu 0269
Timişoara 0256

To call abroad from Romania, dial 00 and then the country code of the country you are dialing. The country code for the United States and Canada, for example, is 1. To call a number in New York with an area code of 212, you would dial 00-1-212 and then the local New York number.

You'll find public telephones —orange in color—scattered throughout towns and cities around major squares and transportation hubs. As mobile phones have grown in popularity, however, public pay phones are not as well maintained, and you may have a hard time finding a working phone. Public phones are card operated, and you can buy cards for 10, 15, and 20 RON at post offices, ROMTELECOM offices, and some magazine and tobacco kiosks. You can use public phones to place local or long-distance calls, depending on how many credits you have on your card. You can also place long-distance calls from your hotel room, though often this will entail a hefty surcharge, and from post offices, which are a lot cheaper.

It's possible to bring your cell phone with you, provided you have activated international roaming (contact your home service provider for details) and your phone is a "tri-band" or capable of working on a GSM network of 900/1800 MHz— which is compatible with most other European countries but different from the band used in the United States. Roaming can be frightfully expensive, so you'll want to keep your international cell phone calls to a minimum. Another option for using your own cell phone is to buy a pre-paid SIM card once you're in Romania. Mobile phone service providers Vodaphone and Orange offer such cards starting at around $10 (25 RON),

though you'll have to buy extra credits to use the phone.

Internet

The Internet is highly popular, although you may occasionally have a hard time finding an Internet café to check your mail. Bucharest, Braşov, and Cluj-Napoca all have several Internet cafés in and around the center of town, but smaller cities may only have one or two. If your hotel does not offer Internet in the room (many of the better places do) or have a small business center with a public computer, ask at the reception desk for the nearest Internet café. Rates are reasonable and generally run about 2.50 RON an hour. Wireless is also making inroads, and some hotels and cafés in Bucharest and other places now offer free Wi-Fi connections that allow you to connect to the Internet automatically by opening up your own laptop. In Buch-arest, some KFC and Pizza Hut restaurants now offer free wireless for customers. Some hotels and restaurants offer what is called Zapp wireless service, entitling you to log on for free for 10 minutes and then requiring you to use a prepaid card ($4 for an hour or $15 for 24 hours) after that.

CONVERSIONS

Romania uses the metric system. Clothing sizes are normally expressed as S, M, L, and XL and correspond approximately to U.S. sizes. Dresses, suits, and shoes are given numbered sizes and their U.S. equivalents are given below.

1 kilo = 2.2 pounds
1 liter = 0.26 U.S. gallons
1 kilometer = 0.62 miles
1 meter = 3.3 feet
1 centimeter = 0.39 inch

Women's clothing

U.S.					
8	10	12	14	16	18
Europe					
36	38	40	42	44	46

Men's clothing
U.S.
36 38 40 42 44 46
Europe
46 48 50 52 54 56

Women's shoes
U.S.
6–6.5 7–7.5 8–8.5 9–9.5
Europe
38 39 40–41 42

Men's shoes
U.S
8 8.5 9.5 10.5 11.5 12
Europe
41 42 43 44 45 46

ELECTRICITY

Romanian appliances, as in the rest of Europe, run on 220V. American appliances will usually need an adaptor and a transformer to function properly. Usually laptop computers have this built in.

ETIQUETTE & LOCAL CUSTOMS

Visitors from North America or western Europe will likely not notice any special rules of etiquette or behavior beyond good manners and common sense. If visiting a private home, it's a thoughtful idea to bring a small gift of flowers, chocolate, or wine. Always offer to remove your shoes when entering a private home. Show special respect when visiting churches and monasteries: Both men and women should wear shirts that cover their shoulders; men should wear long pants and women long skirts. Women should cover their hair if possible.

HOLIDAYS

Businesses, banks, and museums, as well as many shops and restaurants, shut down on national holidays. Many Romanians traditionally take off for the seashore on May 1, and depending on when the holiday falls, businesses may be closed for more than one day.

January 1, 2—New Year's Day
April—Orthodox Easter
May 1—Labor Day

December 1—National Day
December 25, 26—Christmas

LIQUOR LAWS

The legal age for purchasing or consuming alcoholic beverages is 18. There are no liquor stores per se. Alcoholic beverages are widely available at supermarkets, kiosks, and little grocery stores scattered around cities and towns.

MEDIA

Romania has several nationwide Romanian-language dailies, but only one in English: a thin broadsheet called the *Nine o'Clock*. The *Nine o'Clock* is a good source of local and financial news, and some cultural information, including Bucharest cinema listings. It's published in Bucharest and can be found at hotels and newsstands for 2.5 RON.

There are several English-language publications aimed at visitors. The most helpful is the *In Your Pocket* guide, with separate editions for Bucharest and Braşov. *In Your Pocket* guides are nearly impossible to find at newsstands, but you can sometimes get them in the gift shops of big hotels. They carry a cover price of 8 RON, but hotels often give them away for free. Another helpful public-ation is the bimonthly English-language *Bucureşti, What, Where, When* magazine, which has a nice city map, informative articles, and a good section on practical advice called "Con-cierge." The same group publishes similar magazines in Timişoara and Constanţa.

Larger newsstands and hotel gift shops usually also carry current (or day-old) editions of the *International Herald Tribune*, the *Wall Street Journal Europe*, and the *Financial Times*, as well as recent editions of *Time*, *Newsweek*, and *The Economist*, among other international publications.

Nearly every hotel will offer in-room television with a cable

or satellite connection, often including several English-language stations, though surprisingly not always CNN or BBC World. The most common English-language networks are Discovery, National Geographic TV, MTV, and VH1.

MONEY MATTERS

LEI

The main unit of currency is the *leu*, more often seen in its plural form *lei* (designated officially at banks and exchange offices as "RON"). Banknotes come in den-ominations of 1, 5, 10, 20, 50, 100, and, less commonly, 500 RON. The leu is divided into 100 *bani*, with coins coming in denominations of 5, 10, and 50 bani. Occasionally you may still see prices listed in "old lei," which were phased out in 2007, following a currency reform that set one "new" leu as equal to 10,000 old lei. All of the old lei notes have been withdrawn from circulation and are no longer legal tender. At the time of this writing, $1 was worth 2.6 RON (meaning that 1 RON was equal to about $0.40).

EURO

Romania is not yet formally a member of the European Union's monetary union and does not use the euro, though many hotels for convenience will also quote room rates in euros. Some larger hotels quote exclusively in euros. Euros are now easier to exchange than dollars, and it's not a bad idea to carry around some euros in your wallet for emergencies. At the time of this writing, 1 euro was worth about 3.4 RON (1 RON was equal to about 0.30 euro cents).

EXCHANGE

You can exchange foreign currency at banks and special foreign exchange kiosks at airports, train stations, and hotels around town. Sometimes you may be asked to show a passport to exchange currency, so keep it handy. Banks generally offer better rates and lower commissions than exchange offices. The best places to obtain lei are at ATM machines, which are ubiquitous around cities and towns at train stations and airports. Most will accept any U.S.-issued Visa or MasterCard credit or debit card assigned a PIN code.

CREDIT CARDS
Visa and MasterCard are widely accepted at hotels, restaurants, and shops, although you may have to purchase goods to a certain value before you can use a card. American Express and other cards, including Diner's Club, are only rarely accepted.

OPENING TIMES
Hours for banks, government offices, and state-run institutions are Monday to Friday from 8:30 or 9 a.m. to 4 p.m. Offices are normally open through the noon hour without pause. Museums are often closed on Mondays. Stores and supermarkets have longer hours and are usually open on Saturdays. Expect large grocery stores to be open from 8 a.m. to 8 p.m., Monday to Saturday. Some larger stores and supermarkets will also open on Sundays, though with shorter hours. Nearly every city or town has a few 24-hour convenience stores scattered around where you can buy small items like nonalcoholic or alcoholic beverages, tobacco products, and sweets late at night or on weekends.

RELIGION
Most Romanians are members of the Romanian Orthodox Church, which is similar to its counterparts in Serbia, Bulgaria, Greece, and Russia. Romanians celebrate Christmas on December 25, but observe Orthodox Easter a week later than western churches. Minority religions include a large number of Hungarian Catholics or Protestants in Transylvania and in the western part of the country.

REST ROOMS
Public toilets are improving but are generally not up to Western standards. Public toilets will usually cost around 1 RON to use. A better bet is simply to seek out a nice hotel or restaurant, and utilizing some discretion or perhaps by purchasing a cup of coffee, use the facilities there.

TIME
Romania is in the Eastern European time zone, 7 hours ahead of the East Coast of the United States, 2 hours ahead of London, and 1 hour ahead of continental cities like Paris and Berlin. Romanians observe Daylight Savings Time, setting clocks forward 1 hour in the spring and back 1 hour in the fall, usually on or around the same week as in the United States.

TIPPING
Tipping is not as widespread as in the United States or western Europe, but waiters at better restaurants will still expect a small reward—up to 10 percent of the bill—for good service. For taxi drivers, round up to the nearest leu. For example, if the taxi bill is 7.50 RON, give the driver 8 RON.

TRAVELERS WITH DISABILITIES
Romania's entry into the EU in 2007 means the country will now have to begin the process of making its streets, buildings, and public transportation accessible to the disabled. This will take some time, and at the moment travelers with disabilities will face considerable difficulties in getting around. These include high curbs, few ramps on stairs, and very narrow elevators. In general, the higher priced four- and five-star hotels will have better facilities for the disabled than smaller, older properties.

VISITOR INFORMATION
Romania does not have a widespread network of national tourist offices, so it's up to each city or town to provide tourist facilities. Many cities, like Tulcea, Brașov, Timișoara, and Sighișoara, have helpful tourist offices that can provide local information and even often give guidance on where to stay or where to eat. Look for a large letter "i"—sometimes written in blue—on buildings. Other places, including Bucharest and Cluj-Napoca, exasperatingly have no tourist office or only substandard facilities.

The Romanian National Tourism Office operates an excellent website for general information at www .romaniatourism.com.

EMERGENCIES

CRIME & POLICE
Romania is a relatively safe country, and violent crime is rare. The only real crimes you'll have to worry about are scams, petty theft, and pickpockets. This is especially true at airports and train and bus stations. Refuse any offers of assistance from strangers and keep a close eye on your wallets and belongings. On long-distance train journeys, keep your compartment door closed and don't leave your bags unattended.

The general nationwide emergency number for police, fire, or to request an ambulance is 112. In theory, the operators have been trained to take calls in English.

EMBASSIES
Most major countries maintain diplomatic representation in Bucharest.

United States
Str. Filipescu 26
tel 021 200 3300

Canada
Str. Nicolae Iorga 36
tel 021 307 5000

United Kingdom
Str. Jules Michelet 24
tel 021 312 0303

EMERGENCY NUMBERS
Nationwide police, fire, or ambulance, 112

WHAT TO DO IN A CAR ACCIDENT
In case of a serious accident, dial 112 for an operator who can dispatch the police and an ambulance. Emergency telephones are not common along highways, so you'll probably have to flag down a passing motorist to use a mobile phone or go to a nearby house to make the call.

In case of a minor accident, it's still a good idea to phone the police, who will come to take statements and make a judgment on fault. Be sure to get copies of any police documentation to be used for insurance purposes. Basic insurance is mandatory on all vehicles, including rentals, so any damage should be covered. If in doubt, inquire at the rental agency before taking possession of the vehicle.

HEALTH
Romania is free of serious infectious diseases, including malaria, and poses no particular health hazards that you wouldn't find in any other European country. Tap water is normally safe to drink, but bottled water is preferable and widely available. In the event of an accident or illness, call 112 to request an ambulance. In Bucharest, there are several private clinics that also maintain 24-hour emergency service. Try Puls (tel 973 or 0749 973 973 or 0720 973 973)

or SOS Medical (tel 9761 or 0722 333 000).

Romania has a well-stocked network of pharmacies, identified by a large green cross on the outside of the building. Pharmacists are well trained and can often dispense medications without a doctor's prescription. Most cities and large towns will have at least one 24-hour pharmacy for medical emergencies. These are often listed in newspapers, so ask at your hotel reception if you need to find one. Bucharest has several 24-hour pharmacies. One is Farmacia Verde (Calea Dorobanților 15, tel 0212 301 451).

FURTHER READING

The most interesting, widely available political book is probably *Red Horizons* by Ion Mihai Pacepa, who was the highest-ranking defector of Romania's former security police, the Securitate. His book is a lurid account of the atrocities committed by Nicolae Ceaușescu, his family, and the Ceaușescu regime in the 1970s and 80s.

Dennis Deletant's *Ceaușescu and the Securitate* is an academic treatment of the nefarious Romanian secret police and its role in containing dissent to the Ceaușescu regime.

Helena Drysdale's *Looking for George* is a more personal and absorbing account of life in Romania in the 1980s and how any perceived disloyalty was brutally prosecuted by the government.

As for travel books, four relatively recent works stand out, although none focuses exclusively on Romania. Jason Goodwin's *On Foot to the Golden Horn* recounts the author's walk from Poland's Baltic seacoast to the Turkish city of Istanbul, with long and colorful accounts of part of the journey through Transylvania.

Patrick Leigh Fermor's 1986 travelogue *Between the Woods and the Water*

describes a journey the author made on foot from the Hook of Holland to Constantinople (Istanbul) in the mid-1930s, with much of the book focused on his time in Transylvania.

Claudio Magris's *Danube*, first published in 1986, is a captivating narrative of life along Europe's second longest river (the longest being the Volga), with passages on Romania and the Danube Delta region.

Ruth Ellen Gruber traces the dramatic changes in Jewish history and culture in *Jewish Heritage Travel: A Guide to Eastern Europe*. This up-to-date and definitive guide to past and present Jewish sites blends insight, information, and travel tips you can use.

In addition, there are several historical novels situated in Romania that weave in elements of fact and fiction. Olivia Manning's *The Balkan Trilogy* tells the story of a young English teacher and his wife who travel to Bucharest just as World War II is breaking out. There is also a BBC-TV adaptation of the novel, starring Kenneth Branagh and Emma Thompson.

Count Miklós Bánffy immortalized his family seat in three romantic novels about pre–World War I Transylvania. They have been translated into English under the title of *The Writing on the Wall: The Transylvanian Trilogy*.

More recently, Philip Ó Ceallaigh's *Notes from a Turkish Whorehouse*, in spite of the title, is actually a thoughtful collection of short stories that recounts life in modern-day Bucharest.

Finally, no list of books on Romania would be complete without reference to Bram Stoker's late 19th-century novel, *Dracula*.

HOTELS & RESTAURANTS

HOTELS

Often on websites, Romanian hotels and pensions (*pensiuni*) are evaluated on a sliding star system, which is only a rough approximation of a property's overall quality. It's best to use the ratings with a grain of salt. Stars are awarded according to an objective assessment of a hotel or pension's amenities, including whether rooms come with air-conditioning or telephones in the bathrooms. Generally, standards are higher for hotels than pensions, and a five-star pension is likely to be nothing more than a nice guesthouse that happens to have amenities like in-room satellite television or doors that lock with magnetic key cards. Typically, what's left out are make-or-break qualities like location, cleanliness, noise levels, and atmosphere.

Five-star hotels, such as the big corporate and luxury chains Marriott and Hilton, are excellent for business trips, but don't hesitate to venture out to try the three- and four-star locally owned hotels. Standards have risen in recent years, and pensions are frequently just as comfortable as five-star properties at less than half the price. Sometimes, hotels will offer a mix of four- and three-star rooms in the same building. In this case, ask to see a couple of each. The price of the three-star room may be as much as 50 percent cheaper than the four-star room and lack only something as simple as a hair dryer.

As a rule, give two-star and lower properties a pass. These are often drafty, unreconstructed holdovers from the communist era or smaller hotels that may lack necessary amenities like 24-hour hot water.

Staying at a pension (*pensiune*) or private apartment is something to consider. Pensions are almost always spotlessly clean and usually a better value than hotels. Tourist towns like Sighişoara are packed with drop-dead-gorgeous guesthouses in the $50-a-night category, and unless you can't live without an in-house gift shop or a full-time receptionist, pensions are definitely the way to go. Short-term apartment rentals also represent good value in towns such as Bucharest and Braşov, where hotels tend to be overpriced. In Bucharest you can rent a full three-room apartment in a modern downtown building, with all the conveniences you'd find in a hotel, for about $70 a night.

Homestays are another option and are gaining popularity. Several organizations can connect you with rural home dwellers and working farmers for stays from a few days to a few weeks. Many of these are in the remote, picturesque villages of Maramureş and upper Transylvania. ANTREC (www.antrec.ro) is a national organization that promotes agro-tourism and ecotourism. Its web page is a good point of departure for seeing what's offered. A private agency, DiscoveRomania (www.discoveromania.ro), comes highly recommended. It offers homestays combined with cult-ure outings, as well as walking, hiking, and adventure trips.

There is a wide range of accommodations in the delta, from guesthouses and land-based hotels to *hoteluri plutitoare* (floating hotels), which must be licenced by ABRDD (see pp. 227–229) and can travel from place to place. Many people also camp but may only do so at approved ABRDD sites.

As you travel around Romania, you'll likely be approached at train or bus stations by private individuals renting out rooms in their homes. In Bucharest, be highly wary of any such offer, but elsewhere these are usually legitimate. Still, weigh the pros and cons carefully. These rooms are often much cheaper than

hotels or pensions, but they may be located in unattractive areas away from the sights or require you to share bathroom facilities with the rest of the family.

Not every city in Romania will have a tourist information office, but those that do—including Braşov, Tulcea, Sighişoara, Sibiu, and Timişoara—can offer invaluable help in finding a place to stay. Most keep a list of public and private accomm-odations on hand and are happy to steer you toward properties they think best meet your budget and preferences. Some offices, like the helpful one in Timişoara, will even call around town for you to check on availability.

If you're quoted a higher-than-expected rate for a room, don't be afraid to negotiate. Reception desks and websites will often offer lower rates on weekends (in cities) and may grant discounts for stays longer than a night or two.

RESTAURANTS

Bucharest, Braşov, and to a smaller extent Cluj-Napoca, all have dynamic dining scenes, and you can eat very well in any of these cities. But this restaurant revolution has not spread much

---

HOTELS

Price categories in the listings are based on high-season rates for a double room with bathroom and breakfast (unless otherwise noted):

$$$$$	over $200
$$$$	$150–$200
$$$	$100–$150
$$	$50–$100
$	under $50

RESTAURANTS

Restaurant prices in the listings are categorized as follows (for a three-course meal for one with some wine):

$$$$$	over $40
$$$$	$30–$40
$$$	$20–$30
$$	$10–$20
$	under $10

to the rest of Romania. Most cities and towns will have one or two decent restaurants, and then a clutch of pizzerias, cafés, and smaller, locally owned fast-food places.

In smaller cities and towns, the best option may still be the restaurant in the local hotel. Pizza, too, is always a possibility. Nearly every Romanian city and town, big or small, has at least one decent pizzeria.

The Romanian word for "restaurant" is simply *restaurant*. As restaurants go, however, appearances can be deceiving; and you will often find better meals at rock-bottom prices at humble-looking establishments. You'll also see places to eat that are marked *crama*. These are usually cellar restaurants, offering traditional atmosphere and live music or entertainment.

Going down the food chain, a *cofetărie*—unlike how it sounds—is not really a coffee shop, but more of a pastry shop, where cakes and nonalcoholic beverages are sold. The best place to buy coffee is simply a *café*. These have proliferated in recent years, and most offer excellent espressos and other coffee drinks, usually in association with major Italian coffee brands such as Illy, Lavazza, and Segafredo. Cafés may have some sweets on the menu, or occasionally sandwiches and salads, but are not usually a good choice for a meal. A *cantina* is a self-serve restaurant, usually open only for lunch or early dinner, where you slide your tray down the line and select entrees from behind the counter. These are popular with students and can sometimes be pretty good; prices are so low, they are still reckoned in bani.

At the bottom of the totem pole are the numerous fast-food options. Among the international chains, you'll see McDonald's restaurants in the larger cities, including at Bucharest's Gara de Nord. KFC is also popular, though not quite as common. Among local varieties, Romanians love Middle Eastern–style kebabs and *shawarma* sandwiches (pita bread stuffed with shaved meat and topped with cabbage, onions, sauce, and whatever else is the local habit). You'll also see take-out pizza places, and stands offering the local versions of hamburgers, cheeseburgers, and hot dogs. In the morning you'll see people lined up at windows to buy French-style baked goods, similar to small croissants, stuffed with chocolate, fruit, or cheese. The most ubiquitous chain is Fornetti, and you'll find these everywhere.

The best Romanian street food is doubtlessly *covrigi*—a mix between a soft pretzel and a bagel, served for pennies hot out of the oven and topped with poppy seeds and salt. Not far behind are *gogoși* (usually sold at stands alongside *covrigi*), which are fried dough topped with sugar.

By law, restaurants must offer nonsmoking seating, though in practice this is often ignored. Still, most of the better restaurants should be able to handle any smoking request if asked. Moves to limit smoking in public are making headway (smoking was recently banned in all trains, for example), but progress has been slow.

Dining hours

Most restaurants are open daily from noon until midnight—though on slow nights, kitchens start closing down earlier. Lunch, traditionally the main meal of the day, is served from noon until about 3 p.m. Between 3 p.m. and 6 p.m., there's generally a lull, and although the restaurant will be open, service may be spotty. Dinner is served from around 6 p.m. until closing (try to arrive before 10 p.m. to avoid disappointment). You will usually not need reservations for small parties, but calling ahead is always a good idea.

Ordering

Although many places have English translation on the menus, or may even offer a separate English-language menu, don't hesitate to consult the waiter for help. He may only be able to speak halting English, but will certainly be able to steer you to what looks good in the kitchen and which sides are appropriate for which mains. In general, meals start with soup and a cold plate of cheeses and meats. Salads are sometimes served ahead of the main meal or together with the main course. If you'd like your salad beforehand, let the waiter know.

Vegetarians will have it rough in Romania. While Romanian cuisine features many possible vegetarian options, in practice vegetarians will be limited to salads, eggs, side dishes, and the ubiquitous polenta (cornmeal mush).

Drinks

Romanians brag about the quality of their wines (and quality is definitely on the rise), but they themselves often prefer to drink beer. Most places will have one or two brands on tap and a full range of bottled beers. There's no nationalism when it comes to beer, and traditional Romanian brands such as Ursus and Ciuc sit calmly alongside the ubiquitous foreign names (made locally under license) like Stella Artois, Heineken, Tuborg, and Carlsberg. After dinner, treat yourself to some of the locally made firewater known as *ţuica* or, even stronger, *palinca*—distilled spirits usually made from plums, grapes, or occasionally apricots. The strength and quality varies from region to region, but it can be surprisingly drinkable. It's traditionally taken neat and drunk in one gulp. *Noroc!*

The check & tip

When you want to pay, ask the waiter for the *nota de plat*—the bill. Feel free to double-check the amounts, but it will usually be in order. It's customary to add a few lei to the tab—but not more than 10 percent—to reward good service. If the bill comes

HOTELS & RESTAURANTS

to 46 RON, for example, you might leave a 50 RON note on the table.

CREDIT CARDS
Visa and MasterCard are widely accepted at Romanian restaurants and hotels. Other credit cards, including American Express and Diner's Club, are only rarely accepted. In the listings below, the presence of the credit card icon means an establishment accepts Visa and MasterCard, but not necessarily any other cards.

ORGANIZATION
Hotels and restaurants are listed first by chapter area, then by price category, then alphabetically.

BUCHAREST

Hotel prices in Bucharest are shockingly high given what's offered. One way to cut down on costs without sacrificing on amenities is to rent a short-term apartment. Apartments are available for stays as short as a couple of nights and the rates—$60–80 a night—are less than half what you'd pay in a hotel. One reliable rental agency in Bucharest is UNID (tel 021 320 8080, fax 021 327 5699, www.accommodation.ro).

🏨 ATHÉNÉE PALACE HILTON
$$$$$
STR. EPISCOPEI 1–3
TEL 021 303 3777
FAX 021 315 2121
www.bucharest.hilton.com
Dating from 1914 and widely considered the city's finest hotel, with a perfect central location overlooking Revolution Square, this hotel is everything you'd expect at five stars and this price. Try booking over the hotel's website for lower rates.
ⓘ 272 🅿 ⓢ 🔃 🅂 ☎ 🖥 ⬥

🏨 CASA CAPŞA
$$$$$
CALEA VICTORIEI 37
TEL 021 313 4038

FAX 021 313 5999
www.capsa.ro
The center of Bucharest's historical area, Capşa (see p. 55) has been restored to its original old-world appeal. Previous guests have included many members of several European royal families.
ⓘ 52 🅿 ⓢ 🖥 ⬥

🏨 HOWARD JOHNSON 🍴 GRAND PLAZA HOTEL
$$$$$
5–7 CALEA DOROBANŢILOR
TEL 021 201 5000
FAX 021 201 1888
www.hojoplaza.ro
This is Bucharest's sleekest five-star palace. The design is stylish, high-concept, bare-bones modern throughout. One of the in-house restaurants is Bucharest's best place for sushi.
ⓘ 285 🅿 ⓢ 🔃 🅂 ☎ 🖥 ⬥

🏨 INTERCONTINENTAL HOTEL
$$$$$
B-DUL NICOLAE BALESCU 4
TEL 021 310 2020
FAX 021 312 0486
www.interconti.com/bucharest
Although it does not come cheap, one can expect a luxurious stay at the Intercontinental. Centrally located in downtown Bucharest near the Universităţii Metro stop, it is the city's only high-rise five-star hotel. There are three restaurants on-site.
ⓘ 283 🅿 ⓢ 🔃 🅂 ☎ 🖥 ⬥

🏨 K+K HOTEL ELISABETA
$$$$–$$$$$
STR. SLĂNIC 26
TEL 021 311 8631
FAX 021 311 8632
www.kkhotels.com
This newly designed hotel offers contemporary furnishings in the lobby and other public areas. One advantage is the prospect of big discounts if you book

early. The hotel also offers special "city break" weekend deals.
ⓘ 67 🅿 ⓢ 🔃 🅂 🖥 ⬥

🏨 DALIN
$$$$
B-DUL MĂRĂŞEŞTI 70–72
TEL 021 335 5541
FAX 021 335 6306
www.hoteldalin.ro
A step down in style from similarly priced properties, this smallish, ordinary-looking hotel is commendable for the excellent, central location. The reception will often drop the rack rate to fill rooms, so try to bargain. Also, the hotel offers lower rates if you book over the Internet.
ⓘ 16 🅿 ⓢ 🔃 🅂 ⬥

🏨 DUKE
$$$$
B-DUL DACIA 33
TEL 021 317 4186
FAX 021 317 4189
www.hotelduke.ro
The Duke is a good compromise for the location, comfort, and feel of a five-star hotel at a lower price. It's a short walk from the center and right on one of the main metro stops.
ⓘ 38 🅿 ⓢ 🔃 🅂 ⬥

🏨 IRISA
$$$$
STR. BANU MANTA 24
TEL 021 223 4965
FAX 021 223 4969
A good northern location makes this small, smart hotel an excellent choice. The cute café restaurant is good spot to relax. The apartments are nice, but the doubles are more attractive and offer better value.
ⓘ 37 🅿 🔃 🅂 ⬥

🏨 OPERA
$$$$
STR. BREZOIANU 37
TEL 021 312 4857
FAX 021 312 4858
www.hotelopera.ro
Tucked away in a quiet

neighborhood not far from Bucharest's main city park, this relatively small, traditional hotel is a good choice if you're looking for something central but quiet. The buffet breakfast gets high marks. The hotel drops rates by about 10 percent on weekends.

🏨 DAN
$$$
B-DUL DACIA 125
TEL 021 210 3958
FAX 021 210 3917
www.hoteldan.ro
The Dan is a stylish three-star hotel with small but comfortable rooms. Each is furnished differently, so ask to see a couple before choosing. The rooms at the back of the hotel are quieter. Rates are lowest in midwinter and midsummer.

🏨 REMBRANDT
$$$
STR. SMÂRDAN 11
TEL 021 313 9315
FAX 021 313 9316
www.rembrandt.ro
This boutique hotel in Bucharest's gentrifying Lipscani area offers high-end touches at mid-range prices. It includes an in-house bar, and the city's best clubs and restaurants are just out the front door. You'll have to book far in advance to get a room.
ⓘ 15 🅂 🅂 🅂

🏨🍴 RESIDENCE
$$$
STR. CLUCERULUI 19
TEL 021 223 1978
FAX 021 222 9046
www.residence.com
This new hotel offers simple, luxurious touches at much lower rates. The hotel is designed in the British colonial style, with natural wood furniture and wrought-iron beds. There are two good restaurants on the premises, with a terrace opening out onto the street in good weather.
ⓘ 35 🅿 🅂 🅂 🅂 🅂

SOMETHING SPECIAL

🍴 LOCANTA JARISTEA
Dinner at this elegant interwar restaurant is about not just eating but also reliving a piece of Bucharest's more glorious past. Forget the enormous menu (in Romanian only) and ask the waiter to advise on food and drink. A floorshow of opera, jazz, cabaret, and dance begins around 8:30 p.m. and unfolds over the course of the evening. Sit back and don't plan on leaving anytime soon. The food, mostly traditional grilled meats, and wines are excellent. Reservations are required.
$$$$$
STR. GEORGE GEORGESCU 50–52
TEL 021 335 3338
www.jaristea.ro
🔼 80 🅿 🅂 🅂 🅂

🍴 CASA DOINA
$$$$
B-DUL KISELEFF 4
TEL 021 222 6717
Set in a restored 18th-century villa, Casa Doina is the perfect spot for a special meal out. The restaurant offers well-prepared Romanian and international dishes, including excellent fresh fish and a special "shepherd's appetizer" made from polenta, pieces of bacon, sheep's cheese, and sour cream. Dress is casual but neat, and reservations are recommended.
🔼 60 🅿 🅂 🅂 🅂

🍴 GOLDEN FALCON
$$$
STR. HRISTO BOTEV 18–20
TEL 021 314 2825
With its excellent selection of delicious grilled meats, the Golden Falcon has the best Turkish food in Romania, bar none. The appetizers are wheeled to your table on a cart practically the moment you sit down.
🔼 50 🅂 🅂

🍴 BALTHAZAR
$$–$$$
STR. DUMBRAVA ROŞIE 2
TEL 021 212 1460
Balthazar fuses French and Asian influences and remains a foodie favorite. If you've had your fill of cabbage rolls and polenta, then feast on salmon tartar with mascarpone or dim sum as a starter. Reservations are a must. Dress is stylish casual.
🔼 60 🅿 🅂 🅂 🅂

🍴 AMSTERDAM CAFÉ
$$
STR. COVACI 6
TEL 021 313 7581
This welcoming bistro is popular with students and at the epicenter of the Lipscani revival. The menu has sandwiches, light main dishes, and great coffee drinks.
🔼 50 🅂

🍴 CARU' CU BERE
$$
STR. STAVROPOLEOS 3–5
TEL 021 313 7560
This highly popular restaurant and beer house has a lovingly preserved 19th-century interior. The menu includes the traditional Romanian staples, but the soups are the high point here. Try the sausages and the national specialty ciorbă de burtă (tripe soup). Eat it like the locals do by adding a spoonful of vinegar. In the evenings, there is Romanian folk dancing to further enhance the atmosphere. Reservations are strongly recommended.
🔼 120 🅂 🅂

🍴 CASA VECHE
$$
STR. GEORGE ENESCU 15–17
TEL 021 312 4119
Casa Veche is one of the best pizzerias in town. In summer, the centrally located streetside terrace is packed, so you'd better book in advance.
🔼 60 🅂 🅂

🍴 DRUMEŢUL
$$
STR. COMPOZITORILOR 28
TEL 021 413 3430
This local spot is well away from the trendy center. If you're not planning on traveling onward in Romania and you want to sample some homemade food at real-people prices (and to hear a Romanian folk band), take a taxi out here (about 15–20 RON from the center). The house specialties include the *sarmale* (stuffed cabbage leaves) and chicken livers, among others.
🔲 120 🅿 🚫

🍴 GRAND CAFÉ GALLERON
$$
STR. NICOLAE GOLESCU 18A
TEL 021 312 4565
www.grandcafegalleron.ro
The café offers freshly made sandwiches, extra-large dinner salads, and very good espresso drinks in a beautifully restored building, located just behind the Atheneum. It's also a free Wi-Fi hotspot if you've got a laptop.
🔲 60 🚫 🚫 🚫

🍴 LA MAMA
$$
STR. BARBU VACARESCU 3
TEL 021 212 4086
Wildly popular, La Mama is an informal local chain of restaurants offering excellent Romanian cooking at reasonable prices. Just about everything is good, but the grilled meats are the best. Ask at your hotel for locations.
🔲 75 🅿 🚫 🚫 🚫

■ MUNTENIA

TÂRGOVIŞTE

🏨 DÂMBOVIŢA
$$
B-DUL LIBERATĂŢII 1
TEL/FAX 0245 213 370, 0245 213 374

www.hoteldambovita.ro
One of the few hotels in Târgovişte, the Hotel Dâmboviţa also offers apartments with terraces, which provide lovely views over the city. Rooms are basic, but comfortable. It also holds 3 restaurants and 2 bars.
🛈 80 🅿 🚫 🚫 🚫
🚫 Visa only

🍴 KAROLINE TOURISTIC COMPLEX
$$
ALEEA MĂNĂSTIRII
TEL 0245 217 975
www.karoline.ro
Dine in a garden-like atmosphere with lush green decorations and plenty of shade. This tourist complex is situated near Mănăstirea Dealu and provides a convenient place to stop for a meal before or after visiting the historic landmark. Indoor/outdoor seating available.
🔲 140 🅿 🚫
🚫 MasterCard only

CURTEA DE ARGES

🏨 POSADA
$$
B-DUL BASARABILOR 27–29
TEL 0248 721 451
Located in the center of town, this hotel is great for those traveling on a budget. There's also easy access to all of the local sights and attractions.
🛈 115 🅿 🚫 🚫

SINAIA

🏨 ECONOMAT
$$
2 PELESULUI
TEL 0244 311 151
FAX 0244 311 150
http://hoteleconomat.apps.ro
Built in the same Saxon style as Castel Peleş, this hotel is in view of the castle and the picturesque scenery surrounding it. The Hotel Economat also has its own restaurant and is in reach of

HOTELS
Price categories in the listings are based on high-season rates for a double room with bathroom and breakfast (unless otherwise noted):
$$$$$ over $200
$$$$ $150–$200
$$$ $100–$150
$$ $50–$100
$ under $50

RESTAURANTS
Restaurant prices in the listings are categorized as follows (for a three-course meal for one with some wine):
$$$$$ over $40
$$$$ $30–$40
$$$ $20–$30
$$ $10–$20
$ under $10

many of Sinaia's spas and historic sights.
🛈 34 🅿 Fee 🚫

🏨 FLOARE DE COLT
$$
PLEVNEI STR. 10
TEL 0244 311 410
www.montania.ro/en_vile_FLC.htm
Only a five-minute walk from Castel Peleş, this villa offers a spectacular view of the Bucegi Mountains. Three apartments are available for reservations, as is the entire villa.
🛈 6 🅿

🍴 TAVERNA SARBULUI
$$$$
CALEA CODRULUI
TEL 0244 314 400
FAX 0244 314 348
http://tavernasarbului.ro
Feast on a traditional Serbian meal with veal or pork, served with fresh vegetables from the local markets. While you dine in the cozy atmosphere, listen to the sounds of the orchestra entertaining guests. There's seating inside, as well as on the terrace with views of the rolling green hills.
🔲 700 🅿 🚫

CAMPULUNG MUSCEL

CASA ANGLIA
$-$$
14 PARCUL MIREA
TEL 0788 128 617
Set in a garden at the foothills of the Carpathian Mountains, this guesthouse offers an at-home feel. It was built in 2005 and the owners offer a variety of accommodation that include airport pickup, breakfast, lunch, and dinner. Not available for families with children.
[i] 4 P S Y

OLTENIA

TÂRGU JIU

ANNA
$$
B-DUL ECATERINA TEODOROIU 17
TEL/FAX 0253 206 333, 0253 206 334
www.hotel-anna.ro
With a simple and slightly modern touch, this hotel in the heart of Târgu Jiu offers a pleasant atmosphere and accommodating staff. The restaurant has a soft ambiance. Good for couples or small groups.
[i] 15 P S ⊗

CRAIOVA

HELIN
$$$
CALEA BUCURESTI U10
TEL/FAX 0251 467 171, 0251 467 172
www.helinstrading.com
One of the newest four-star hotels in Craiova, Hotel Helin offers a wide range of accommodations from single/double rooms to a studio. If participating in the nightlife is of interest, there is also a nightclub located inside the hotel.
[i] 25 P ⊖ S ⊗

REX
$$

STR. FAGARASI 3A
TEL 0351 404 637, 0723 204 039
TEL/FAX 0251 416 328
www.restaurantrex.ro
Indulge in another part of Romanian culture through its traditional meals, specifically Transylvanian cuisine. The atmosphere here successfully combines the modern look with a rustic quality.
⊞ 300 P S

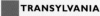 TRANSYLVANIA

CLUJ-NAPOCA

OPERA PLAZA
$$$$
STR. G-RAL TRAIAN MOŞOIU 10–12
TEL 0364 403 600
FAX 0364 403 607
www.operaplaza.ro
This nicely renovated former candy factory opened its doors in 2006 as Cluj's only five-star hotel. The rooms are unexciting, yet decently sized with all the modern conveniences. The indoor pool and fitness rooms are the best around. The hotel's location is ideal, in a quieter part of town, yet just 5–10 minutes by foot from central Piaţa Unirii.
[i] 52 P S ⊖ S ⊠ Y ⊗

PENSION DÉJÀ VU
$$$
STR. ION GHICA 2
TEL 0264 354 941
FAX 0264 354 939
www.deja-vu.ro
Déjà Vu is the most attractive of several pensions around town, though the location—a 20-minute walk from the center—is a big drawback. This pension is more popular with visiting businessmen than with tourists.

AGAPE
$$-$$$
STR. IULIU MANIU 6
TEL/FAX 0264 406 523
www.hotelagape.ro

This upscale hotel is operated by the Hungarian Catholic Church, which renovated the 19th-century neoclassic building. The spotless rooms (most nonsmoking) on the second and third floors open onto an enclosed courtyard and are roomier than the fourth-floor attic rooms. The hotel complex includes eight restaurants.
[i] 64 P S ⊖ S ⊗

FULLTON
$$
STR. SEXTIL PUŞCARIU 10
TEL 0264 597 766
FAX 0264 597 898
www.fullton.ro
Small and trendy, this boutique hotel appeals mainly to visiting businessmen. Each room is different and priced according to room and bed size. The corridors are cramped, but the rooms on upper floors are slightly larger and airier.
[i] 12 P S ⊗

MELODY-CENTRAL
$$
PIAŢA UNIRII 29
TEL 0264 597 465
FAX 0264 597 468
www.centralmelody.com
Judging from the faded, neoclassic exterior, this centrally located hotel looks like it's seen better days, but the inside turns out to be clean and well run. Rooms are priced according to size, so ask to see a couple before deciding.
[i] 60 P S ⊖ S ⊗

METEOR
$$
B-DUL EROILOR 29
TEL/FAX 0264 591 060
www.hotelmeteor.ro
The Meteor is an acceptable budget option for the central location and reasonably priced rooms. The rooms, furnished in a nondescript contemporary style, have white walls and big double beds. The bathrooms could use an upgrade, but they're all clean.
[i] 30 P S ⊗

HOTELS & RESTAURANTS

VILA EUNICIA
$$
STR. EMILE ZOLA 2
TEL 0264 431 950
FAX 0264 594 067
www.vilaeunicia.ro
On a quiet side street just a stone's throw away from the central square, this intimate, family-run pension offers small but well-appointed rooms, with clean carpets, hardwood beds, and built-in armoires. The intimate public areas are sensibly nonsmoking, and there's free Wi-Fi.
🛈 9 ⬡

HANUL URSITA
$
VALEA NEGRILESEI 860
ALBA
TEL 0723 230 790
www.ursita.ro
Tucked in the Apuseni Mountains in the village Bucium, this converted farmhouse has self-catering rooms. You can order meals from local village women, who will cook traditional meals and bring them to you.
🛈 10

HUBERTUS
$$$–$$$$
B-DUL 21 DECEMBRIE 22
TEL 0264 596 743
Offering one of the handsomest tables in town, Hubertus is ideal for a quiet dinner or a family night out. The theme is game, but the menu runs from international standards like steaks and seafood to original takes on traditional Romanian specialties. The wine list is the best in town, and the waiters are happy to advise.
⬒ 60 🅿 ⬡ ⬡ ⬡

MATEI CORVIN
$$$
STR. MATEI CORVIN 3
TEL 0264 597 496
For years, this was widely regarded as Cluj's top restaurant, and it's still one of the best. Hungarian dishes predominate. Order the fabulous "country goulash," a thick stew of beef, potatoes, pasta dumplings, and peppers. Reservations are strongly recommend for both lunch and dinner.
🛈 35 ⬡ ⬡ ⬡

ERNESTO
$$–$$$
PIAȚA UNIRII 23
TEL 0264 596 909
This romantic cellar restaurant offers classical French cuisine with Edith Piaf belting out tunes in the background. A buffet lunch priced at 20 RON ($8) offers fresh salads, soups, cheeses, and three mains, all cooked to order.
🛈 40 ⬡ ⬡ ⬡

HANUL CETĂȚII
$$
STR. FORTĂREȚEI 6
TEL 0264 594 091
Located close to the central Piața Unirii, this restaurant offers excellent traditional Romanian cuisine. The "innkeeper's stew"—a thick and flavorful mush of marinated beef and vegetables served with a side of mashed potatoes—is especially good. The restaurant is small, so reservations are a must, particularly in the evening.
⬒ 20 ⬡ ⬡

CREMA
$
PIAȚA UNIRII 25
TEL 0723 161 002
This trendy café just off the main square, Piața Unirii, serves the best coffee and fresh juice in town. Ignore the attitude and gilded decor, and simply enjoy your drink. There's not much in the way of food, except for some sweets and ice cream desserts.
⬒ 40 ⬡ ⬡ ⬡

FLOWERS
$
PIAȚA UNIRII 24
Next door to Crema, this student-oriented teahouse is more laid-back, though still style conscious. The teas are great; the coffee is nothing special. Flowers is a free Wi-Fi hot spot.
⬒ 25

BISTRIȚA

COROANA DE AUR
$$–$$$
PIAȚA PETRU RAREȘ 4
TEL 0263 232 470
FAX 0263 232 667
www.hotel-coroana-de-aur.ro
This decent, modern hotel is probably the best in-town option. In Bram Stoker's fictitious *Dracula*, the protagonist, Jonathan Harker, spends a night here on his way to complete a property deal at Dracula's castle on the Borgo Pass (Borgo is the Hungarian name for the Tihuța Pass). In the hotel's restaurant, you can eat a "robber steak" just as Harker does in the novel.
🛈 110 🅿 ⬒ ⬡

CASTEL DRACULA
$$
PIATRA FÂNTÂNELE
TIHUȚA PASS
TEL 0263 264 010
FAX 0263 266 119

www.hotelcasteldracula.bn.ro
It's not actually Dracula's castle, but a modern, three-star hotel pitched near the mountain site where Stoker placed his fictionalized castle. Since it's outside Bistrița, you'll need a taxi or your own wheels to get here. The rooms have nice period furnishings. The view from the hotel is lovely, and you can dine in the atmospheric wine cellar.
🛈 62 🅿 🛗 🗝

SIBIU

Sibiu has two decent tourist information offices that can help find accommodations. The municipal Tourist Information Center (Str. Samuel Brukenthal 2, tel 0269 208 913, fax 0269 208 811, www.sibiu.ro) has a list of hotels and is a good place to pick up maps of the area and leaflets for smaller pensions. Kultours (Piața MICĂ 16, tel/fax 0269 216 854, www.kultours.ro) is a youthful, energetic travel agency that will find and book rooms for you, as well as rent cars and bikes and organize sightseeing tours.

🏨 CONTINENTAL
$$$
CALEA DUMBRĂVII 2–4
TEL 0269 218 100
FAX 0269 210 125
www.continentalhotels.ro
This is a refurbished communist-era high-rise that offers standard-sized rooms and all of the usual three-star amenities at a moderate price. The rooms are priced as "standard" and "executive," with the latter offering in-room air-conditioning (a must during the summer) and robes and slippers.
🛈 182 🅿 🚭 🛗 🗝 🗝

🏨 ÎMPĂRATUL ROMANILOR
$$$
STR. N. BĂLCESCU 2–4
TEL 0269 216 500
FAX 0269 213 278
www.imparatulromanilor.ro

This renovated 18th-century hotel, with period furnishings in the lobby and the rooms, is one of the nicest places near the historic center. Many rooms occupy two levels, a sleeping chamber above and a sitting room below. Some of the rooms are being remodeled, so ask to see several before choosing.
🛈 93 🅿 🚭 🗝 🗝 🗝

🏨 PALACE
$$$
STR. PĂDUREA DUMBRAVA 1
TEL 0269 218 086
FAX 0269 242 222
www.hotelpalace.ro
The Palace is a very nice hotel, though the location (3 miles/5 km outside of town along a busy highway) is a drawback. That said, the standard doubles are enormous, and some even come with fully separate sitting rooms. The furnishings and carpets are nothing short of luxurious.
🛈 25 🅿 🗝 🚭 🗝 🗝 🗝

🏨 CASA LUXEMBURG
$$
PIAȚA MICĂ 16
TEL/FAX 0269 216 854
www.kultours.ro
This clean, historic guesthouse offers plain rooms with no real amenities or services to speak of. Nevertheless, to be this close to the historic core at this price means you'll have to book well in advance.
🛈 12 🗝 🗝 🗝

🏨 GASTHOF CLARA
🍴 **$$**
STR. RÂULUI 24
TEL 0269 222 914
FAX 0269 206 071
www.gasthofclara.ro
This upscale pension, situated on a busy street across the river from the old town, is about a 10–15 minute walk from the main square. The spotless, warm-hued rooms have modern furniture. The on-site German restaurant is a good choice for a meal, even if

you aren't staying here.
🛈 6 🅿 🗝 🗝 🗝

🏨 PENSION DANIEL
$$
STR. MĂSARILOR 1
TEL 0269 243 924
FAX 0269 215 197
www.ela-hotels.ro
The Daniel's rooms are light and airy, furnished in a mix of modern and 19th-century styles. The location is ideal, just across from stone steps leading into the old town.
🛈 11 🅿 🗝 🗝

🏨 PENSION PODUL MINCIUNILOR
$–$$
STR. AZILULUI 1
TEL 0269 217 259
www.ela-hotels.ro
Plain, but probably the nicest of several two-star pensions in town. The rooms are clean, and it's relatively close to the center.
🛈 7 🗝

🍴 CRAMA SIBIUL VECHI
$$–$$$
STR. PAPIU ILARIAN 3
TEL 0269 210 461
This atmospheric, Transylvania-themed cellar restaurant is an absolute must. Try the "shepherd's bag," a grilled chicken breast stuffed with cheese and sausage and trussed up to make a little sack. Book ahead.
🍴 60 🗝 🗝

🍴 LA TURN
$$–$$$
PIAȚA MARE 1
TEL 0269 213 985
La Turn is a busy grill restaurant right off the main square that specializes in traditional soups, as well as grilled meats and vegetables. Here you can choose from three national soup favorites: tripe, pork, and meatball. Pork ribs are a house specialty.
🍴 135 🗝 🗝 🗝

🍴 LA PIAZZETTA
$$

PIAȚA MICĂ 15
TEL 0269 230 879
This Italian pizzeria serves the best pizzas in Sibiu and possibly all of Romania. Only 25 seats, so reservations are necessary on weekends.
🔧 25 🅂 🅰

🍴 IL CAPPUCCINO
$
PIAȚA MICĂ 14
TEL 0788 299 807
Not far from the Casa Luxemburg, this small Italian café serves excellent coffees and small sweets and desserts.
🔧 20 🅂

SIGHIȘOARA

Sighișoara has some truly beautiful private pensions, so if you don't require the full services of a hotel, this is one place to take the guesthouse option. Unusually for Romania, breakfast is usually not included in the price of pension rooms, but must be ordered separately for about $6–8 a person. Aside from the choices below, the tourist office (Str. Octavian Goga 8, tel 0265 770 415) maintains a list of hotels and guesthouses and can help find a room. You may need the tourist office's services if you turn up in town in July or August without a room reservation in hand.

🏨 KORONA
$$$
STR. ZAHARIA BOIU 12–14
TEL 0265 770 480
FAX 0265 770 483
www.hotelkorona.ro
This is probably the best of the standard hotels in Sighișoara in terms of service and facilities, but you'll sacrifice location and charm, since the hotel lies outside the citadel. You'll need to take a taxi to get here from the train or bus station.
🛏 30 🅿 🅂 🔁 🅂 📺 🅰

🏨 SIGHIȘOARA
🍴 $$–$$$
STR. ȘCOLII 4–6

TEL 0265 771 000
FAX 0265 777 788
www.sighisoarahotels.ro
Sighișoara's best-known hotel is a rambling affair right in the center of the citadel. The rooms are a bit of a disappointment. Faded carpets and worn-out spreads and drapes cry out for an update. The cellar restaurant is considered by some to be the best in the city.
🛏 32 🅿 🅂 🅰

🏨 CASA CU CERB
$$
STR. ȘCOLII 1
TEL 0265 774 625
FAX 0265 777 349
www.casacucerb.ro
This lovingly reconstructed pension has a good restaurant and is just on the citadel's main square. The rooms are bright and clean, with hardwood floors and wrought-iron beds. Britain's Prince Charles stayed here in 2002. Book early for summer since rooms fill up fast.
🛏 10 🅿 🅰

🏨 CASA EPOCA
$$
STR. TÂMPLARILOR 4
TEL 0265 773 232
FAX 0265 772 237
www.casaepoca.com
A rare treat, this 17th-century house has been remodeled so that each of the ten rooms is different. Most rooms sport furnishings from the time the house was built, with drop-dead-gorgeous views over the town and surrounding hills.
🛏 10 🅿 🅰

🏨 CASA SĂSEASCĂ
$–$$
PIAȚA CETĂȚII 12
TEL/FAX 0265 772 400
www.casasaseasca.com
Casa Săsească is a decent choice because of the prime citadel location. The walls are painted in the Saxon peasant style. The rooms and baths are spotless. Breakfast is not included in the room price, but

HOTELS
Price categories in the listings are based on high-season rates for a double room with bathroom and breakfast (unless otherwise noted):

$$$$$	over $200
$$$$	$150–$200
$$$	$100–$150
$$	$50–$100
$	under $50

RESTAURANTS
Restaurant prices in the listings are categorized as follows (for a three-course meal for one with some wine):

$$$$$	over $40
$$$$	$30–$40
$$$	$20–$30
$$	$10–$20
$	under $10

available for about 20 RON per person.
🛏 9 🅿 🅰

🏨 CLAUDIU
$–$$
STR. ILARIE CHENDI 28
TEL/FAX 0265 779 882
www.hotel-claudiu.com
Rather ordinary and minimal, this family-run hotel is in a quiet area of the new city. If other places are full, the spotless rooms here are perfectly adequate. The lower-level rooms are cooler in summer. The in-house restaurant gets high marks.
🛏 16 🅿 🅰

🏨 GUESTHOUSE CRISTINA
$
STR. COJOCARILOR 1
TEL 0744 119 211
Don't be surprised if Cristina, the owner of this small, basic family home in the citadel, approaches you in the train station offering rooms. In July and August, she might just be a lifesaver. It's not much, but it's clean, comfortable, and close to the action.
🛏 5

PENSION VILA FRANKA
$
STR. I DEC. 1918 1
TEL 0265 771 515
FAX 0265 775 901
www.sighisoara-tourism.com
At this, the most attractive pension outside the citadel area, the decor feels slightly dated, but the rooms and baths are clean and cozy. Breakfast is not included. Try the breakfast at the nearby Rustica restaurant (see below) after 9 a.m.
🚹 10 🅿 🏧

CASA VLAD DRACUL
$$–$$$
STR. COSITORARILOR 5
TEL 0265 773 304
This attractive, tourist-oriented restaurant occupies the corner house in the citadel where Dracula was allegedly born in 1431. The Dracula theme is ever present on the menu, but the food is genuinely good.
🍴 70 🆒 🆓 🏧

CONCORDIA
$$
PIAȚA HERMANN OBERTH
Conveniently located near the steps leading up to the citadel, this new and trendy pizza and pasta joint is aimed at Sighișoara's upwardly mobile. The pies are better than average.
🍴 40 🆒 🏧

RUSTICA
$–$$
STR. I DEC. 1918 5
TEL 0742 012 889
Perfect for a quick bite, Rustica is a great traditional restaurant in the newer part of the city. The *sarmale* (stuffed cabbage leaves) are excellent, and served with a healthy dollop of polenta.
🍴 40 🆒

TÂRGU MUREȘ

The provincial capital of Târgu Mureș (sometimes printed on maps as Tîrgu Mureș) unexpectedly has two of the country's nicest hotels, either of which would make an excellent stopover. If you arrive in summer and are looking for where the locals hang out, tell the taxi driver to take you to "Weekend," a generic name for a clutch of outdoor restaurants and bars perched along the banks of the Mureș River outside of town.

CONCORDIA
$$$–$$$$
PIAȚA TRANDAFIRILOR 45
TEL 0265 260 602
FAX 0265 269 666
www.hotelconcordia.ro
It's an eye-opener to see a hip designer hotel in this most workaday of Transylvanian towns. The rooms are designed with a 60s minimalist aesthetic. The design quality extends to top-of-the-line amenities, including beautifully tiled bathrooms with extra-thick white cotton towels. The hotel has free Wi-Fi throughout, including in the trendy streetside bar.
🚹 34 🅿 🆒 🆓 🆒 ☎ 🎮 🏧

PRESIDENT
$$$
STR. GHEORGHE DOJA 231
TEL 0365 410 420
FAX 0365 410 418
www.presidenthotel.ro
The location, about 3 miles (5 km) from town along the main road to Cluj-Napoca, makes it close to the bus station, but don't consider staying here unless you have your own wheels or are willing to pay for cabs every time you want to go into town. That said, it has enormous, regally appointed rooms with all conveniences imaginable, including new Jacuzzis in the bathrooms.
🚹 70 🅿 🆒 🆓 🆒 🎮 🏧

CONTINENTAL
$$–$$$
PIAȚA TEATRULUI 6
TEL 0265 250 416
FAX 0265 250 116
www.continentalhotels.ro
The Continental is a decent, cheaper alternative to the President and Concordia, with a nice location just a couple minutes' walk from the central square. The rooms are small but clean and comfortable.
🚹 110 🅿 🆒 🆓 🆒 🎮 🏧

TRANSILVANIA
$$
PIAȚA TRANDAFIRILOR 46
TEL/FAX 0265 265 616
Ideally located right on the central square, Transilvania is in the midst of a renovation. Many of the formerly two-star rooms have been upgraded to three and four stars. The renovated rooms have comfortable double beds and sleek modern baths. The older, two-star rooms are an acceptable budget option.
🚹 120 🆒 🆓 🆒 🏧

VILLA HELVETIA
$$
STR. BORSOS TAMÁS 13
TEL. 0265 216 954
FAX 0265 215 099
www.villahelvetia.ro
As ordinary pensions go, the rooms here are expectedly plain, but clean. There's an in-house restaurant and little bar for after hours. The location is good, about a 10-minute walk from the central square, although you'll need to take a taxi if you arrive from the bus or train station.
🚹 11 🅿 🆒 🆒 🏧

PENSION TEMPO
$–$$
STR. MORII 27
TEL/FAX 0265 213 552
www.tempo.ro
You'll need a taxi to find this hidden family-run pension about a half-mile (1 km) from the center of town. The rooms are plain but clean and quiet. The pension also has one of the city's best restaurants on the premises, Tempo Laci Csarda (see below).
🚹 12 🅿 🏧

🆒 Nonsmoking 🆓 Elevator 🆒 Air-conditioning 🏊 Indoor/🏊 Outdoor pool 🎮 Gym 🏧 Credit cards **KEY**

🍴 TEMPO LACI CSARDA
$$–$$$
STR. MORII 27
TEL 0265 213 552
Reflecting Târgu Mureş's
Hungarian history, this
restaurant, which is connected
to the Pension Tempo (see
above), features mostly well-
done Hungarian dishes like
chicken *paprikas*, served in a
traditional, rustic atmosphere.
Try the *gombot cu prune* for
dessert, plum-filled fruit
dumplings sprinkled with sugar
and cinnamon.
🚻 120 🅿 🚭 ❄ ⬛

🍴 PIZZERIA LA TEA
$
STR. PAPIU ILARIAN 1
TEL 0265 212 244
This local pizzeria does both a
thriving in-house and take-out
business. The informal dining
room is not a place for that
romantic candlelit dinner. It's
better suited to a fast, no-frills
lunch or dinner.
🚻 20 🅿 🚭 ❄

BRAŞOV

🏨 ARO PALACE
$$$$
B-DUL EROILOR 27
TEL 0268 478 800
FAX 0268 478 889
www.aro-palace.ro
This art deco landmark is
slowly being refurbished to
its once glittering state. It's
the city's best hotel by a wide
margin. The enormous and
elegant glass lobby could easily
hold a high school marching
band. However, for all the
amenities, the daily rates still
feel overpriced. Check the
web page for weekend and
holiday deals.
ⓘ 200 🅿 🚭 ❄ 🛗 ⬛

🏨 CASA HEIDI
$$$$
BRAN
TEL 0235 256 228
FAX 0257 797 40 43
www.casa-heidi.com
The nightly rate covers rent for
the entire villa—three double

bedrooms and two attic
bedrooms. Ideal for families
traveling together, this cozy
guesthouse is set in the
picturesque village of Bran
within walking distance of
Dracula's Castle.
ⓘ 5 🅿 🚭 ⬛

🏨 AMBIENT
$$$
STR. IULIU MANIU 27A
TEL 0268 470 856
FAX 0268 474 210
www.hotelambient.ro
Though just a short 5 to 10-
minute walk from the old
town, this newish hotel is in
an unattractive area of the
new town. The suites and
apartments come with Jacuzzi
tubs; the standard singles and
doubles have showers only.
Friendly, English-speaking
staff and a high standard of
cleanliness offset the stark,
simply furnished rooms and
grim location.
ⓘ 39 🅿 🚭 ❄ 🛗 🍴
⬛

🏨 LA RESIDENZA
$$$
STR. GRĂDINARILOR 18
TEL 0268 473 377
FAX 0268 473 378
www.residenza.ro
One of the most beautiful
pensions in Braşov, La
Residenza has elegant rooms
in a quiet 1930s villa about
a 10-minute walk from the
old town. Most rooms have
a view onto Tampa Mountain;
some have a small terrace
overlooking the garden.
The bountiful breakfast is
a major draw.
ⓘ 7 🅿 🚭 ❄ 🛗 ⬛

🏨 PENSION CURTEA BRAŞOVEANA
$$–$$$
STR. BAILOR 16
TEL 0268 472 336
FAX 0268 472 145
www.curteabrasoveana.ro
This charming and well-run
pension has 14 motel-like
rooms all facing a small garden
out the back. The location, in

the atmospheric, pleasantly
tumbledown neighborhood
of Fichei just a couple minutes'
walk from the historic core, is
a big plus.
ⓘ 14 🅿 ⬛

🏨 CAPITOL
$$
B-DUL EROILOR 19
TEL 0268 418 920
FAX 0268 472 999
www.aro-palace.ro
A communist-era, concrete
high-rise hides a perfectly
decent three-star hotel with
clean, modern rooms and an
excellent location, just on the
edge of the old town. This is
a nice balance between price,
amenities, and location.
ⓘ 184 🅿 🚭 ❄ 🛗 ⬛

🏨 COROANA
$$
B-DUL REPUBLICII 62
TEL 0268 477 448
FAX 0268 418 469
www.aro-palace.ro
This badly faded, once elegant,
turn-of-the-century hotel
might be for you if you
favor the Marlene Dietrich
atmosphere and can tolerate
the threadbare carpets and
quirky plumbing.

ⓘ 80 🅿 🔁 🅢

🏨 PENSION AMALFI
$$
STR. PAUL RICHTER 7
TEL/FAX 0268 511 883
www.pensiunea-amalfi.ro
This small, private house has
five individual apartments, each
with its own bedroom, bath,
living area, and kitchen. The
location couldn't be better, on
a quiet alley behind the Black
Church.
ⓘ 5

🏨 PENSION AMBIENT
$$
STR. IULIU MANIU 62B
TEL 0268 410 622
FAX 0268 410 387
www.pensiuneambient.ro
The Pension Ambient is cozier,
quieter, and slightly cheaper
than the hotel of the same
name. All rooms have free
Internet access.
ⓘ 18 🅿

🏨 TRANSYLVANIAN CASTLE
$$
MICLOŞOARA
TEL 0742 202 586
FAX 0267 314 088
www.transylvaniancastle.com
Located in a village north of
Braşov, Count Kálnoky's
restored, 19th-century Saxon
guesthouses are furnished
exclusively in antique
Transylvanian furniture. The
main 16th-century castle is also
a bed-and-breakfast, serving
Transylvanian cuisine and
offering a variety of culture,
nature, and hiking tours.
🅢

🍴 COLIBA HAIDUCILOR
$$$
POIANA BRAŞOV
TEL 0268 262 137
This tavern-style restaurant is
one of the best known in the
country, and no visit to Poiana
Braşov would be complete
without a stop here to sample
some traditional Romanian
dishes in a hunting lodge
atmosphere. Vegetarians are
likely to be put off by the
animal skins on the walls
and the lamb soup, served in
half a lamb's skull. Reservations
are a must.
ⓘ 100 🅿 🅢 🅢

🍴 ŞURA DACILOR
$$$
POIANA BRAŞOV
TEL 0268 262 327
This large, family-run
restaurant specializes in
evoking the history of the
Dacians with traditional fare
and folk music. You can choose
from contemporary dishes or
entrees that go back centuries
like *Dacian chunk*, which is
oven-baked polenta served
with sour cream.
🔁 300 🅢

🍴 BELLA MUZICA
$$–$$$
PIAŢA SFATULUI 19
TEL 0268 477 946
Bella Muzica is a cellar
restaurant that serves an
eclectic mix of international
and Romanian dishes in a
secluded, intimate setting. First
the waiter brings a
complimentary shot of
palinca—high-octane plum
brandy. You'll get three
menus—one for food, one for
drinks, and the last for music.
You'll need reservations.
🔁 40 🅢 🅢 🅢

🍴 CASA HIRSCHER
$$–$$$
PIAŢA SFATULUI 12–14
TEL 0268 410 533
www.casahirscher.ro
Casa Hirscher sets the mood
with romantic candlelit tables,
excellent service, and an Italian
menu that runs the gamut
from fresh salads to pastas to
excellently rendered chicken,
beef, and fish.
🔁 54 🅢 🅢

🍴 ŞIRUL VĂMII
$$–$$$
STR. MURESENILOR 18
TEL 0268 477 725
Popular with locals for its
innovative takes on traditional
dishes, the space is casual but
intimate. Try the Viennese-
inspired boiled beef with
horseradish. End the meal with
the "horn of plenty," a fresh
pastry, stuffed with fruit and
cream and covered with
chocolate.
🔁 45 🅢 🅢 🅢

🍴 DEANE'S IRISH PUB
$$
B-DUL REPUBLICII 19
TEL 0268 411 767
www.deanes.ro
Many rave about this place,
but truth be told, the food is
average. The real draw may be
the Irish "fry up" breakfast. It's
also a good spot to meet local
expats, listen to live music, and
sing karaoke.
🔁 50 🅢 🅢

🍴 LA FIFI
$
STR. PAUL RICHTER 4
TEL 0722 581 638
Tucked away from the crowds
and popular with students, this
small, intimate café is perfect
for a drink.
🔁 20

▮ BANAT & CRIŞANA

TIMIŞOARA

The unofficial capital of western
Romania has a large number of
hotels and pensions to suit all
budgets. Oddly, the better places
tend to be located outside the
center of town, though there
are a couple of acceptable in-
town options.
    If you turn up without
a room, consult the friendly
staff at the Tourist Information
Center (Str. Alba Iulia 2, tel/fax
0256 437 973).

🏨 LA RESIDENZA
$$$–$$$$
STR. INDEPENDENŢEI 14
TEL 0256 401 080
FAX 0256 401 079
www.laresidenza.com
This Timişoara town house is

HOTELS & RESTAURANTS

simply one of the nicest and most welcoming hotels in the country. The pluses include beautifully furnished rooms, inviting public areas, high-end fitness equipment, and a sauna. An outdoor pool and lush garden round out the charms. The small number of rooms make advance booking an absolute must.

🛏 20 🅿 🔲 🔲 🏊 📺 🚫

🏨 BEST WESTERN AMBASSADOR
$$$
STR. MANGALIA 1–3
TEL 0256 306 880
FAX 0256 306 883
www.ambassador.ro

After a look at the stately lobby and reception area, filled with 19th- and early 20th-century period chairs and works of art, the plainly furnished rooms are a bit of a letdown. On the other hand, everything is squeaky clean, and the pool and patio are nice places to while away a hot afternoon.

🛏 40 🅿 🔲 🔲 🔲 🏊 📺 🚫

🏨 NH TIMIȘOARA
$$$
STR. PESTALOZZI 1/A
TEL 0256 407 440
FAX 0256 407 441
www.nh-hotels.com

The NH chain is an excellent choice for anyone looking for a modern, well-run hotel at relatively moderate prices. Breakfast is not included. The location is just outside the historic center, about 15 minutes by foot from Piața Victoriei.

🛏 80 🅿 🔲 🔲 🔲 📺 🚫

🏨 NORTH STAR CONTI-NENTAL RESORT
$$$
B-DUL REVOLUȚIEI 3
TEL 0256 494 144
FAX 0256 204 038
www.hotelcontinental.ro

In spite of the name, this hotel is not a member of the Continental chain, and not really a resort, either. Rather, it's a well-maintained, in-town, high-rise hotel with clean, ordinary-looking rooms and business-oriented amenities.

🛏 164 🅿 🔲 🔲 🔲 🏊 📺 🚫

🏨 SAVOY
🍴 $$$
SPL. TUDOR VLADIMIRESCU 2
TEL 0256 249 900
FAX 0256 275 500
www.hotelsavoy-tm.com

About a 10-minute walk from Piața Victoriei, this boutique hotel is housed in a 1930s, art deco villa. The rooms in the newly built wing at the back are quieter, but the front rooms are quirkier and more interesting. There is also an excellent on-site restaurant.

🛏 55 🅿 🔲 🔲 🔲 📺 🚫

🏨 TIMIȘOARA
$$–$$$
STR. MĂRĂȘEȘTI 1–3
TEL 0256 498 851
FAX 0256 499 450

Acceptably clean and in-town, this high-rise hotel has snug, well-appointed rooms, marred slightly by some wear and tear in the carpets and drapes. The hotel offers decent breakfasts.

🛏 152 🅿 🔲 🔲 🔲 🚫

🏨 CENTRAL
$$
STR. LENAU 6
TEL 0256 490 091
FAX 0256 490 096
www.hotel-central.ro

Just off the main square Piața Victoriei, this hotel appears drab from the outside, but offers clean and bright rooms for excellent value. The rooms also provide in-room climate control and hair dryers in the bathrooms.

🛏 84 🅿 🔲 🔲 🔲 🚫

🍴 RISTORANTE AL DUOMO

HOTELS
Price categories in the listings are based on high-season rates for a double room with bathroom and breakfast (unless otherwise noted):

$$$$$	over $200
$$$$	$150–$200
$$$	$100–$150
$$	$50–$100
$	under $50

RESTAURANTS
Restaurant prices in the listings are categorized as follows (for a three-course meal for one with some wine):

$$$$$	over $40
$$$$	$30–$40
$$$	$20–$30
$$	$10–$20
$	under $10

$$$–$$$$
STR. PAUL CHINEZU 2
TEL 0256 437 199

This formal, high-end Italian restaurant just a few feet away from the large, central Piața Unirii has a superb range of pastas and main courses. Prized by local foodies, the Italian chef has even appeared on national cooking shows.

🪑 35 🔲 🔲 🚫

🍴 LLOYD
$$–$$$
PIAȚA VICTORIEI 2
TEL 0256 294 949

The food in this atmospheric restaurant gets a bad rap in some guides, but truth be told, it's pretty good. Don't stray too far, however, from the traditional chicken and pork offerings. The terrace, on the central Piața Victoriei, is a delight in nice weather.

🪑 65 🔲 🚫

🍴 CASA CU FLORI
$$
STR. ALBA IULIA 1
TEL 0256 435 080

Sample some of the traditional cooking from the local Banat region at this quiet and refined spot. The downstairs café is

---

great for coffee and cakes. In summer, the terrace is the ideal spot to relax and people-watch.

⬚ 40 Ⓢ Ⓢ ⬟

DA TONI
$$
STR. DALIEI 14
TEL 0256 490 298
This authentic Tuscan-style pizza place is one of the best pizzerias in Romania. It gets popular at lunch, so time your arrival for between meals to have the run of the place to yourself.

⬚ 30 Ⓢ Ⓢ ⬟

TIMIȘOAREANA CLUB XXI
$$
PIAȚA VICTORIEI 2
TEL 0256 295 421
Live folk music and dancing make this traditional Romanian restaurant popular with patrons. Sample authentic *sarmale* and *mămăligă*, as well as other standard Romanian dishes.

⬚ 60 Ⓢ Ⓢ ⬟

ORADEA

CONTINENTAL
$$$
AL. ȘTRANDULUI 1
TEL 0259 418 655
FAX 0259 411 280
www.continentalhotels.ro
This refurbished high-rise attracts people looking for good value. The selling point is the outdoor hot springs pool, which allows you to take a dip in the dead of winter.

ⓘ 168 🅿 Ⓢ ⊟ Ⓢ ⬚
⬚ 🎽 ⬟

ELITE
$$$
PARCUL I. C. BRĂTIANU 26
TEL 0259 414 924
FAX 0259 419 759
www.hotelelite.ro
Though the location isn't too convenient, this small hotel is widely considered to be the best in the city. The rooms are elegant with comfortable

mattresses. The slick lobby has a little bar that opens onto a terrace.

ⓘ 32 🅿 Ⓢ Ⓢ 🎽 ⬟

VULTURUL NEGRU
$$$
STR. INDEPENDENȚEI 1
TEL 0259 450 000
FAX 0259 450 045
www.vulturulnegru.ro
Built in 1906, this massive art nouveau complex has seen better days, but the owners are trying hard to restore the hotel's luster. The rooms are clean, enormous, and well appointed. Corner rooms are larger. The hotel offers discounts for stays longer than one night.

ⓘ 47 🅿 Ⓢ ⊟ Ⓢ ⬟

ATLANTIC
$$
STR. IOSIF VULCAN 9
TEL/FAX 0259 426 911
www.hotelatlantic.ro
Small, intimate, and centrally located, this house has a faded art nouveau exterior. The interior is modern, and the amenities are aimed at mostly business clientele.

ⓘ 4 🅿 Ⓢ ⬟

ATRIUM
$$
STR. REPUBLICII 38
TEL 0259 414 421
www.hotelatrium.ro
Though similar in price and amenities to the Scorilo (see below), the Atrium lacks the homey atmosphere and excellent restaurant. The lobby atrium is impressive, and the rooms are plain, clean, and quiet.

ⓘ 20 🅿 Ⓢ ⬟

SCORILO
$$
PARCUL PETOFI 16
TEL 0259 470 910
FAX 0259 470 952
www.hotelscorilo.ro
The rooms of this conveniently located, family-run hotel occupy three floors of an 18th-century bishop's

residence. The hotel has two restaurants—one in the original cellar—and both are among the best in the city. Reserve the cellar in advance.

ⓘ 16 🅿 Ⓢ Ⓢ 🎽 ⬟

LA GALLERIA
$$$–$$$$
STR. MADACH IMRE 1–5
TEL 0259 475 490
www.lagalleria.biz
La Galleria is one of the best Italian restaurants around for fish, including a mouth-watering tuna carpaccio and a mixed fish grill with scampi, swordfish, and salmon. Book ahead.

⬚ 40 Ⓢ ⬟

KELLY'S IRISH PUB & PIZZERIA
$$
STR. MADACH IMRE 1–5
TEL 0259 413 419
This Irish-themed pizzeria is not as bad as it sounds and gets very popular on weekend evenings. In addition to pizzas, the menu offers a range of sandwiches and bar food like chicken wings.

⬚ 90 ⬟

MARAMUREȘ

BAIA MARE

HOTEL CARPAȚI
$$$
STR. MINERVA 16
TEL 0262 214 812
FAX 0262 215 461
www.hotelcarpati.ro
This impressive hotel lies on the Săsar River bank in downtown Baia Mare. Its serene gardens make it an oasis of tranquility in a busy city.

ⓘ 94 🅿 ⊟ Ⓢ 🎽 ⬟

COMPLEX LOSTRIȚA
$
STR. BLIDARI 13B
TEL 0744 471 692
www.complexlostrita.ro
Set about 11 miles (18 km)

from Baia Mare at the base of Igniş Mountain, this unique complex houses both a hotel and restaurant. For those who love to eat trout, the Complex Lostriţa's restaurant may be just the place, as its specialty dish comes fresh from its own trout farm.
25 (plus 1 villa) P

MOLDAVIA

IAŞI

SOMETHING SPECIAL

LITTLE TEXAS

The American owners have spared no expense in constructing this Texas-style roadhouse, which includes thick mattresses from the United States. In summer, the backyard terrace comes alive with guests and locals alike enjoying beers and barbecue around a big hot tub. The adjoining restaurant (see p. 258) serves excellent Tex-Mex food year-round. Little Texas lies about 3 miles (5 km) from the center of Iaşi along the road to the airport. A taxi will cost about 8 RON.

$$$
MOARA DE VÂNT 31–33
TEL 0232 272 545
FAX 0232 216 995
www.littletexas.org
32 P

TRAIAN
$$$
PIAŢA UNIRII 1
TEL 0232 266 666
FAX 0232 212 187
www.grandhoteltraian.ro
This late 19th-century neoclassic building, designed by Alexandre Gustave Eiffel (of Eiffel Tower fame), was thoroughly renovated in 2006 and is now Iaşi's top address.
60 P

UNIREA
$$–$$$
PIAŢA UNIRII 5
TEL 0232 205 000
FAX 0232 205 026
www.hotelunirea.ro
With an excellent central location and just a 10-minute walk from the train station, this enormous communist-era skyscraper has crisp, clean, and fully modernized rooms.
186 P

ASTORIA
$$
STR. LĂPUŞNEANU 1
TEL 0232 233 888
FAX 0232 244 777
www.hotelastoria.ro
The Astoria dates from the 1920s, but a relatively recent renovation has left it without much character. The clean, nondescript rooms are fine, and the location is excellent.
60 P

CASA LAVRIC
$$$
STR. SF. ATANASIE 21
TEL. 0232 229 960
You'll find some of the best local Moldavian and Romanian specialties in this intimate setting, including grilled pork served in cream sauce, with polenta on the side. Sample a bottle of Grasă de Cotnari, one of the country's best white wines, produced not far from Iaşi.
40 P

LITTLE TEXAS
$$–$$$
MOARA DE VÂNT 31–33
TEL/FAX 0232 272 545
www.littletexas.org
Here at the Moldovan border, you'll find very good Mexican food, including burritos, fajitas, and quesadillas, as well as steaks on the grill, twice-baked potatoes, and even decent cheeseburgers. To finish it off, choose from brownies, apple pie à la mode, or even a piece of Texas mud pie.
60 P

PHENICIE
$$–$$$
STR. LASCĂR CATARGIU 9
TEL 0232 222 239
This well-reviewed Lebanese restaurant, serving upscale appetizers (hummus, tabouleh) and main courses (mostly grilled meats), offers both casual and formal settings. Don't leave without trying one of the pastries.
50 P

PIZZA PAZZO
$$
B-DUL TUDOR VLADIMIRESCU
TEL 0232 210 442
The pizzas are decent at this hole-in-the-wall pizzeria which never seems to slow down. You can order in three sizes (S, M, or L) depending on your appetite, but the real draws are the oven entrees. Try the chicken Viennese: chicken cooked in a cream-and-mushroom sauce and then baked au gratin.
40 P

CORSO
$
STR. AL. LĂPUSNEANU 11
TEL 0232 276 143
www.corsoterasa.ro
The spot in the center of town to hang out and drink a beer on a hot summer day, Corso also has a good

HOTELS
Price categories in the listings are based on high-season rates for a double room with bathroom and breakfast (unless otherwise noted):

$$$$$	over $200
$$$$	$150–$200
$$$	$100–$150
$$	$50–$100
$	under $50

RESTAURANTS
Restaurant prices in the listings are categorized as follows (for a three-course meal for one with some wine):

$$$$$	over $40
$$$$	$30–$40
$$$	$20–$30
$$	$10–$20
$	under $10

KEY Hotel Restaurant No. of guest rooms No. of seats P Parking Closed Metro stop selection of nonalcoholic beverages, though not much in the way of food. There's free Wi-Fi here.

🕂 120 💲

SUCEAVA

Though an unattractive industrial city, Suceava is an important rail junction and the biggest city near the painted monasteries, making it a suitable base for exploration. If you arrive in Suceava early enough, you might consider traveling onward by car or bus to Gura Humorului, a small town about 20 miles (32 km) away that has one very nice hotel and several decent pensions and is just a couple miles (3 km) from two monasteries (Humor and Voroneț). Both of Suceava's train stations are a hike from the center, so you'll need to take a taxi (about 8 RON).

🏨 CONTINENTAL
$$$
STR. MIHAI VITEAZUL 4–6
TEL 0230 210 944
FAX 0230 216 266
www.continentalhotels.ro
This central, upscale, and modern hotel offers basic rooms, comfortable beds, and a good restaurant that stays open until midnight. Some services advertised online, like in-room Internet access, are in fact not available. Nevertheless, the hotel is commendable for cleanliness and maintenance standards.

🛈 96 🅿 🚫 ➡ 💲 ◈

🏨 VILLA ALICE
$–$$
STR. SIMION FLOREA MARIAN 1
TEL/FAX 0230 522 254
www.villaalice.ro
Situated close to the center, this family-run hotel offers both standard and deluxe rooms, the latter coming with free Internet access and air-conditioning. Rooms are plain but clean. The hotel is

connected to a health clinic and offers additional services like sauna, fitness, and massage.

🛈 10 🅿 🚫 💲 💪 ◈

🍴 LATINOS
$$–$$$
STR. CURTEA DOMNEASCĂ 3
TEL 0230 523 627
On weekend evenings, this upscale trattoria functions as the de facto center of Suceava social life. The restaurant opens daily at 9 a.m. for breakfast.

🕂 50 💲 ◈

GURA HUMORULUI

🏨 BEST WESTERN BUCOVINA
$$$
GURA HUMORULUI
TEL 0230 207 000
FAX 0230 207 001
www.bestwesternbucovina.ro
This impressive Best Western lodge strikes a nice balance between comfort and rusticity. Rooms on the upper floors open onto terraces, affording lovely views on the hills and surrounding town. The staff can help arrange tours to the monasteries.

🛈 130 🅿 🚫 ➡ 💲 ♿ 💪 ◈

🏨 CASA ELENA
$$
VORONEȚ
TEL 0230 230 651
FAX 0230 235 326
www.casaelena.ro
The handsome and well-run guesthouse, located not far from the monastery at Voroneț, offers simple but clean rooms. The restaurant is superb and an excellent spot to sample Moldavian specialties like *pomana porcului*, small pieces of smoked pork and sausage.

🛈 30 🅿 🚫 💲 ◈

🏨 CASA IOANA
$$
VORONEȚ

TEL 0745 610 317
Essentially a couple of rooms in a tidy farmhouse, Casa Ioana is situated close to the monastery. Taxi drivers usually know it, but if you're driving, head toward the Voroneț monastery and look for a sign with Ioana's name and a picture of a young girl in peasant garb.

🛈 5 🅿

◼ DOBROGEA

CONSTANȚA

Constanța is rediscovering its identity and redeveloping its historic core. That said, if you're coming to the Black Sea coast in July or August with the main idea to swim and lie on the beach, choose a property in Mamaia over Constanța. The surf in Mamaia is cleaner, and the resorts are better geared toward summer vacationers. Rates in both towns rise accordingly in midsummer; in winter, hotel traffic slows to a trickle and many hotels are willing to cut deals on rates.

🏨 ROYAL
$$$
B-DUL MAMAIA 191
TEL 0241 545 570
FAX 0241 545 882
www.hotelroyal.ro
The pleasant and well-run Royal might make a nice compromise choice if you don't want to be too far from Constanța's historic center and beach, and if you don't mind its location on a slightly depressed strip. The rooms are a step up from the Ibis and Class, and it has sauna and fitness facilities. Book well in advance in season.

🛈 50 🅿 🚫 ➡ 💲 💪 ◈

🏨 FERDINAND
$$–$$$
STR. FERDINAND 12
TEL 0241 617 974

FAX 0241 617 924
www.hotelferdinand.ro
The Ferdinand may have a slight advantage in that it's closer than the Ibis or Class to Constanța's city beach. The rooms are upscale and contemporary, and some have views over the sea. The bathrooms are spotless.
🛈 20 🅿 🔁 🔄 ⬙

🏨 **IBIS**
$$–$$$
STR. MIRCEA CEL BĂTRÂN 39–41
TEL. 0241 508 050
FAX 0241 508 051
www.ibishotel.com
A short walk from the city's beach and close to the historic center, this nondescript, high-rise building offers clean, cubicle-size rooms with all the modern conveniences at excellent prices.
🛈 154 🅿 🔁 🔄 📺 ⬙

🏨 **CLASS**
$$
STR. RĂSCOALA DIN 1907 1
TEL 0241 660 766
FAX 0241 660 909
www.hotelclass.ro
Within walking distance to Constanța's old city and port, the Class has simply but tastefully furnished rooms and spotless bathrooms. This isn't a great choice if swimming is high on your list. The better beaches at Mamaia are a good 3–4 miles (5–6 km) down the road.
🛈 26 🅿 🔁 🔄 ⬙

🍴 **MARCO POLO**
$$$
STR. SARMISEGETUZA 2
TEL 0241 617 357
This centrally located pizza joint serves proper sit-down meals, with a menu that goes well beyond pizzas and includes steaks, seafood, and very good salads.
🍴 90 🅿 🔄 🔄 ⬙

🍴 **EL GRECO**
$$–$$$
STR. DECEBAL 18
TEL 0241 554 032
The menu features the traditional starters and salads you'd expect at a Greek restaurant, perhaps slightly altered to suit Romanian tastes. If you can't decide, choose chicken *kaftero*, a spicy mix of grilled chicken, tomatoes, and green peppers. It might be the best meal in Constanța.
🛈 50 🅿 🔄 ⬙

🍴 **COLONADELOR**
$$
STR. TRAIAN 53
TEL 0241 618 058
The real draw here is the terrace in summer, where if you're lucky you can catch a rare cool breeze off the harbor. The Colonadelor is open year-round and remains a strong draw for its decent pizzas and good Romanian specialties.
🍴 200 🅿 ⬙

🍴 **IRISH PUB**
$$
STR. ȘTEFAN CEL MARE 1
TEL 0241 550 400
www.irishpub.ro
Not quite what you'd expect from an Irish pub, since this upscale, dark-wooded bistro, serves excellent steaks, chops, and seafood as well of a range of cocktails and coffee drinks. The pub opens at 9 a.m. and lays on a full menu of omelets.
🛈 60 🅿 🔄 ⬙

🍴 **AMSTER'S**
$–$$
B-DUL TOMIS 55
TEL 0241 511 499
This atmospheric coffee shop just a block from the town center is a good spot for hot beverages or a light lunch. Amster's has free Wi-Fi.
🍴 70 🔄 ⬙

MAMAIA

Don't arrive in Mamaia during

HOTELS
Price categories in the listings are based on high-season rates for a double room with bathroom and breakfast (unless otherwise noted):

$$$$$	over $200
$$$$	$150–$200
$$$	$100–$150
$$	$50–$100
$	under $50

RESTAURANTS
Restaurant prices in the listings are categorized as follows (for a three-course meal for one with some wine):

$$$$$	over $40
$$$$	$30–$40
$$$	$20–$30
$$	$10–$20
$	under $10

high season (mid-June–August) without room reservations in hand. The entire 3-mile (5 km) strip of shoreline is booked solid end to end. Room rates rise accordingly in summer, and only begin to drop around mid-September. By October the season is largely over, and many hotels close down for the winter. A note on addresses: There are no street addresses in Mamaia; properties are listed by name, not number. Maps showing the names and locations of the various resorts are available at the hotels.

🏨 **GRANDHOTEL REX**
$$$$$
MAMAIA
TEL 0241 831 520
FAX 0241 831 690
www.grandhotelrex.ro
Open year-round, this palatial interwar resort (the original hotel was built in 1936) has been restored to its former luster and is once again the leading property on Romania's Black Sea coast. The interior is crisp and clean, with white woods and dark blue carpets. The hotel is still undergoing

some reconstruction.

ⓘ 102 🅿 Ⓢ ⊟ Ⓢ
🌊 🌴 ⬡

 IAKI

$$$$

MAMAIA

TEL 0241 831 025

FAX 0241 831 169

www.iaki.ro

This sprawling pink resort complex has excellent sports facilities, including an indoor pool and fitness club. The rooms are generously proportioned, with high ceilings and all modern conveniences, including Internet access. Iaki is open year-round.

ⓘ 98 🅿 Ⓢ ⊟ Ⓢ 🌊
🌴 🐡 ⬡

TULCEA

Tulcea is the biggest city in the Danube Delta area, making it a natural base for organizing tours into the delta. That said, it's little more than a homely port town, and if you have time, you'll want to move further into the delta itself. Try to book private accommodations on arrival through one of the many travel agencies in Tulcea or through the local tourist information office (Str. Garii 26, tel/fax 0240 519 130).

SOMETHING SPECIAL

🏨 **DELTA NATURE RESORT**

The Danube Delta has spawned a new generation of eco-friendly resorts that promise to cater to your every whim and safeguard the environment at the same time. The nicest and most expensive of these is the Danube Nature Resort, near the village of Parches, about 12 miles (20 km) inland from Tulcea. The resort is built around 30 private bungalows, each designed in local materials and with a riverside view. The staff will take care of planning

boating and birding adventures in the delta. The resort is reachable from Tulcea by car, minibus, or taxi (about 50 RON).

$$$$$

SOMOVA-PARCHES

TEL 0213 114 532

FAX 0213 114 533

www.deltaresort.com

ⓘ 30 🅿 Ⓢ Ⓢ 🌊 🐡
⬡

🏨 **REX**

$$$

STR. TOAMNEI 1

TEL 0240 511 351

FAX 0240 511 354

www.hotelrex.ro

The only four-star hotel within the city limits of Tulcea, the Rex has generously sized rooms with polished, modern decor. A drawback is the inconvenient location (about half a mile/1 km from the town center).

ⓘ 38 🅿 Ⓢ ⊟ Ⓢ 🐡 ⬡

🏨 **DELTA**

$$

STR. ISACCEI 2

TEL 0240 514 720

FAX 0240 516 260

www.deltahotelro.com

This standard, communist-era high-rise has been retrofitted with plush carpets and modern bath fixtures to make a comfy, snug hotel, fully deserving of its three stars. Pluses include a decent restaurant, kind staff, a big indoor pool, and an ideal riverside, portside location.

ⓘ 120 🅿 Ⓢ ⊟ Ⓢ 🌊
⬡

🏨 **EGRETA**

$$

STR. PĂCII 3

TEL 0240 506 250

FAX 0240 517 103

The lower room prices at the Egreta reflect the slight step down from the accommodations at the Delta. Nevertheless, the Egreta is a clean and well-maintained hotel with a

central location not far from the river and a friendly, English-speaking staff.

ⓘ 98 🅿 Ⓢ ⊟ Ⓢ ⬡

🏨 **EUROPOLIS**

$

STR. PĂCII 20

TEL 0240 516 649

FAX 0240 512 443

This communist-era housing block aims more at budget travelers. Its strong points are nonstop hot water and heating during the winter. The on-site tourist agency can help book Danube cruises and tours of the delta.

ⓘ 25 🅿 ⬡

🍴 **SELECT**

$$

STR. PĂCII 6

TEL 0240 506 180

This tavern offers traditional fare. For main dishes, go with the fish; the local favorite is *somn* (a relative of the catfish). For dessert, the *papanași* (fried doughnuts with a dollop of jam and cream on top) are excellent.

🍴 65 🅿 Ⓢ ⬡

🍴 **TRIDENT**

$–$$

STR. UNITATEA 3

TEL 0240 519 502

Trident is a cheerful pizzeria in the center of town that cooks its pies in a clay oven. It also serves decent pastas and coffee drinks.

🍴 40 ⬡

SHOPPING & ENTERTAINMENT

SHOPPING

For the visitor, the most interesting items to buy are high-quality handicrafts, including traditional lace, wood carvings, jewelry, and pottery. Romania has several organizations dedicated to promoting quality crafts. They can give you a list of craftspeople in the area you want to visit and put you in direct contact with the makers.

Fundația Meșteșuguri Românești (Romanian Crafts Foundation), based in Bucharest, has a nationwide database of craftspeople. In Sibiu, Artefact Biertan sells good quality, newly made crafts from all over Romania (Str. Nicolae Balcescu 2, tel 0269 868 494).

In Bucharest, try the excellent crafts store in the Romanian Village Museum (Șoseaua Kiseleff 28, tel 021 317 9110, www .muzeul-satului.ro). Another decent shop is at the nearby Museum of the Romanian Peasant (Șoseaua Kiseleff 3, tel 021 650 5360). You can also inquire locally at your hotel or nearest tourist information office about what is made locally and where to find it.

On one side of the square in Biertan, Transylvania is an imaginative crafts shop, Artefact Biertan. As well as displays of furniture and textiles belonging to its enthusiastic proprietor, the shop sells good quality, new hand-made pottery, textiles, paintings, icons and jewelry from all over Romania. (tel 0269 868 494, closed Nov.–Mar.)

Books are another excellent souvenir. All around the center of the city, particularly in the neighborhood around the university (Piața Universității) you'll see stalls selling all manners of used books, some in English, ranging from 60s and 70s dross to real finds. For new books, try the stunning bookstore/teahouse Cărturești (Str. Arthur Verona 13, tel 021 317 3459 or 078 875 8408; info@carturesti.ro), which houses great art and architecture books, many in English, as well as one of the best collections of music CDs in Bucharest.

Bucharest is also home to some of the country's most interesting antique, secondhand, and junk shops. The center of this universe is the gentrifying Lipscani district. A good place to begin would be at Hanul cu Tei (Str. Lipscani 63–65, tel 021 313 0181). Just follow your nose around the tiny streets until you find what you're looking for.

In terms of other souvenirs, Romania is home to some excellent reproductions of religious icons and religious art. Outside of the monasteries, particularly the painted monasteries around Suceava, you'll usually find several dealers in handicrafts and religious artifacts. Be sure to shop around, since quality can vary.

Most of the big cities, including Bucharest, Brașov, Constanța, Timișoara, and Iași, now have at least one shiny, modern shopping mall. In addition, the highways leading out of the cities are lined with big-box retailers and hypermarkets that you'd see outside any American or western European city. Most cities and towns still have a central fruit and vegetable market—and these are definitely worth searching out—but the supermarkets are starting to exert their inevitable pull.

In terms of what to buy, the malls and hypermarkets are not likely to offer much. Most of what's available is similar to what you can find at home, and contrary to common sense, prices in Romania for items like high-end clothing, cosmetics, shoes, and leather goods are likely to be higher than what you're used to.

ENTERTAINMENT

OPERA & CLASSICAL MUSIC

You'll find lively cultural scenes in all of the major cities. Opera is popular. Bucharest, Brașov, Cluj-Napoca, Constanța, Iași, and Timișoara all support full-time opera companies. Cluj has opera for both its Romanian and Hungarian communities. In Bucharest, the main opera house is the Bucharest National Opera (B-dul Kogălniceanu 70–72, tel 021 314 6980, www.operanb.ro). You can check the schedule as well as reserve tickets through the website, which has an English translation.

Classical music is equally beloved, and wherever you are in Romania, you'll have the chance to take in a concert. Hotels and tourist information offices should be able to point you in the right direction. Also be on the lookout for two Romanian-language what's-going-on publications, Șapte Seri (Seven Evenings) and Zile și Nopți (Days and Nights), both of which carry excellent local cultural listings. While in Bucharest, don't pass up the chance to catch a classical concert at the beautiful Romanian Atheneum (Str. Benjamin Franklin 1–3, tel 021 315 8798), home of the Romanian Philharmonic George Enescu.

FOLK MUSIC

Interest in Romanian folk music and tradition is still strong, and in many places this interest is growing among younger people as a way to reconnect with the country's cultural roots. Occasionally, you'll see notices of folk performances, but your best chance of seeing some traditional song and dance is at summer festivals in Transylvania or Maramureș or at traditional restaurants, such as Bucharest's Caru' cu Bere, Poiana Brașov's Coliba Haiducilor, or Timișoara's Timișoareana Club XXI.

NIGHTLIFE

Romanians love to party, and unsurprisingly the centers for after-hours drinking and dancing are in big university towns such as Bucharest, Iași, Brașov, Cluj-Napoca, and Timișoara. In the summer, the action shifts to the Black Sea port of Constanța and the adjoining resort of Mamaia. In

July and August, Mamaia becomes a long strip of dance clubs, discos, and raves. The most popular clubs change with the season, so you're best off consulting the cultural guides Şapte Seri and Zile şi Nopți, both of which issue local editions for the major cities. The In Your Pocket guides, which cover Bucharest and Braşov, are also excellent for checking out what's hot at the moment.

Casinos are big business, too, and you'll find them in all the major cities. A note about other forms of after-hours entertainment: You'll see plenty of questionable-looking nightclubs and "gentlemen's clubs," usually scattered around the outskirts of major cities. Such adult-oriented dance clubs and massage parlors may be unsavory, but they are legal. However, prostitution is not, and fines can be heavy.

ACTIVITIES & FESTIVALS

ACTIVE SPORTS
Boating, fishing, & bird-watching
The Danube Delta, a meandering marshland where the Danube River meets the Black Sea, is a beautiful and relatively remote wilderness that offers miles of waterway for canoeing, boating, fishing, and bird-watching.

The town of Tulcea makes for a good base to arrange tours, accommodation, and boat rentals. Private tourist agencies can set you up with anything you might need. A first stop should include a visit to the small but helpful tourist information office, just along the waterfront in Tulcea (Str. Gării 26, tel 0240 519 130). The staff maintains an updated list of the tour operators and can advise on what's offered, as well as suggest possible itineraries given your budget and preferences. Several private operators can book trips in advance. Go Romania Tours (www.goromaniatours.com), for example, offers an 8-day "Discover the Danube Delta" tour, with a focus on bird-

watching.

To push farther into the delta, you can take the regular ferry services along the three main channels or hire a boat. Several kinds of boats are available, but all boats in the delta must be driven by local boatmen licensed by the Danube Delta Biosphere Reserve Administration. The boatmen are good local guides, often with a knowledge of birds, but few speak English and some like to speed, which damages the birds' habitat. To find responsible and experienced guides, contact Asociația de Ecoturism din România (Str. Gabroveni 2, et. 4, sector 3, Bucharest, tel 074 431 9742; 026 832 6271). Tioc Nature and Study Trips (www.tioc-reisen.ro/en), based in Sibiu, specializes in conservation, bird-, and wildlife-watching tours for individuals and small groups.

Fishing in the delta is allowed only with a permit from Asociația Rezervației Biosferei Deltei Dunării (Str. Portului 34A, Tulcea, tel 0240 518 945).

Cycling & mountain biking
Cycling has yet to take off in a serious way in Romania, but that doesn't mean you can't bring your own bike and enjoy the literally thousands of miles of country roads, byways, logging roads, and paths that crisscross the country. Off the main highways, traffic is relatively light, making for excellent biking terrain, though probably better suited to a wider-tire hybrid or mountain bike than to a pure road cycle. Unfortunately, you'll find little in the way of bike rental outfits or good cycling infrastructure, including bike repair shops, along the way. It's possible to transport bikes on trains, provided the train has a baggage car and the bike is tagged as checked luggage. On other trains, it may be possible to bring a bike at the discretion of the conductor.

In general, forget about cycling around Romania's cities. Most, including Bucharest, Cluj-Napoca, Braşov, and Constanța, are simply too busy and the roads too poor

to allow for enjoyable biking. One area that seems better suited to cyclists would be around the city of Sibiu and the surrounding Transylvanian countryside. Kultours (Piața Mică 16, tel/fax 0269 216 854, www.kultours.ro) rents bikes and sells decent cycling maps of the area.

If you'd like to leave the planning to others, several private operators arrange guided and self-guided cycling tours. Adventure Transylvania (www.adventuret ransylvania.com) offers an 8-day mountain-biking tour of the Bucegi Mountains, with transfers to and from Bucharest and bike rental included in the price. A U.K.-based operator, Hooked on Cycling (tel 1501 744 727, www.hookedoncycling.co.uk), offers a similar self-guided 7-day trip, with a focus on Transylvania and winding up in Sibiu. Cycle rental is available but not included in the base price.

Golf
Still largely seen as an elite sport, golf has been relatively slow to get going in the years since 1989. Still, there are a couple of nice courses around. You'll find a delightful and tourist-friendly nine-hole course, Lac de Verde (www.lacdeverde.ro), in the picturesque Prahova Valley, not far from Braşov. The course offers various packages, including overnight stays, greens fees, and club rentals.

Hiking & walking
With its miles of unspoiled countryside, gently rolling hills, and occasionally rugged mountaintops, Romania is a hiker's paradise. The best areas for hiking are in Transylvania, in the Bucegi Mountains around Sinaia and the high Făgăraş range. Here you'll find well-marked hiking trails plus decent hiking maps. The best strategy is to simply choose a town (Sinaia, Predeal, Braşov, Sighişoara, and Sibiu are all good bases), buy some maps from the local tourist information office, and select suitable routes. You can do day hikes or arrange stays

in a mountain shelter *(cabane)*. The hiking season generally runs from early June through September. Romania's mountains are not tall by world standards—the tallest peaks are in the 7,000–8,000 foot (2,000-2,500 m) range—but they still require a measure of respect. Remember to wear sturdy shoes with ankle support, and be sure to pack water, sunscreen, sunglasses, and something waterproof for a late afternoon shower.

You can easily plan hikes on your own, but if you'd like some guidance, several private tour operators offer hiking/walking tours of Romania.

U.S.-based Wilderness Travel (tel 1-800-368-2794, www .wildernesstravel.com) offers a 12-day walking tour of Romania, covering much of the Transylvanian hillsides, including visits to Braşov, Sighişoara, and Sibiu, and two nights in a mountain cabin. Another U.S. company, Pure Adventures (tel 1-800-960-2221, www.pure-adventures.com), offers a similar 8-day Transylvania trip, with more of a focus on the area around Predeal and Bran Castle. Canada-based Hidden Trails (tel 1-888-987-2457, www.hidden trails.com) focuses primarily on horseback riding trips, but also offers self-guided hiking trips in Romania through Transylvania and the painted monasteries in the area around Suceava.

A company based in Romania, Adventure Transylvania, offers a series of walks, hikes, and treks to meet all difficulty levels (tel 0727 394 727, www.adventuretransyl vania.com).Caliman Club, a Romanian company operating from Bistriţa in northern Transylvania, specializes in activity holidays in the beautiful Someş Valley and other little-known areas of the Carpathian Mountains. Tours include canoeing, hiking, riding, and cycling (tel 0263 235 046). Roving Romania (www.roving-romania.co.uk) based in Braşov is oriented toward nature and hiking tours with an emphasis on conservation. Transylvania

Uncovered (www.beyondthe forest.com) has a helpful hands-on approach and arranges group and custom-made tours.

A young Romanian company based in Braşov, DiscoveRomania organizes guided and unguided tours to many of the country's less well picked-over places (www.discoveromania.ro).

Corbet Transair travel agency (www.corbet-transair.ro) operates from Târgu Mureş and helps travelers find quirky little places that make a visit memorable.

NordNordVest Turism (tel 0262 226 508) of Baia Mare will get you around the Maramureş efficiently if you're in a hurry.

For more information about the many other exciting possibilities for hiking, touring, and riding in the Apuseni Mountains, see www.buciumland. ro, www.buciumanii.ro, and www.greenmountainholidays.ro.

Paragliding, rock climbing, kayaking, & adventure sports
Adventure sports are only now developing in Romania. The center for these kinds of activities is Braşov, where you'll find several small private tour operators offering trekking trips and outings for climbing, paragliding, free-ride mountain biking, etc. The place to start would be the Braşov tourist information office (Piaţa Sfatului 30, tel 0268 419 078, www.brasovcity.ro). There you'll find plenty of brochures and catalogues of local agencies. Another region where adventure sports, hikes, and treks are gaining in popularity is around Oradea in western Romania. One of the best companies for organizing outings there is the local Apuseni Experience (tel 0259 472 434, www.apuseniexperience.ro).

Skiing
Romania's mountains offer decent skiing from about mid-December until early March, though you may be disappointed if you're accustomed to the superior facilities in Austria, Switzerland, or France. The most popular ski

resort is Poiana Braşov, about 9 miles (15 km) away and easily reachable from Braşov by car or bus. The resort is relatively small, but has several good runs and a usually reliable snowpack. Most of the other major resorts are not far from Braşov. Sinaia, about an hour south by train, also offers decent skiing; those in the know say its runs are the most challenging in Romania. Another popular ski resort is Predeal, which is situated along the main train route between Sinaia and Braşov. You can rent skis and equipment and take skiing lessons at all of the resorts. If you're flexible with time, try to arrive on a weekday, when lines at the lifts are not nearly as long.

Swimming & sunbathing
Romania's best beaches are along the Black Sea coast, just to the north and south of Constanţa. Don't come expecting a gorgeous, unspoiled seacoast. Popular playgrounds like Mamaia, north of Constanţa, look more like a canyon of high-rise hotels than a pristine getaway. On the other hand, if you're looking for some lively, fun discos and a chance to do some sunbathing while you are here, you needn't look any farther.

If you are serious about spending time on the coast in summer, you'd be well advised to try to book a package. During the summer, the beaches and promenades are packed, and trying to organize rooms and meals independently can be a headache. Packages here work out cheaper in the long run anyway. Several tour operators can set you up with a package. For example, the U.K.-based Romania Travel Centre (www.romaniatravelcentre.com) books one- and two-week trips to Mamaia and other Black Sea destinations. Prices generally include breakfast and, if needed, air transfer to and from London. Packages can also include excursions to the Danube Delta just up the coast.

FESTIVALS
Some of the highlights of the festival calendar are listed below; local tourist offices will have complete lists of festivals in their areas.

December/January
Many cities and towns plan massive Christmas and New Year's Eve celebrations, and then shut down for the first two or three days of the year.

April
Orthodox Easter is a major holiday, celebrated sometimes a week after the western Easter.

May/June
Fertility festivals abound in spring. In early May the village of Hoteni in Maramureș holds its annual Tânjaua de pe Mara festival to celebrate the sowing of seeds. Bucharest holds an annual crafts fair at the Village Museum to recognize traditional skills like wood carving, glassblowing, and egg painting.

In June, Sibiu plays host to an International Theater Festival. Also in June, Cluj-Napoca is the main venue for the annual Transylvania International Film Festival, and Bucharest hosts the annual Francophone international music festival. Târgu Mureș, in the last week of June, hosts its popular Marosvásárhely Napok, the Târgu Mureș Days festival.

July/August
The Bucharest Festival of Old is held to celebrate the city as it was in the 19th century. You'll find parades, period costumes, and traditional food and music.

The Sighișoara Medieval Arts Festival in early July entails three days of arts, crafts, and music from the Middle Ages. This festival draws huge crowds, and you'll need to plan well in advance to attend.

The Girls' Fair (Târgul de Fete) in the Găina Mountains is a matchmaking festival where villagers dress in folk costumes and go through the rituals of choosing a mate.

In July, the village of Vadu Izea in Maramureș holds a four-day folk music Maramuzical Festival.

In August, Sf. Gheorghe holds

Festival Anonimul, a film festival founded in 2004 which is also a competition for feature films, fiction and animation shorts. Bizarre as its location sounds, the festival has attracted an enthusiastic, international following. (For more information visit www.deltasfantugheorghe.ro)

The Black Sea coastal resort of Mamaia hosts an annual summer music festival in August, and Sibiu holds an International Folk Music Festival. The annual Dance at Prislop festival links Romania's regions of Transylvania, Moldova, and Maramureș with

traditional dances and foods at the Prislop Pass in the Carpathians.

September/October
Sibiu hosts jazz musicians from around Europe and the rest of the world during the International Jazz Festival.

In odd-numbered years, Bucharest hosts the 10-day George Enescu Music Festival.

November/December
National Unity Day celebrations are held in Bucharest and Alba Iulia on December 1.

The northern city of Sighet holds its Winter Customs Festival in the days following Christmas.

LANGUAGE GUIDE
Romanian is a Latin-based language that has been influenced over the centuries by Slavic languages, Turkish, Hungarian and other languages. Its closest linguistic cousin is Italian, though French and Spanish speakers also will be able to read store signs and newspaper headlines. English is compulsory in grade schools and widely understood, although you may have to resort to your high school French or use sign language when communicating with taxi drivers and ticket sellers at train and bus stations. If you speak German or Hungarian, this will help you in parts of Transylvania and the west of the country.

Romanians are proud of their Latin linguistic roots, so any effort on your part to learn a few words, like "thank you" or "good day," will be greeted by appreciative laughter.

Basic words & phrases
Yes/No	Da/Nu
Please	Vă rog
Thank you	Mulțumesc
Good day	Bună ziua
Good evening	Bună seara
Good night	Noapte bună
Hello	Salut/Servus (in Transylvania)
Goodbye/See you	La revedere
Excuse me	Scuzați-mă
How are you?	Ce mai faceți?
Very well, thanks	Bine, mulțumesc
Cheers! Good luck!	Noroc!
Bon appétit!	Poftă bună
Open/Closed	Deschis/Închis
Entrance/Exit	Intrare/Ieșire
No entry	Intrare interzisa
Men/Women	Bărbați/Femei
Town center	Centru
Train station	Gara
Arrival/Departure	Sosire/Plecare
What's your name?	Cum vă numiți?
Do you speak English?	Vorbiți englezește?
I would like ...	Aș vrea ...
How much?	Cât costă?
The check/bill, please	Nota, vă rog

ILLUSTRATIONS CREDITS

All images by Steven Weinberg unless otherwise noted. Abbreviations for terms appearing below: (UP) Upper; (LO) Lower. Cover: left, Steven Weinberg; center, D. Mosel; right, Dinu Lazar

1, 4, Alexandra Avakian; 2–3, G. Kerr; 9, Gavin Hellier/Getty Images; 12-13, Alexandra Avakian; 14-15, Dinu Lazar; 16-17, Alexandra Avakian; 18, Richard l'Anson/LPI/Getty Images; 21 (LO), Mihal Radu Baluta; 22-23, Dinu Lazar; 25, AFP/Getty Images; 28-29, Tibor Mester; 30, Hulton Archive/Getty Images; 33, Joel Robine/Getty Images; 34-35, Daniel Mihailescu/Getty Images; 38, Dinu Mendrea; 40, 41, G. Kerr; 42, Pascal Guyot/Getty Images; 43, Time & Life Pictures/Getty Images; 44, 47, Dinu Lazar; 48, age fotostock/SuperStock; 61, G. Kerr; 62 (UP), Joe Mabel; 62 (LO), G. Kerr; 69, Zediu Felix/Fotolia; 70, Bogdan Morar; 74, Marian Curelaru; 75, Ioana Bancos; 77, Tibor Bognar/Alamy Ltd; 78, 79, Civic Academy Foundation, Bucharest, 2007; 89, G. Kerr; 91, Romanian Tourist Office; 92, Romanian Tourist Office; 93, © 2006 Artists Rights Society (ARS), New York/ADAGP, Paris; 94, Catalin Rotaru/www.rotaru.com; 96, Cristina Mitroi; 103, Dinu Mendrea; 104, David Toase/Getty Images; 106, Pablo Corral Vega/CORBIS; 111 (UP), O. Louis Mazzatenta; 112, Craig Pershouse/Getty Images; 115, Opriscan Romulus Ioan; 117, Dan Tataru/Shutterstock; 118-119, 119, Alexandra Avakian; 120, Oana Vinatoru/ iStockphoto.com; 122, Alin Popescu/Shutterstock; 124, Falk Kienas/Shutterstock; 127, Kathy Kavalec; 128, Dinu Mendrea; 129, Radu Mendrea; 130, Romanian Tourist Office; 131, Radu Mendrea; 132, Alan Grant; 134, Andrei Dragomir; 135, allOver photographer/Alamy Ltd; 137, Radu Mendrea; 138, Russell Young/CORBIS; 140, Sandu Mendrea; 142, Dorling Kindersley/Getty Images; 143 (LO), Falk Kienas/iStockphoto.com; 143 (UP), Holger Ehlers/Alamy Ltd; 144, Kathy Kavalec; 146, Radu Mendrea; 154, G. Kerr; 155, D. Mosel; 164, Seth Brush http://cender.net; 166, Paul Carstairs/Alamy Ltd; 169, Gregory Wrona/Alamy Ltd; 172, allOver photographer/Alamy Ltd; 175, G. Kerr; 176, D. Mosel; 183, Ioana Bancos; 184, Alexandra Avakian; 187 (UP), D. Mosel; 188, Kristen Soper/Alamy Ltd; 189, Bogdan Cristel/CORBIS; 194, G. Kerr; 198-199, Page fotostock/SuperStock; 200, G. Kerr; 206, D. Mosel; 216, Tortocan Alexandru; 218, Romanian Tourist Office; 220, 221 (UP), Tomasz Tomaszewski; 221 (LO), Michael Chen/iStockphoto.com; 224, Sorin Cristescu; 228-229, Ed Kashi; 232, Sandu Mendrea; 234, Ceban Cristi.

A NOTE ON RESPONSIBLE TOURISM: National Geographic encourages rewarding, mindful travel—mindful of the relationship between the traveler and the quality of the destination. To retain and improve its sense of place, Romania has signed on to the principles listed in National Geographic's Geotourism Charter, which defines geotourism as tourism that sustains or enhances the geographical character of the place being visited—its environment, culture, aesthetics, heritage, and the well-being of its residents. By being a geo-savvy traveler, you'll sustain and enhance your own trip as well. For a more authentic travel experience, and to gain an in-depth appreciation for Romania, realize the power you wield in making your touring choices. To be a geo-savvy traveler:

· Recognize that your presence has an impact on the places you visit.
· Indulge responsibly, spending your time and money in ways that sustain local character. (Besides, it's more interesting that way.)
· Value the aspects of Romania's natural and cultural heritage.
· Respect the local customs and traditions.
· Show appreciation to Romanians about things unique to Romania: its nature, scenery, music or food, historic villages, and buildings.
· Separate historical myth from reality; many people in Wallachia do not appreciate the way their land and history are portrayed in Dracula fiction.
· Vote with your wallet: Support the people who support the place, patronizing businesses that make an effort to celebrate and protect what's special about Romania. Seek out small shops, local restaurants, and tour operators who love the place—who love taking care of it and showing it off.
· Avoid businesses that detract from the character of the place.
· Enrich yourself, taking home more memories and stories to tell, knowing that you have contributed to the preservation and enhancement of Romania.

For more about geotourism, and to learn about National Geographic's Center for Sustainable Destinations, visit www.nationalgeographic.com/travel/sustainable/

APPRECIATION

The author would like to thank the following people and institutions for their help with her research for this guide:

Jean Blajan
Corneliu Bucur
Primăria Câmpulung Muscel
Ioana Bogdan Cataniciu
Horia Ciugudean
Mirela and Sorin Ciutacu
Jean-Michel Corbet
Niculiță Dărăfltean
Crina Draghici
Ştefan Enache
Cristina Enescu
Caroline Fernolend
Reghina Ghiţiu
Ioan Godea

Vichi Guţa
Institutul de Cercetări Eco-
    Muzeale Tulcea
Vasile Ionescu
Anamaria and Georgeta Iuga
Mike Joseph
Anca and Gabi Jugănaru
Tibor Kálnoky
Valeria Lehene
Kathleen Laraia McLaughlin
Fundaţia pentru Meşteşuguri
    Româneşti
Ramona Mitrica
Angela and Mike Morton

Adrian Munteanu
Doru Munteanu
Sorin Negrea
Pro Patrimonia
Cristina Popescu
The Rai Family
Reuniunea Mărginimii Sibiului
Done Şerbanescu
Kit Shann
Colin Shaw
Livia Stoia
Nora Stroe
Ecaterina Tantareanu

Founded in 1888, the National Geographic Society is one of the largest nonprofit scientific and educational organizations in the world. It reaches more than 285 million people worldwide each month through its official journal, NATIONAL GEOGRAPHIC, and its four other magazines; the National Geographic Channel; television documentaries; radio programs; films; books; videos and DVDs; maps; and interactive media. National Geographic has funded more than 8,000 scientific research projects and supports an education program combating geographic illiteracy.

For more information, please call 1-800-NGS LINE (647-5463) or write to the following address: National Geographic Society, 1145 17th Street N.W.,Washington, D.C. 20036-4688 U.S.A.

Visit us online at: www.national geographic.com/books

For information about special discounts for bulk purchases, please contact National Geographic Books Special Sales: ngspecsales@ngs.org.

Order *Traveler* today, the magazine that travelers trust. In the U.S. and Canada call 1-800-NGS-LINE; 813-979-6845 for international. Or visit us online at www.national geographic.com/traveler and click on SUBSCRIBE.

Printed in Spain

National Geographic Traveler: Romania

Published by the National Geographic Society
John M. Fahey, Jr., *President and Chief Executive Officer*
Gilbert M. Grosvenor, *Chairman of the Board*
Nina D. Hoffman, *Executive Vice President;*
    President, Book Publishing Group

Prepared by the Book Division
Kevin Mulroy, *Senior Vice President and Publisher*
Leah Bendavid-Val, *Director of Photography Publishing*
    and Illustrations
Marianne R. Koszorus, *Director of Design*
Elizabeth Newhouse, *Director of Travel Publishing*
Carl Mehler, *Director of Maps*
Cinda Rose, *Art Director*
Barbara A. Noe, *Series Editor*
R. Gary Colbert, *Production Director*
Mike Horenstein, *Production Manager*
Jennifer Thornton, *Managing Editor*

Staff for this book:
Lawrence M. Porges, *Project Editor*
Kay Kobor Hankins, *Designer*
Jane Sunderland, *Text Editor*
Vickie Donovan, *Illustrations Editor*
Cristina Rai and Florin Filip, *Researchers*
Lise Sajewski, *Editorial Consultant*
XNR Productions, *Map Research and Production*
Marshall Kiker, *Illustrations Specialist*
Connie D. Binder, *Indexer*
Jack Brostrom, Olivia Garnett, Lynsey Jacob, Michael McNey, Nida
    Sophasarun, Rob Waymouth, Meredith Wilcox, *Contributors*

Artwork (pp. 86–87 & 148–149) by Maltings Partnership, Derby, England

National Geographic Traveler: Romania (2007)
ISBN: 978-1-4262-0147-9

Printed and bound by Arnoldo Mondadori, Toledo, Spain.
Color separations by North American Color, Portage, MI.

The information in this book has been carefully checked and to the best of our knowledge is accurate. However, details are subject to change, and the National Geographic Society cannot be responsible for such changes, or for errors or omissions. Assessments of sites, hotels, and restaurants are based on the author's subjective opinions, which do not necessarily reflect the publisher's opinion. The publisher cannot be responsible for any consequences arising from the use of this book.

NATIONAL GEOGRAPHIC
TRAVELER
A Century of Travel Expertise in Every Guide

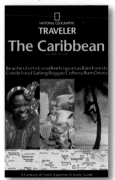

- **Alaska** ISBN: 978-0-7922-5371-6
- **Amsterdam** ISBN: 978-0-7922-7900-6
- **Arizona** (2nd Edition) ISBN: 978-0-7922-3888-1
- **Australia** (2nd Edition) ISBN: 978-0-7922-3893-5
- **Barcelona** (2nd Edition) ISBN: 978-0-7922-5365-5
- **Berlin** ISBN: 978-0-7922-6212-1
- **Boston & environs** ISBN: 978-0-7922-7926-6
- **California** (2nd Edition) ISBN: 978-0-7922-3885-0
- **Canada** (2nd Edition) ISBN: 978-0-7922-6201-5
- **The Caribbean**
  (2nd Edition) ISBN: 978-1-4262-0141-7
- **China** (2nd Edition) ISBN: 978-1-4262-0035-9
- **Costa Rica** (2nd Edition) ISBN: 978-0-7922-5368-6
- **Cuba** (2nd Edition) ISBN: 978-1-4262-0142-4
- **Egypt** (2nd Edition) ISBN: 978-1-4262-0143-1
- **Florence & Tuscany**
  (2nd Edition) ISBN: 978-0-7922-5318-1
- **Florida** ISBN: 978-0-7922-7432-2
- **France** (2nd Edition) ISBN: 978-1-4262-0027-4
- **Germany** (2nd Edition) ISBN: 978-1-4262-0028-1
- **Great Britain**
  (2nd Edition) ISBN: 978-1-4262-0029-8
- **Greece** (2nd Edition) ISBN: 978-1-4262-0030-4
- **Hawaii** (2nd Edition) ISBN: 978-0-7922-5568-0
- **Hong Kong**
  (2nd Edition) ISBN: 978-0-7922-5369-3
- **India** (2nd Edition) ISBN: 978-1-4262-0144-8
- **Ireland** (2nd Edition) ISBN: 978-1-4262-0022-9
- **Italy** (2nd Edition) ISBN: 978-0-7922-3889-8
- **Japan** (2nd Edition) ISBN: 978-0-7922-3894-2
- **London** (2nd Edition) ISBN: 978-1-4262-0023-6
- **Los Angeles** ISBN: 978-0-7922-7947-1

- **Madrid** ISBN: 978-0-7922-5372-3
- **Mexico** (2nd Edition) ISBN: 978-0-7922-5319-8
- **Miami & the Keys**
  (2nd Edition) ISBN: 978-0-7922-3886-7
- **New York** (2nd Edition) ISBN: 978-0-7922-5370-9
- **Naples & southern Italy**
  ISBN 978-1-4262-0040-3
- **Panama** ISBN: 978-1-4262-0146-2
- **Paris** (2nd Edition) ISBN: 978-1-4262-0024-3
- **Piedmont & Northwest Italy**
  ISBN: 978-0-7922-4198-0
- **Portugal** ISBN: 978-0-7922-4199-7
- **Prague & the Czech Republic**
  ISBN: 978-0-7922-4147-8
- **Provence & the Côte d'Azur**
  ISBN: 978-0-7922-9542-6
- **Romania** ISBN: 978-1-4262-0147-9
- **Rome** (2nd Edition) ISBN: 978-0-7922-5572-7
- **St. Petersburg** ISBN 978-1-4262-0050-2
- **San Diego** (2nd Edition) ISBN: 978-0-7922-6202-2
- **San Francisco**
  (2nd Edition) ISBN: 978-0-7922-3883-6
- **Shanghai** ISBN: 978-1-4262-0148-6
- **Sicily** ISBN: 978-0-7922-9541-9
- **Spain** ISBN: 978-0-7922-3884-3
- **Sydney** ISBN: 978-0-7922-7435-3
- **Taiwan** (2nd Edition) ISBN: 978-1-4262-0145-5
- **Thailand** (2nd Edition) ISBN: 978-0-7922-5321-1
- **Venice** ISBN: 978-0-7922-7917-4
- **Vietnam** ISBN: 978-0-7922-6203-9
- **Washington, D.C.**
  (2nd Edition) ISBN: 978-0-7922-3887-4